Designing•
Brain-
Compatible
Learning

THIRD EDITION

OTHER CORWIN PRESS BOOKS BY GAYLE H. GREGORY

GAYLE H. GREGORY • **TERENCE PARRY**

Designing •
Brain-
Compatible
Learning

Foreword by
Pat Wolfe

THIRD EDITION

CORWIN PRESS
A SAGE Publications Company
Thousand Oaks, California

For information:

Corwin Press
A Sage Publications Company
2455 Teller Road
Thousand Oaks, California 91320
www.corwinpress.com

Sage Publications Ltd.
1 Oliver's Yard
55 City Road
London EC1Y 1SP
United Kingdom

Sage Publications India Pvt. Ltd.
B-42, Panchsheel Enclave
Post Box 4109
New Delhi 110 017 India

Printed in the United States of America.

Library of Congress Cataloging-in-Publication Data

Gregory, Gayle.
Designing brain-compatible learning / Gayle H. Gregory, Terence Parry.—3rd ed.
    p. cm.
Includes bibliographical references and index.
ISBN 1-4129-3716-7 (cloth) — ISBN 1-4129-3717-5 (pbk.)
    1. Instructional systems—Design. 2. Learning, Psychology of. 3. Learning—Physiological aspects.
4. Educational innovations. I. Parry, Terence. II. Title.
LB1028.38.P37 2006
370.15′23—dc22

                                                      2006002890

This book is printed on acid-free paper.

06   07   08   09   10   10   9   8   7   6   5   4   3   2   1

Acquiring Editor:	Faye Zucker
Editorial Assistant:	Gem Rabanera
Project Editor:	Astrid Virding
Copyeditor:	Linda Gray
Typesetter:	C&M Digitals (P) Ltd.
Indexer:	Naomi Linzer
Cover Designer:	Rose Storey

To my family—my mom and dad,
who provided nature and nurture; my children,
Jodie and Jennifer, for love and support; and
my husband, Joe, my cheerleader.

G.G.

To my wife, Susan, my companion, friend, and
soul mate.

T.P.

CONTENTS

FOREWORD

(to the Original Edition)

Everyone agrees that what teachers do in classrooms should be based on what we know about how people learn. However, until recently, we have had few clues to unlock the "black box" that holds the secrets of the brain. New research from the neurosciences is changing this scenario. Our understanding of the neurological underpinnings of the learning process has increased tremendously in the past few decades. We now have a much more solid foundation on which to base educational decisions.

But while the theoretical information is readily available, the translation of this information has not been. How do teachers sift through the enormous amount of available information and determine what applies and what doesn't? What does a brain-compatible classroom look like? Gayle Gregory and Terence Parry have tackled this challenging job of translating the research into classroom practice and provided teachers with what they've been looking for, a guide to brain-compatible instruction.

The book begins with a very understandable synthesis of cognitive research, pulling from the work of leading neuroscientists, psychologists, and educators. An introduction to brain organization and architecture, the role of emotion in attention, and memory systems leads to a listing of general principles of how the brain works. This leads to a discussion of pedagogical theory and how pedagogical researchers and other education professionals have identified a number of powerful instructional techniques that enhance learning.

Intelligence has become a major topic for discussion in recent years. With the publication of Daniel Goleman's *Emotional Intelligence* and Howard Gardner's proposal of multiple intelligences, educators have come to realize that intelligence is much broader than we had previously thought. We have come to understand that IQ measures a very narrow band of intelligence, yet most of our assessment has been based on this measure. Gregory and Parry provide an excellent overview of alternate theories of intelligence, not only looking at Coleman's and Gardner's work but also weaving in Art Costa's description of intelligent behaviors.

Three major instructional methodologies are the focus for a large part of the book. Cooperative group learning (and the collaborative skills students need to work cooperatively), thinking skills, and graphic organizers are presented in a format that offers first a brain-based rationale and description of the method, followed by a discussion of why it is needed and how to do it. Readers will find guidelines for using each of the strategies along with numerous examples of what they look like in the classroom.

Instruction that fits well with how the brain learns best is an admirable goal, but it will be difficult to reach if the way we measure attainment doesn't match the instruction. Gregory and Parry address this issue by including an excellent section on assessment. Again, they use the format of describing authentic/performance assessment strategies, discuss why they are needed, and finally, address the practical issue of how to move from the more traditional forms to alternate and more authentic assessments.

Human brains remember what they've seen, and the authors make good use of this finding by including numerous charts, diagrams, and other types of visual tools in this book to increase not only understanding but also retention of the strategies they discuss.

There's a strong possibility that this will become one of the most used books on the educator's bookshelf, and that's all to the good because ultimately it will be the students (and their brains) who benefit.

Pat Wolfe, EdD
Napa, California

INTRODUCTION

This book is about designing learning experiences that combine the best of what we know about how the brain learns with the best of what we know about teaching. Our primary goal is to make sense of the wealth of information that exists and condense it into a format that is both teacher friendly and practical.

There is a growing sense of frustration among teachers regarding the sheer number of educational innovations that bombard them on a regular basis. We believe this frustration will be decreased when teachers can make sense of the mass of information by focusing on a limited yet powerful set of research-based instructional strategies.

In the first two chapters, we delve into the research of how the brain learns based on the works of Robert Sylwester, Gerald Edelman, Daniel Goleman, Marian Diamond, Renate Nummela Caine, Geoffrey Caine, David Sousa, Marilee Sprenger, and Pat Wolfe and then establish a link between this information and current educational theories as proposed and described by Howard Gardner, David Perkins, Jacqueline Brooks, Martin Brooks, Robin Fogarty, Jay McTighe, and Art Costa. Using cognitive research and pedagogical theories, we have developed a set of skills and strategies that fall under the general rubric of brain-compatible instruction.

In chapter 3, we share a framework for designing units and lessons. This framework offers teachers multiple strategies to "paint" a brain-compatible lesson. The artist's palette is used as a metaphor for selecting colors (instructional strategies) and mixing them in a unique lesson.

In chapter 4, we examine three theories of intelligence: multiple intelligences (Gardner 1983), emotional intelligence (Goleman 1995), and intelligent behavior (Costa 1995). We include suggestions for applying the theories to classroom practice.

In chapters 5 and 6, we discuss cooperative group learning and collaborative skills, which are presented as master strategies that facilitate the implementation of all the other teaching suggestions in this book.

Chapters 7 and 8 cover thinking skills and graphic organizers. For the purpose of clarity, these are presented as separate topics; however, in practice they often are used in combination with each other.

The final chapter provides suggestions for assessment in the brain-compatible classroom. It includes tips on using alternate forms of assessment (such as projects, performances, and portfolios), establishing criteria, and using assessments to promote student growth.

In effect, we have created a tool kit for teachers that contains a comprehensive set of best teaching practices. Many of these strategies are familiar to teachers— some may have been forgotten, others may not have been used in a while. This book calls the strategies back to mind, organizes them, provides a rationale for their use, and gives some suggestions for integrating them into the classroom.

The strategies in the tool kit may be transferred to the classroom by using a framework for designing brain-compatible learning through lesson planning. The framework is designed so that all the strategies are on display at all times during the lesson design process. This is to remind us of the range of options available, therefore increasing the chances that we will use an expanded repertoire of instructional skills in our day-to-day teaching.

The public, in general, and parents, in particular, are sometimes skeptical of educational innovation. Oftentimes, this is because no one has explained the innovations to them or not enough information has been provided to make clear the purpose of the innovations. As teachers, we are often so busy implementing new ideas that we do not have time to achieve a thorough understanding of the research that supports them. This can lead to situations where we are at a loss to define what we are doing and why we are doing it. For this reason, we have organized the information in each chapter under three general headings: What Is It? Why Do We Need It? and How Do We Do It?

The What Is It? section of each chapter introduces the key concepts related to the chapter topic, provides a working definition of the skills or strategies, and presents research findings related to these ideas.

The Why Do We Need It? section provides the rationale for the skills or strategies and states why they are important and how they are connected to the concept of brain compatibility. The importance of the rationale cannot be overstated, because it is as important to understand why we are adopting a particular strategy as it is to know how to do it.

The How Do We Do It? section provides a step-by-step approach to using particular skills as well as examples of how they may be applied in the classroom.

Reflections are included at the end of many chapters to enhance individual or group learning.

Blackline masters (including Reflections) are provided in several chapters and may be reproduced for use with your students.

Note the glossary and bibliography for clarification of strategies and brain-related terms and additional readings.

ACKNOWLEDGMENTS

W e would like to acknowledge the following people who have devoted their lives to the improvement of education and have helped and inspired us, and many others, to become better teachers:

Pat Wolfe, whose lucid presentations and writing first turned us on to brain-compatible learning.

Barrie Bennett and Carol Rolheiser, who opened up the world of instruction for us and made us realize just what makes teaching go.

Jay McTighe, who provided the link between cognitive research and pedagogical theory that is the foundation of this book.

Michael Fullan, for his support over the years and his dedication to the proposition that education is worth fighting for.

PUBLISHER'S ACKNOWLEDGMENTS

Corwin Press thanks the following reviewers for their contributions to this book:

William Fitzhugh, Second Grade Teacher, Reisterstown Elementary School, Reisterstown, MD

Steve Hutton, Educational Consultant, Kentucky Department of Education, Villa Hills, KY

ABOUT THE AUTHORS

 **Gayle H. Gregory** has been a teacher in elementary, middle, and secondary schools. For many years, she taught in schools with extended periods of instructional time (block schedules). She has had extensive districtwide experience as a curriculum consultant and staff development coordinator. She was course director at York University for the Faculty of Education, teaching in the teacher education program. She now consults internationally (Europe, Asia, North and South America, Australia) with teachers, administrators, and staff developers in the areas of managing change, differentiated instruction, brain-compatible learning, block scheduling, emotional intelligence, instructional and assessment practices, cooperative group learning, presentation skills, renewal of secondary schools, enhancing teacher quality, and coaching and mentoring.

Gayle is affiliated with many organizations, including the Association for Supervision and Curriculum Development and the National Staff Development Council. She is the author of *Differentiated Instructional Strategies in Practice: Training, Implementation, and Supervision* and the coauthor of *Designing Brain-Compatible Learning; Thinking Inside the Block Schedule: Strategies for Teaching in Extended Periods of Time; Differentiated Instructional Strategies: One Size Doesn't Fit All; Data Driven Differentiation in the Standards-Based Classroom; Differentiated Literacy Strategies for Student Growth and Achievement in Grades K-6;* and *Differentiated Literacy Strategies for Student Growth and Achievement in Grades 7-12.* She has been featured in Video Journal of Education's bestselling elementary and secondary videos *Differentiating Instruction to Meet the Needs of All Learners.*

Gayle is committed to lifelong learning and professional growth for herself and others. She may be contacted by e-mail at gregorygayle@netscape.net. Her Web site is www3.sympatico.ca/gayle.gregory.

 **Terence Parry** has taught at the elementary, secondary, and university levels, and he is now a full-time staff developer and educational consultant in Waterloo, Ontario. He truly believes that the key to educational changed depends on what teachers do in the classroom. He has traveled all over the world and has received international recognition for his lively and engaging workshops, which offer a wealth of practical experience to help teachers cope with the overwhelming number of changes that bombard schools on a daily basis.

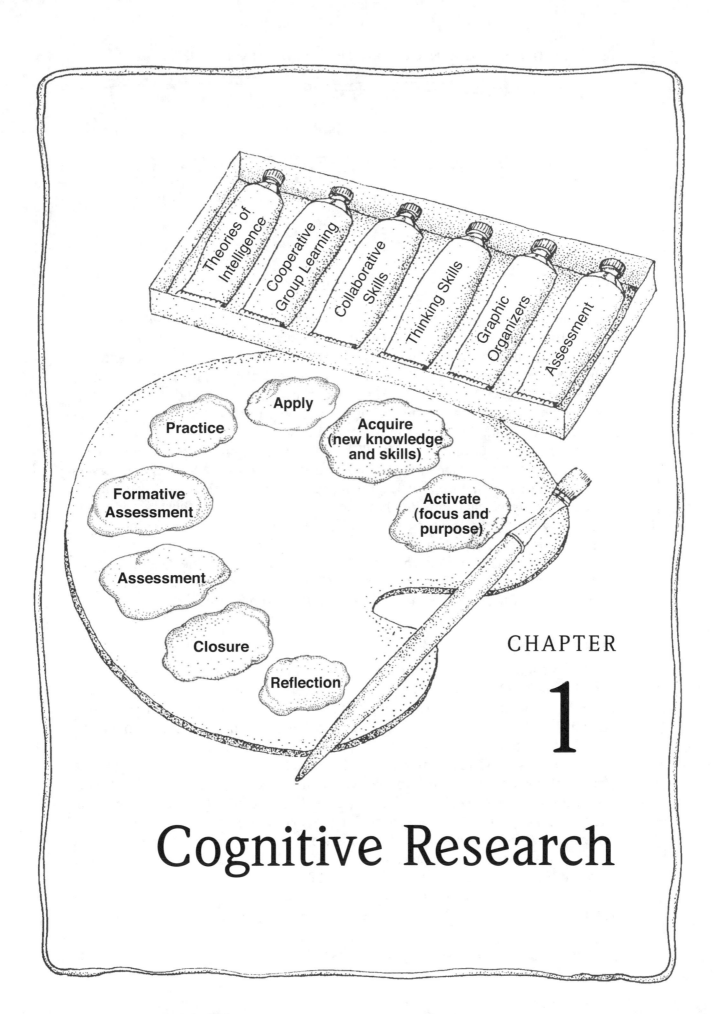

Theories of Intelligence

Cooperative Group Learning

Collaborative Skills

Thinking Skills

Graphic Organizers

Assessment

Practice

Apply

Acquire (new knowledge and skills)

Formative Assessment

Activate (focus and purpose)

Assessment

Closure

Reflection

CHAPTER

1

Cognitive Research

CHAPTER 1

COGNITIVE RESEARCH

WHAT IS IT?

Much of what is known about how the brain learns has been discovered in the past twenty-five years. For the first time, scientists are able to examine the internal organization and working of the brain as opposed to merely observing the external behavior that results from brain activity. The advent of brain-imaging technology has provided a window into the skull that allows scientists and researchers to observe how and where information is manipulated in the process we call learning. The CAT (computerized axial tomography) scan can create a graphical three-dimensional image of the brain. The PET (positron-emission tomography) scan can monitor the pattern of blood flow to various parts of the brain and allows observers to see which parts "light up" as the brain processes information.

Cognitive researchers are just beginning to understand how the brain interacts with the external environment to acquire information, to manipulate and process it, to store it as memory, and to retrieve it on demand. Educators, neuroscientists, cognitive psychologists, and researchers such as Renate Nummela Caine, Geoffrey Caine, Marian Diamond, Gerald Edelman, Howard Gardner, Jane Healy, Eric Jensen, Robert Sylwester, and Pat Wolfe have provided a variety of theories of how the brain learns.

The Brain Is Like . . .

The organization and functions of the brain are predicated on a number of very complex ideas. One way to understand these complex ideas is through the use of metaphors and analogies. These comparisons afford us a place to begin our understanding of the brain, and although they provide somewhat distorted representations, they give us approximations that simplify complex ideas.

One discovery from research is that the brain makes sense of the world by constructing meaning from the information around it (Caine and Caine 1994). One way it does this is by connecting information about something it already knows to the new concept that it is trying to understand. For example, we can use the computer (something we know about) as an analogue for the brain (something we are trying to learn about). We then can take our knowledge about computers and apply it to the brain in an attempt to understand it.

The computer analogy works well for most people when trying to learn about the networks of brain cells and the ways in which they are connected, especially if they already understand networks, connections, and wires. However, the analogy breaks down when we use it to explain how the brain is organized or how it transmits information.

To explain these concepts we need another analogy—the jungle. Neurobiologist Gerald Edelman (1992) proposed that the organization and functions of the brain are more analogous to a jungle or a rain forest than they are to a computer. According to his theory, the brain is a rather messy and disorganized place. Like a jungle, it has no external controller and few predetermined goals other than to survive. In fact, survival is its primary function. Survival also is the main reason that the brain engages in learning. In a jungle, no outside agency or group is in control; each species of plant and animal goes about its own business, never thinking that it is part of a master plan. However, each organism is, in fact, part of a system within other interdependent systems, which together form one giant ecosystem. All the animals and plants have the capacity to thrive and reproduce, but some do and some don't; this is natural selection at work. The jungle does not tell the individual species *how* to survive; it merely supports the survivors.

The brain is organized in a similar fashion. No one part of the brain is in charge, and the brain is made up of myriad interconnecting systems. Each system goes about its own business but also contributes information that allows the brain to survive.

All systems in the brain have the capacity to survive. As in the jungle, some systems thrive, some don't. The brain supports the winners, which are the neural systems that are stimulated by their environments and frequently used. This process operates similarly to the way in which we retain many of our physical capabilities— we either use them or lose them. Just as muscles become stronger through use and weaker through disuse, neural networks that are used strengthen and those that are not used weaken. When a neural network weakens, the cells within it may become rededicated to other uses. This is called neural pruning.

An example of neural pruning is evident in the process of language acquisition. We are born with the capability to make all the sounds and learn the vocabularies and grammatical structures of every language spoken by humans. In many cases, however, we learn only one. The networks not found in one's native tongue eventually weaken through a lack of use and, in some cases, are lost forever.

The "double 1" sound in the Welsh language, found in words such as Llangollen and Llewelyn, is a case in point. If one does not learn the sound early, the chance of being able to acquire it later is not very promising. Similarly, native speakers of Cantonese who learn English as adults often have difficulty with the "th" sound in English words, whereas Chinese children raised in English-speaking environments have no such difficulty.

The brain has two primary kinds of cells: nerve cells and glial cells. The nerve cells, called neurons, form a complex network that transmits information to all parts of the brain/body system. To visualize a neuron, imagine an old-fashioned floor mop with a wooden handle and a head made from twisted cotton fibers. Now imagine that the handle has begun to split apart. The dense part of the mop represents the cell body, and the individual strands of the mop are the dendrites. The stick is the axon, which is an extension of the cell body, and the split ends of the stick represent the axon terminals (see Fig. 1.1).

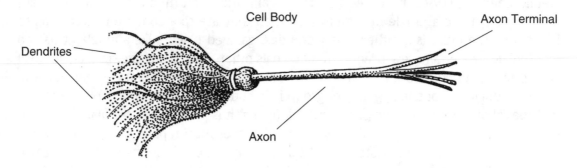

Figure 1.1

In reality the dendrites are a complex array of filaments like hairs that grow out of the cell body. The axon is a snake-like projection that can vary in length from a few millimeters in the brain to several feet in the spinal cord, and the axon terminals are the staging area for the chemical messengers called neurotransmitters. An actual neuron would look more like Figure 1.2.

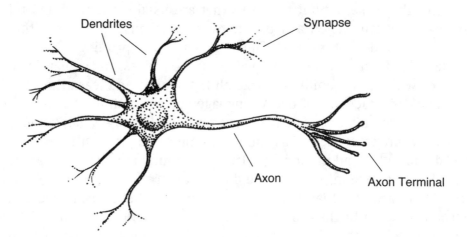

Figure 1.2

Now imagine that our floor mop representation is matched up with a series of other floor mops arranged head to tail. When neurons connect like this, they begin to form a neural network. The axon terminals of the first neuron send a message, which is passed on to the dendrites of the second neuron. The second neuron passes the message on to the next cell in line until the message gets to its final destination. The message is carried by molecules called neurotransmitters, which are, in fact, chemical messengers. Neurotransmitters cross the space between one neuron and the next. This space, or gap, is called a synapse (see Fig. 1.3).

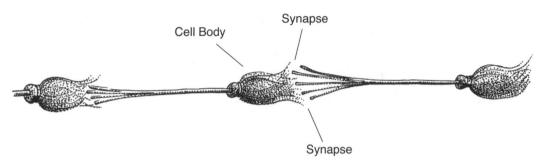

Cell Body

Synapse

Synapse

Figure 1.3

More than fifty different kinds of neurotransmitters have been identified (Sylwester 1995), but they all have one of two basic functions—they either excite the system or calm it. For example, glutamate, an amino acid compound, stimulates the system, whereas gamma-aminobutyric acid (GABA), also an amino acid compound, inhibits it.

One large group of neurotransmitters is made up of peptides. Peptides travel along a chain of neurons to all parts of the brain and the body. They elicit a wide range of responses from pleasure to pain. Peptides have a powerful effect on our emotional lives because they control our feelings and, hence, our responses to the outside world. They also control the internal regulating mechanisms of the body by telling them things such as when to shed excess heat, when to conserve it, when to eliminate fluids, when to store them, and so on. In general terms, the peptides tell all bodily systems and functions what to do, when to do it, and how to do it (see Fig. 1.4, page 6).

Cortisol and endorphins are two neurotransmitters that are peptides. Cortisol activates the body's defense systems as a reaction to the stress caused by a perceived threat. For example, when the body perceives a threat, the adrenal glands distribute cortisol, which elevates the cholesterol level and releases clotting agents into the blood. This was useful for our ancestors, who often faced physical dangers such as broken bones and flesh wounds. In modern times, however, stress more often is a result of emotional causes than physical ones. Because the body responds to both emotional and physical threats in the same manner, this can result in inappropriate responses to stress. In situations of chronic stress, high levels of cortisol can cause feelings of extreme despair and, in some cases, can cause the destruction of neurons related to both learning and memory (Vincent 1990).

Endorphins are a class of peptides that can decrease pain and increase pleasure. They are released both when a person is in pain and when a person is engaged in pleasurable activities such as games, dancing, and other social interactions.

Close-Up of a Synapse

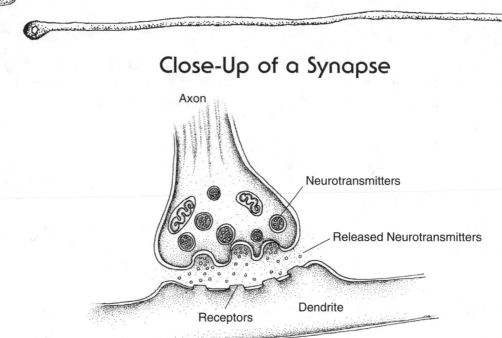

Figure 1.4

Endorphins are often released when a person receives overt signs of support, affection, and positive regard. Classrooms that encourage a relaxed, enthusiastic, and cooperative approach to learning are usually perceived as enjoyable because they stimulate the release of endorphins (Sylwester 1995).

Glial cells, the other primary type of brain cells, perform a number of support functions for the nerve cells. One of these is to provide insulation in the form of a myelin sheath that prevents a short circuit of information between one nerve cell and the next.

Although the brain weighs only about three pounds, it is responsible for the cathedrals of Europe, the mobile home, the works of Shakespeare, *Sesame Street*, Beethoven's sonatas, and punk rock. In fact, everything that defines human culture is a product of the brain.

Brain Organization and Architecture

The brain is enormously complex. Some scientists speculate that there are more possible connections in the brain than there are pieces of matter in the universe. The brain has about 100 billion neurons, each of which can produce up to 20,000 connections in the form of dendrites. Each neuron, therefore, is capable of connecting with other cells in an almost infinite variety of ways. This profusion of connections gives the brain its amazing powers to think, learn, and create.

The brain can be divided into three parts, lower, middle, and upper, but in effect, it functions as a highly interactive and profusely connected whole. Because the functions of the lower and middle brain are so elaborately connected, they are often described as one unit called the emotional brain. This unit is responsible for monitoring many of the physical processes of the body, including heartbeat, respiration, digestion, sexual activity, and body temperature. It also controls many of the functions associated with the emotions and the formation of memories. The emotional brain has many other functions critical to our survival. Apart from its ability to recognize and react to sudden changes that signal danger, it also monitors all the other more gradual or subtle changes going on around us, such as room temperature, hunger, hormone cycles, and the waking and sleeping cycles. It also evaluates all the incoming information provided by the senses—sight, hearing, touch, taste, and smell. It then decides which information is important enough to be singled out for attention by the rest of the brain. The third and most complex part of the brain is the cerebral cortex, which handles language, perceives patterns, decodes symbols, and performs all the functions associated with higher-order thinking and reasoning. The cells of the cortex are organized into several million interconnecting and overlapping systems, or networks, each of which processes a small piece of information. Each piece of information is then connected to other pieces in a system that allows us to think, solve problems, remember past experiences, and plan for the future. The cortex is the most complex part of the brain and the least understood. The individual systems of the cortex interact not only with each other but also with the systems of the emotional brain. They work together to form a comprehensive alerting or arousal system that establishes the degree of emotion and/or attention. That sets the stage for the ways in which we respond to both danger and opportunity. Sometimes the response may be a slow and well-considered action that results from thinking through a problem. At other times, it may be a hasty and seemingly ill-considered reaction to a highly charged emotional stimulus. Sometimes the response is a life-or-death decision to jump out of the way of a speeding truck before the thinking parts of the brain have even registered the problem.

Left and Right Hemispheres

The right and left hemispheres of the brain perform different but totally interdependent functions. In simple terms, the right hemisphere takes in great gulps of information, and the left hemisphere analyzes and sorts that information. Working together, the right and left sides of the brain deal with information as both wholes and parts. The right brain is global or panoramic in its approach to information. The left brain is more logical and linear; it controls activities such as speech, logical thinking, and the manipulation of symbols and numbers. The section on Creative and Critical Thinking in chapter 7 shows how both sides work together in decision making and problem solving. Two strategies called *concept formation* and *concept attainment,* also discussed in chapter 7, illustrate how the brain seeks patterns and makes wholes from parts. Elkhonon Goldberg (2001) provides us with an alternate theory of right brain/left brain organization. He suggests that the right hemisphere is organized to confront new challenges and deal quickly with situations that the brain has not previously encountered. He postulates that this is all part of the brain's primary mandate, which is survival. For example, the face of a stranger represents a novel situation that may pose a threat. The right side of the brain therefore quickly processes this information. Familiar faces, which presumably pose no threat, are processed on the left.

Both hemispheres are active in learning situations. When we are learning new skills, information processing is principally a right-hemisphere operation. As we come closer to mastery of the skill, more of the processing is transferred to the left side. The right hemisphere responds to new situations with a solution, which is typically rapid but not necessarily appropriate. The left hemisphere selects the most promising responses and devises strategies and systems to deal with similar situations in the future.

Whole Brain Theory

Because the right and left sides of the brain continually interact in much more complex and interactive ways than previously thought, many scientists now believe in what is called a whole-brain approach to learning; this theory says, in effect, that nearly every part of the brain is involved in nearly every activity of the brain (Goldberg 2001). This modifies many of the earlier notions of brain organization, such as Sperry's (1968) right brain/left brain theory and MacLean's (1978) theory of the triune brain.

WHY DO WE NEED IT?

In the past, schools have often been accused of teaching "the facts, the whole facts, and nothing but the facts." The "facts" then were memorized, trotted out for the test, and promptly forgotten. Even when they were not forgotten, the facts were rarely connected and often were misunderstood. Nevertheless, some people still define education as the ability to recall a vast number of facts.

A more rational definition of education maintains that what counts is not the sheer number of facts a person knows but what a person does with those facts. Facts become useful when they are used to solve problems or extend knowledge. This does not mean that schools should give up teaching facts. Nor does it mean that students should not train their memories to recall important information. It does suggest, however, that we need to spend more time in teaching students to sort and classify discrete facts into categories and to deal with information at a conceptual level. Both the process of memorizing facts and the process of forming concepts are necessary elements of learning.

Learning is a search for meaning, yet most of us have only a rudimentary notion of how meaning is created. According to Eric Jensen (1996), meaning is created when new information is connected at the neural level to information that already has meaning or relevance for the learner. The more closely the new information conforms to what the learner perceives as interesting, useful, and emotionally stimulating, the more likely it is to be integrated and learned.

Nearly everything we learn has an emotional element. Whenever the emotions are engaged, the brain releases a battery of chemical messengers (neurotransmitters) that mark the event and signal its importance to the brain. This focuses the learner's attention and, in doing so, facilitates learning. The emotional context, thus, becomes part of the matrix or pattern to which the new learning is attached. What has in fact been created is a neural organizer, or a place where information sticks—a kind of Velcro for the mind.

By understanding how the brain, the body, the emotions, and learning are interdependently connected, we can get a sense of how these ideas relate to the concept called brain-compatible learning. If we consider the work of Daniel Goleman (1995) on emotions and learning, the work of Marian Diamond (1988) on the effects of experience and learning, and the work of Renate Nummela Caine and Geoffrey Caine (1994) on the connection of information and learning, we can see how these theories not only support each other but also support and extend the concept of brain compatible learning. By adding information from the work of Gerald Edelman (1987) about his notion of neural Darwinism, which describes the brain as a richly interconnected whole in which the parts that are successful are retained and nurtured while other parts die off, and backing this up with Robert Sylwester's (1995) lucid overview of current research in *A Celebration of Neurons,* the characteristics that define brain compatible learning become even clearer.

Understanding how the brain learns—by actually capturing, sorting, and holding on to information—enables teachers to implement the kinds of instruction and develop the kinds of classrooms that capitalize on the brain's natural abilities and thus promote student learning.

HOW DO WE DO IT?

The field of cognitive research is vast, complex, and continually expanding. New discoveries are being made and old theories are updated or discarded almost on a weekly basis. Although many prior assumptions have been reinterpreted, based on more current information, a central core of knowledge about how the brain learns remains unchallenged.

The following pages contain a digest of just some of the current theories in the fields of cognitive science, cognitive psychology, and educational research. The underlying premise of these theories is that if we understand how the brain learns, we can use that information to improve classroom practice.

Emotion and Learning

The connection between the thinking parts of the brain and the emotional or survival-oriented parts of the brain is of particular importance to teachers. When a human being experiences stress, the body reacts by producing a battery of hormonal and electrochemical changes.

If the level of stress is perceived as critical, the brain may go into a survival mode by transferring the locus of control to more survival-oriented part of the brain. In the past, this phenomenon was referred to as "downshifting"; psychologist Daniel Goleman (1995) referred to it as "emotional hijacking." In a recent article, Robert Sylwester (1998) made a proposal that rather than downshifting, the brain transfers control to part of the brain that is better equipped to deal with the situation at hand. In situations that pose a clear-and-present danger, the body reacts before the cerebral cortex (the thinking part of the brain) has had a chance to review what's happening and process all the information. This is why we are able to jump out of the path of a speeding truck before we have consciously registered its presence. Before incoming information is processed by the cerebral cortex, it is filtered through the reticular formation, the brain's gatekeeper. The reticular formation monitors incoming information and decides if it is life threatening or potentially dangerous. This information is transmitted to the amygdala, the brain's alarm system. The amygdala is connected to other parts of the brain in a way similar to how many home alarm systems are connected to the police and fire services (Sylwester 1995). In a threatening situation, these parts of the brain respond to the amygdala's message by causing a release of hormones. These, in turn, alert those parts of the body needed for survival, such as the cardiovascular system, the digestive system, and the muscles. This results in a heightened state of physical preparedness in which so much attention is focused on survival that the thinking parts of the brain may relinquish much of their control and allow the emotional brain to take over. There are educators who believe that stress is an effective motivator for learning. Psychiatrist Arnold Scheibel (1994) maintained that lessons learned under stress are remembered better than those learned in nonthreatening environments. He bases this on the fact that the neurotransmitters and hormones released under duress result in a heightened state of being. This allows the brain and body to function more effectively because they are now on alert status.

As teachers, we need to differentiate between eustress, the positive feelings of enjoyment or excitement that one experiences when engaging in something new and different, and distress, the negative feelings that may cause one to panic or revert to survival behaviors. Eustress comes from the same root word as euphoria it puts us into a state of heightened awareness in which our ability to learn is at its optimum level. Distress has the opposite effect and triggers the release of neurotransmitters, such as cortisol, that may cause the thinking parts of the brain to function below peak efficiency (Vincent 1990). It appears, then, that a certain amount of stress may be beneficial, whereas acute or prolonged stress may have negative effects on learning.

If students are to learn efficiently, stress needs to be kept within tolerable levels so that their self-esteem and personal efficacy remain intact. Strategies such as cooperative group learning and metacognitive reflection, which promote social interaction and allow students to discuss their emotions, are effective tools for creating a tolerable level of stress and, hence, a climate conducive to learning.

Assignments that create a challenge without imposing a threat are essential for learners to feel confident and committed to a task. This creates a sense of "relaxed alertness" (Kohn 1993). In classrooms where teachers differentiate the instructional process by using "adjustable assignments" (Gregory and Chapman 2002), students are challenged at their level of ability or abstraction.

If we reflect, most of us can recall situations that may have caused students to react with a visceral rather than a cognitive behavior. In extreme cases, this may lead to the fight-or-flight response in which a student may exhibit aggressive behavior or language (fight) or even run from the room (flight). As far as the brain is concerned, actions speak louder than words. Everything that happens in the classroom is monitored by three parts of the brain, two of which have no spoken language but are very adept at reading body language and tone of voice. Every gesture, every inflection, and every invasion of personal space is monitored by the emotional brain and evaluated in terms of its threat potential. These skills allowed our ancestors to survive, and they are still alive and well in all of us.

The implications of emotion in the teaching and learning process seem too important to be left to chance. It seems vital that teachers understand the physiological processes operating and are cognizant of how these forces act on the students. The classroom environment, the ways in which questions are asked of students, and the amount of wait time between question and response may all represent a perceived threat and thus cause the brain to react at an emotional level. Figure 1.5 lists some indicators that help create and support a positive learning environment.

Indicators for Classroom Climate

Positive	Negative
Provide attractive surroundings	Sterile surroundings
Include plants and decorative walls	Student work not displayed
Student work displayed	Poor, inappropriate lighting
Low-stress lighting	Negative attitude of teacher
Encouraging teacher	"One size fits all" mentality
Offer choice and variety	Unnecessary pressure
Provide wait time	Little or no feedback
Provide think time	Challenge inappropriate
Offer constructive feedback	Teaching to the "middle"
Offer appropriate challenge	Everyone does the same task
Ensure safety	regardless of style or multiple
Ensure relaxed alertness	intelligence strengths
Consideration of learning styles	

Figure 1.5

Everything else teachers do, in terms of curriculum or instruction, may be irrelevant if the students cannot remain in a state where the functions of the emotional brain are integrated and harmonized with the capabilities of the thinking, reasoning parts of the brain.

Emotion, Attention, and the Formation of Memories

The cortex is the seat of higher-order thinking, but it relies on its connections with the emotional brain for a number of vital functions in the learning process. These functions are concerned with the engagement of emotions, the focusing of attention, and the formation of memories. The human mind can consciously focus on only one thing at a time, and it is our emotions, mediated by the emotional brain, that dictate to what we pay attention. There is an emotional component to all learning and it seems to work like this:

> **Emotion focuses our attention,**
> **and attention sets the stage for learning.**
> **Even people who appear to be multitasking are,**
> **in reality, switching their attention from one task to another.**

Emotion also plays a role in the formation of memories. Events with a high degree of emotional impact seem to stay in most people's minds with no conscious effort. Most of us can recall with clarity and precision the pivotal events of our lives. Among the more famous examples of emotionally charged events are the assassination of President Kennedy, the *Challenger* disaster, the death of Diana, Princess of Wales, and the events of September 11, 2001. It seems that everyone alive at the time of these events can remember in some detail where they were and what they were doing when they first heard about them.

Information that has an emotional context seems to be more readily recalled, and by recalling the emotional context, we also can usually recall the details of the event. This is why strategies that engage the emotions are such powerful learning tools. Activities such as role plays, simulations, debates, and discussions all provide emotional hooks that facilitate the recall of information.

Memory Systems

Memory has been described as being both like a sponge that soaks up information and like a muscle that gets stronger with use. Neither of these metaphors is particularly accurate. A more apt description is that memory is a process, not a thing. Pat Wolfe, a noted educational consultant, described how the processes of memory and learning are inextricably linked in the following way: "We say we have learned something. We also could say we have gotten something into memory" (Wolfe 1998).

The way the brain processes memory can be compared to the memory processing model shown in Figure 1.6 (page 14), which shows how sensory memory, working (or short-term) memory, and long-term memory are processed. The strategies at the bottom can be used at different stages in the learning process to garner, rehearse, or access stored memory.

Sensory Memory

Sensory memory acts like a sieve, or filter, to screen out much of the input that comes from our senses and internal organs. Without this filter, we would drown in a sea of information. Sensory memory decides which information should be passed on to short-term memory and which information should be discarded. The decisions are influenced by three additional processes: perception, expectation, and attention.

Perception is the process whereby the brain attaches meaning to what the senses perceive. This is affected by the patterns of experience that the brain previously has acquired and therefore what it expects to see. For example, if you were told that the figure below was a number, you would perceive it as a thirteen.

13

However, if you were told to expect a letter you would see it as a **B**. Even though the figure remained the same, what you expected to see altered your perceptions. The way that the brain interprets information depends on neural networks that have been built up as a result of experience.

The structures in the brain related to sensory memory also determine whether or not we pay attention to incoming information. Our attention is focused by anything that the brain finds new, exciting, pleasurable, or threatening. In the classroom, we can capitalize on this by introducing information in new and exciting ways, making the learning experience enjoyable, and providing enough of a challenge to maintain the students' interest within a climate of low stress.

It is difficult to pay conscious attention to two things at once. We may think we can, but what we often do is rapidly cycle our attention from one thing to another. This effectively screens out a lot of sensory input. To illustrate this point, read the following paragraph (adapted from Wolfe and Sorgen 1990) and concentrate on the words in bold type.

Inductive teaching house **strategies involve the presentation** window **of a data set** door **from which the students** step **form categories,** house **generalizations and** window **concepts. The power of the strategy** door **is in the discussion** step **that takes place as** house **the students make** window **their decisions.**

What do you remember of the words in non bold type? They are, in fact, a series of words repeated over and over. Although you saw them and they entered your sensory memory, they were discarded because you were not paying attention to

Memory Processing Systems and Classroom Strategies

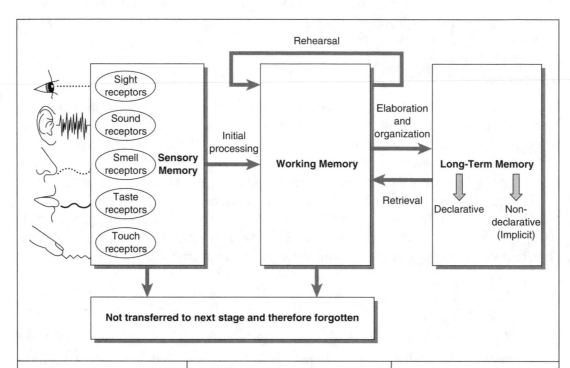

Not transferred to next stage and therefore forgotten

SENSORY MEMORY TO GARNER ATTENTION	WORKING MEMORY TO REHEARSE & ELABORATE	LONG-TERM ACCESS TO STORED MEMORY
Novelty **Relevance/meaningful** **Pique curiosity** **Emotion** • An interesting story • A question or problem • Pictures or video • A role play or drama • A unique object • A guessing game • A personal anecdote • A question • Focus on activities related to the standard	**Rote: for procedural memory** • Practice and recitation **Elaborative rehearsal** **Declarative memory** Using the new knowledge and skills in context • Mnemonics and memory pegs • Graphics/visual representations • Cooperative groups & structures • Simulations and role plays • Centers and projects • Using multiple intelligences • Problem-based inquiry • Performances & exhibitions • Raps, rhythm, song • Synectics • Integrated studies	• KWL • People search • Brainstorming • Carousel • Graffiti • Give one, take one • Yes, no, maybe • I have, who has? • Four corners • Journaling • 3-2-1 • Graphic organizers • Advance organizers • Think-pair-share

Figure 1.6

SOURCE: Parts of this illustration have been adapted with permission from *Building the Reading Brain* by Pat Wolfe and Pamela Nevills. Thousand Oaks, CA: Corwin Press, 2004.

them. We see this phenomenon in action when someone says, "You've got your head stuck in that book; you haven't heard a word I've said." In fact your ears did pick up the sound, but you didn't "hear" because you weren't paying attention. Similarly, people who live near highways filter out road noise. And, yes, hard as it may be to believe, students filter out their teachers.

The key point about sensory memory is that we are not consciously aware of the information processing that takes place. This is a crucial point for teachers, because students' attention will wander if they do not consciously select the information to which they should be attending. If they do not actively decide to concentrate on what the teacher is presenting, sensory memory takes over and selects what it finds relevant and interesting (Wolfe and Sorgen 1990). This is one of the reasons the lecture method may not be a particularly effective way of teaching. One thing we can do to make a lecture more effective is to stop every ten to fifteen minutes and allow the students to discuss the presentation's main ideas. This not only refocuses the students' attention but also helps them to understand the concepts being presented.

Short-Term, or Working, Memory

When information manages to capture the attention of the sensory memory, it is transferred into short-term memory. Information that does not capture our attention is discarded. Most people use their short-term memories to describe events from the past week, the past day, or earlier in the day. In the cognitive sciences, short-term memory is measured in seconds (Peterson and Peterson 1959).

Short-term memory sometimes is called the primary, or working, memory. Before you can begin to process information, it must be in your short-term memory. Think of it as your desktop. Unless the work is on your desk, you cannot begin to deal with it. This process of calling information into short-term memory is synonymous with conscious thought. When you consciously think about something, it remains in your short-term memory; when you stop thinking about it, the information either disappears or is transferred into long-term memory, where it is stored until you recall it at some other time.

Short-term memory can process a limited amount of material for a short time. Information fades quickly and is forgotten unless there has been enough impact or processing to transfer it to long-term memory. Without rehearsal or other forms of processing, information remains in short-term memory for less than twenty seconds (Peterson and Peterson 1959). Although this may seem short, it allows us enough time to process information without the added burden of remembering the details of every piece. For instance, it is enough time for most people to decode written text and to make sense of what they are reading.

Memory Spaces and Chunking

The other limitation of short-term memory is its capacity. It can handle only about seven separate pieces of information (plus or minus two) at one time (Miller

1956). To demonstrate this, read the following set of numbers, one time, and then try to recall them: 6324578.

You probably did quite well on that one. Now try another: 4785169657. This second set probably was much more difficult because it exceeded the capacity of your short-term memory.

Let's see what happens with another one. Read the following string of letters WTCFDNYSEPNYCUSA This string also exceeds the capacity of most people's short-term memories. However, if you group the information into chunks—WTC-FDNY-SEP-NYC-USA—it is much easier to recall, because there are now only five chunks. The fact that the chunks are well-known acronyms also helps in their recall,

Five chunks of information are well within the capacity of most people's short-term memories. Our retention of the jumbled list of letters may have been poor because the letters were seen as unrelated. When they were grouped, or chunked, we could handle them more easily. You also may have noticed a narrative thread, which has to do with events in New York City on September 11, 2001. This helps, because embedding information in a story or context aids in recalling it.

Information can be remembered in two ways: through rote learning or contextual learning. Of the two, contextual learning, or embedding, is the more powerful.

The way we create meaning by chunking information is neither random nor arbitrary. We do it by forming groups that make sense to us based on our previous experiences, which means that one person's way of forming chunks or categories may be different from another person's. Although they may be different, both ways of grouping are valid. Grouping information together in classes, categories, or chunks allows us to process greater amounts of information more easily.

Rehearsal

Making connections between separate pieces of information aids the formation of concepts or generalizations, which increases the probability the material will be transferred into long-term memory and made available for recall.

Although unrelated information disappears from short-term memory in less than twenty seconds, it can be held for much longer if it is given conscious and continuous attention. This process is called rehearsal. We rehearse information for two reasons: (1) when we need to retain it in short-term memory and (2) when we want to transfer it into long-term memory.

To understand the process of rehearsal for short-term memory, consider what happens when you look up a telephone number to order a pizza. You may rehearse by repeating the number to yourself until you have finished dialing. As soon as someone answers your call, you forget the number. If the number is busy, you may put the phone down and try again, but by this time you may have forgotten the number and might have to look it up again. However, if the number is important enough, or if you eat a lot of pizza, you may keep rehearsing it until it is transferred into long-term memory. This is an example of rote rehearsal.

Rote rehearsal is the capability of a person to retain information for extended periods in short-term memory, but it is not very effective in transferring information to long-term memory. When information learned through rote is transferred to long-term memory, it usually fades after a short time. Most of us have "rote memorized" information for an exam. How long did it last? For many of us, perhaps two weeks, but in some cases, we were lucky if it followed us out the door of the examination room.

Another form of rehearsal is called elaboration, or integrated rehearsal. It increases the probability that material will be transferred to long-term memory and held for significant periods of time. It does this by creating a context into which the learning is embedded.

Integrated rehearsal is the basis on which inductive teaching strategies work. Inductive learning means that students are encouraged to form concepts and generalizations from separate pieces of data through discussion. Inductive strategies, therefore, increase the probability that students will elaborate on what they already know by connecting new information to existing information.

Long-Term Memory

Among the capabilities of the human species is the ability to profit from prior experience and to plan for the future. This depends on two functions of long-term memory: information storage and information retrieval.

Information Storage

The storage capacity of long-term memory is, for all practical purposes, infinite. We have more capacity than we can possibly use in a lifetime. It also is hypothesized that information stored in long-term memory remains there indefinitely. We may not be able to recall much of this information, but it is there nevertheless. Because of the sheer volume of information, long-term memory is arranged and stored differently than short-term memory. Short-term memory is usually limited to seven separate pieces of information. This means that we can scan the pieces one at a time. Long-term memory holds so much information that scanning one piece at a time literally would take forever.

Theorists hypothesize that information in long-term memory is set up like a supercomplex filing system with the information chunked into categories and classifications. Long-term memory also has a cross-indexing system in which the individual files of information are elaborately interconnected. Furthermore, the system is continually updated as new information is integrated with existing knowledge. Every time we learn something new, the brain files it in the appropriate place. In fact, it stores the same information in a number of places as a backup system.

The sophistication and complexity of our "filing systems" give the brain its awesome powers to retrieve and process information. We all understand that the brain does not have a metal filing cabinet lurking about in the cranial cavity. But many people think that short- and long-term memory are specific places in the brain. Not true. Memories are not stored as pictures, which can be taken out and looked at occasionally. Instead, it is believed that the brain stores information in a number of different places: sounds in one place, sights in another, and color someplace else (Sylwester 1995). Whenever we wish to recall an event, the brain reconstructs it from the emotions, locations, sights, sounds, tastes, and smells associated with it. Each time, the sequence of recall may be different—smell before sound one time, color before smell another. This may be the reason that our recollections of an event often change over time.

We have the ability to recall information by delving into a number of files. In one instance, a particular sound may trigger the process of recollection; another time, a particular color may set in motion the process that reconstructs the same memory. As we recall one piece of the memory, it triggers another piece and soon we have retrieved the entire event.

We usually recall a piece of learning by remembering the context of emotions, sounds, smells, and locations associated with it. Information embedded in a context is stored in the same "file" as the context. This means that when we recall the circumstance (context) in which the learning took place, we also can recall the content of that learning. Location has a powerful effect both on the formation and the recall of memory.

As an example, when asked to recall what they had for dinner the previous night, most people first recall the location—I was at home or I was at a restaurant. Next, they recall the other people present—Elsie, Gran, and the kids. Finally, they zero in on their dinner plates and find the answer. Now, most people do not go around repeating, "Meatloaf, cabbage, meatloaf, cabbage," over and over, memorizing their dinners on the off chance that they will be held accountable. However, location has such a powerful influence on memory that once it is recalled, we are able to recall related information even though we did not deliberately try to remember it.

Classrooms and Long-Term Memory

In the classroom, we can capitalize on this by changing the location in which learning takes place (Jensen 1996). This might mean changing the seating arrangement, going to a different room, moving outside to sit under a tree, or going on an extended field trip.

We also can create a context for learning by engaging the other memory contexts—visual, auditory, tactile, and emotional. To do this, we might consider using masks and other props, performing role plays and dramatic presentations, telling stories, producing simulations, presenting analogies or metaphors, and manipulating concrete material, all of which tend to create a context for both learning and the formation of memories. By actively structuring multisensory experiences, we also can enhance learning in other ways. This is because these types of activities tend to alter learners' mental states by releasing endorphins that give rise to emotions such as joy, wonder, curiosity, and anticipation (Jensen 1996).

Barbara Given (2002) suggests that the brain uses five natural systems (Restak 1994) for attending and processing new information and skills.

- The emotional learning system (sense of cognitive and physical safety and well-being)
- The social learning system (sense of belonging and trust)
- The physical learning system (making sense through physical involvement)
- The cognitive learning system (engagement of the neocortex)
- The reflective learning system (metacognition and goal setting)

Given suggests that these are like theaters of the mind and the more "multiplex" the theaters are, the more senses that are tapping into the learning.

Because the connections between information stored in different parts of the brain are so comprehensive, we are able to process information very quickly; because each piece of information is connected with other pieces, we are able to make great leaps of insight and creativity. This leads us to the second capacity of long-term memory, its ability to retrieve and process information.

Information Retrieval and Processing

Another useful analogy to describe memory is an office that has an enormous filing system but only a very small desktop. Because the desk has limited space, we cannot have all the files out at one time. Therefore, we bring out the ones that we need to work with and leave the others in storage. When we have finished with one file, we put it back into storage to make room for another file to be brought to the desktop.

Although we may hold only seven pieces of information in short-term memory for a limited time, we can increase our memory's capacity by chunking the information into concepts. Short-term memory can hold seven facts or seven concepts. Seven concepts contain far more information than seven facts and, thus, we can increase the capacity of our working memory.

This discussion of memory systems may seem remote from the issue of student learning. However, if we are to proceed to higher-order thinking, such as comprehension, application, analysis, and synthesis, then our students need to be able to recall information and bring it on to their desktops before they can work with it. This is what learning is all about. It is a process whereby long-term memory is modified in some way. In other words, learning may be said to take place when new information is linked to existing or prior learning. If there are no links or hooks, no neural networks, to grab on to the information, it is lost and not learned. This is why the cramming of unrelated facts for an exam seldom has many long-term benefits. As soon as the exam is over, the information may be forgotten because it was not connected to prior learning in meaningful or useful ways.

Encoding Systems for Declarative Memories

People often use the term *memory* to describe or explain information they have stored over time. Neuroscientists refer to this as explicit or declarative memory. Declarative memories are formed in the hippocampus and then transferred to the temporal lobe of the cortex where they are stored for future use. When students answer questions or write exams, they are using declarative memory. Declarative memories come in a number of forms, all of which are encoded (i.e., processed and retrieved) in different ways. They include semantic or word-related memories and procedural or movement-related memories as well as episodic, automatic, and emotional memories (see also Sprenger 1999).

Semantic Memory

Semantic memory refers to the type of memorization associated with "book learning" or school learning. It is sometimes called *taxon* memory because it is used to recall lists, or taxonomies, of dates, names, places, and sundry other facts. It is word-related and tends to remember facts by seeking out associations, similarities, and differences among pieces of information and then chunking them together as groups of related ideas. It is the ability to associate or chunk ideas that allows us to recall facts more efficiently. Of all our information processing systems, the semantic memory is the least efficient and requires a high degree of intrinsic motivation. Despite this, it is the basis for many of the instructional strategies that schools favor most.

Episodic Memory

Episodic memory is sometimes called spatial or contextual memory because it is usually recalled by focusing on the context or event that caused the memory to be formed. Events that create a high emotional charge, such as the *Challenger* disaster or the events of September 11, 2001, are instantly and indelibly etched into our long-term memories by the release of a neurochemical marker that tells the brain, "This is important, remember it." Events that are less highly charged but perceived as novel, exciting, or pleasurable are marked in a similar manner and transferred to long-term memory with relatively small effort on the part of the learner. As in the example "What did you have for dinner?" we first recall the context: the location, the people, the smells and sounds. Once we recall the contextual information, the attached details are readily brought to mind. Episodic memory has a seemingly unlimited capacity and requires very little intrinsic motivation. However, instructional strategies that capitalize on this memory system, such as role plays, masks, and group investigations, are often regarded with skepticism by schools.

Procedural Memory

Procedural memory is associated with motor learning and is sometimes called muscle memory. Playing the piano, typing, and riding a bike are all skills in this category. The pathway to the formation of memories that allow us to perform complex physical skills involve the basal ganglia (which is located in the middle of the brain) and part of the cerebellum known as the motor strip.

The learning of physical skills involves the brain and the body in highly complex and integrated ways. This dual processing of information gives rise to extremely complex cognitive maps, which may be difficult to acquire, but once they are learned they are rarely forgotten. Learning situations that involve movement, such as conducting an experiment or building a model, require a greater variety of sensory input than do activities that involve only paper and pencil. As Robert Sylwester (2000) reminds us, we are a body/brain system:

> This suggests that it is also important to think beyond multiplicity in intelligence. Most body/brain systems are multiple. We obviously have multiple sensory/motor systems, and we now know that we have multiple emotional and attentional systems. We have known for some time that we have multiple memory and problem-solving systems. What we have is a multiple-everything bodybrain, and intelligence is only one part of the quite intricate equation. (p. 13)

Active learning situations are therefore remembered as being enjoyable and are recalled with a wealth of ancillary information attached to them. Procedural memory has an unlimited capacity and requires only moderate intrinsic motivation. Yet hands-on experiences are often regarded as frivolous and a waste of time unsuited to academic learning in many schools.

Automatic Memory

Automatic memory is a relatively recent discovery that is sometimes equated with conditioned response because a specific stimulus always triggers the same reaction. If you learned your multiplication tables in elementary school, you have already stored up a number of automatic memories. The equation 9×8 always triggers the same answer, 72. The alphabet, the rules of grammar, and the words of songs are all stored in automatic memory along with any other information that was learned through repetition or drill.

Automatic memory is often the key that opens up pathways to other types of memory. A song from our teenage years sometimes opens up episodic memories of summer days and the procedural memories of beach volleyball. The process then may lead to a list of names of all the players involved, which is stored in semantic memory.

The endless drilling of "facts and nothing but the facts" has gone out of fashion. However, certain pieces of factual information are crucial to all learning. For example, students who have not been drilled in number facts are always at risk in math. Students who cannot decode words are similarly hampered with regard to reading. Teachers must become more selective about the essential facts their students require and then, using rehearsal and repeated interaction with the information, ensure that these facts are acquired and understood.

Emotional Memory

Emotional memory is extremely powerful; it can override all other memories. Any experience with an emotional component, such as happiness, sadness, fear, or loathing, is processed by the amygdala, which is the emotional center of the brain. When an emotional memory is recalled, it may be strong enough to interfere with other memory systems, thereby causing the body to go into survival mode. This mode triggers the release of stress hormones and sundry other chemical messengers. In extreme cases, these may interrupt the brain's information processing system and render learning all but impossible.

Figure 1.7 lists some instructional processes that capitalize on the different ways in which the brain forms and encodes memories.

Instructional Processes Suited to Particular Memory Pathways

Semantic	Episodic	Procedural	Automatic	Emotional
• Graphic Organizers • 3 Step Interview • Jigsaw • I have . . . who has • Mnemonics • Acronyms • Acrostics • Raps, Songs	• Cooperative Groups • Role Plays • Props/Costumes • Bulletin Boards • Room Location • Case Studies • Simulations	• Practice • Rehearsal • Debate • Role Plays • Dance • Raps, Songs	• Word Association • Drill • Cues • Mnemonics • Poems, Rhymes	• Music • Personal Anecdotes • Experiences • Empathy Encouraged

Figure 1.7

The Brain Learns by Recognizing and Constructing Patterns

As we have seen, the brain can increase the capacity of its short-term memory by chunking facts and creating concepts. It does this by engaging its pattern-seeking abilities.

Caine and Caine (1994) noted that we make sense of the world around us by recognizing and constructing patterns. All new information is compared with these patterns to see if it matches with what the brain already knows. We are genetically programmed to seek patterns in the world around us—patterns in nature, patterns of behavior, patterns of speech, patterns in numbers and symbols. These patterns form the concepts, or mental maps, we use to organize and make sense of information in both formal and informal learning situations. The brain learns by constantly updating its mental maps. New information is integrated with previous learning to form larger and more complex mental maps. If the information doesn't make sense, it is discarded. If no previous map exists, then the information has no place to go and the brain goes about creating a brand new map.

This is similar to setting up a filing system to accommodate a new category of learning. Opening a new file or creating a new mental map is much more difficult than adding information to an existing file, which is why totally new concepts are usually hard to grasp at first. Part of the learning process, then, is about creating new maps.

Mental Maps

To visualize mental maps, picture a table on which a vast array of maps is displayed in an apparently random manner. Some maps are large and complex and others are small and simple. Some maps touch at the edges, others are in layers on top of one another. Now, imagine that the roads, rivers, and railway lines on these maps begin to grow and connect with similar features on other maps. This enables the maps to communicate with each other and share information. This networking of information is what complex learning is all about. The more complex the information on the map and the more profuse the connections to other maps, the more meaning we are able to derive from the learning.

In reality, a mental map is a network of neurons linked by synaptic connections. Each time we learn something, a series of new connections is made.

Once a connection has formed, it remains open for use as a conduit for long-term memory or other kinds of learning. Every time the connection is used, it becomes stronger, which makes it easier for neurotransmitters to bridge the synaptic gap and pass their message on to the next neuron in the chain. Rehearsal, repetition, and elaboration of new learning strengthen neural connections and thus make recall and further elaboration of learning easier.

Pattern Recognition and Probability

Another advantage of the brain's ability to recognize and construct patterns is that it allows us to make decisions quickly and flexibly on the basis of probability. This allows us to recognize a pattern, make rapid and efficient judgments, and come to an appropriate decision quickly, often before all the evidence is in. For example, the human face is a pattern. The ability to recognize faces is a survival behavior, which allows us to recognize friends and identify potential foes instantly. For most of us, this is a simple task and yet computers have a great deal of difficulty with it. Computers have individual processors that allow them to manipulate huge numbers in a fraction of a second; however, they have only recently begun to recognize faces, and some forms of disguise still confuse the average computer.

We have billions of processors and, although ours are slower and fuzzier than a computer's, the sheer number and complexity of our connections allow us to identify patterns very quickly. Computers have to work out every detail before making a decision; the brain does this based on previous experience and probability. As far as the brain is concerned, if someone looks like Aunt Gladys and walks like Aunt Gladys, it's probably Aunt Gladys. The brain jumps to this conclusion even when Aunt Gladys is wearing a Halloween costume and a false mustache. The computer, on the other hand, would focus on these details and would search its memory banks for information about people with mustaches and costumes. Not only would this take a long time, it is doubtful the computer would identify Aunt Gladys correctly.

Sometimes, the brain jumps to the wrong conclusion, but generally it does very well. For example, good readers do not sound out every word and examine every letter before deciphering a page of text. To do so would overload the working memory's capacity to handle information. When we read, our eyes scan up, down, and across the page looking for patterns in the form of context and syntax clues. These chunks of information are enough "probable cause" for the brain to make sense of the text. For example, the statement *The man ran his car into the garage* makes sense based on most readers' previous experience. However, the statement *The man ran his car into the garbage* is more unusual, and the reader might not grasp the accurate meaning at first. The brain then would scan the following lines of text and read *and it spilled all over the sidewalk.* Now, the reader detects an anomaly in the pattern of information and revises his or her previous conclusion.

There are a number of implications here for how we design curriculum and present information to our students. Schools are one of the few places where information is compartmentalized into subject disciplines. In the real world, most information comes at us as an integrated whole and we are able to deal with it. In schools, conventional wisdom dictates that we break learning into small, bite-sized pieces, or manageable chunks. This sounds plausible, but if we don't make explicit connections between these bite-sized pieces and expose students to the overall pattern, it should not surprise us when they "don't get it."

The mind is programmed for survival in a complex world where data are delivered as whole chunks of integrated information (Jensen 1996). In natural learning situations (as opposed to structured learning situations), the information is not broken down into specific bits, and yet we are able to cope with it. When schools oversimplify or apply a rigid structure to the teaching-learning process, they may inhibit the natural working of the mind and restrict the students' ability to learn (Jensen 1996).

Parallel Processing

The human brain is capable of handling enormous amounts of information simultaneously. This is called parallel processing. The ability of the brain to process information down multiple paths, using multiple modes simultaneously, is what gives us our enormous capacity for detecting patterns and forming mental maps. For example, sights, sounds, and smells may combine to provide information that is processed in various parts of the brain and then cross-referenced to see if it conforms to previously acquired patterns. Based on this information, the brain makes decisions about what action to take.

The linking and cross-referencing of information simultaneously along multiple pathways is what allows us to learn, gain understanding, and make decisions. On the other hand, processing information along one path at a time produces very few insights or moments of discovery when the person says "Aha."

To picture both linear and parallel processing, imagine a large multinational corporation with a worldwide network of interconnected businesses. The company has a chief executive officer (CEO) who is responsible for running the company and a team of advisers from each business unit who provide various kinds of information, such as financial, legal, geopolitical, security, and technological. The advisers report directly and individually to the CEO, who, based on their input, makes all executive decisions. This is an example of linear processing, an often slow and cumbersome process.

An alternative would be for the advisers to report to the CEO as a group, in a somewhat chaotic free-for-all, with no formal agenda, and with each adviser vying for the CEO's attention. The CEO receives, links, and cross-references the information, assigns meaning to it, and decides what to do with it.

This simultaneous, or parallel, processing of information is more aligned with how the brain operates. In real terms, much of the information that goes into making a decision is below the threshold of the conscious mind and thus we are unaware of it. However, once a decision is made, it quickly captures our attention.

Parallel processing may appear to be somewhat random and chaotic, but it is very fast—and it works. Parallel processing allows the brain to receive information, sort it, and make decisions quickly, thus enabling an individual to learn quickly and effectively.

Learning through parallel processing works very well, but it is somewhat "messy." The acquisition of knowledge and skill is different for all of us and is, for the most part, nonlinear and somewhat disorganized. Learning often is recursive, which means that we appear to be covering the same ground over and over as we grope our way toward understanding. One thing is certain. In the thinking-learning process, the journey from point A to point B is rarely a straight line, and each of us may take a different, winding path to get to a similar destination.

Complex Learning and the Brain

As teachers, we need to be aware that what appears logical and simple to us may make absolutely no sense to our students. This is especially true when we break the information into smaller pieces and then deliver the pieces in a logical progression. The students may not have the neural networks in place that allow them to make sense of the small, unconnected bits of information, and the progression may be logical only to the teacher. This is why activating prior learning at the start of any lesson is beneficial—it allows the teacher to find out what the students know, and it enables the students to bring information up to the level of conscious thought, or working memory.

The second part of any lesson should be devoted to "painting the picture on the box." The teacher does this by telling the students where the current lesson is going and how it is connected to previous lessons. Just as assembling a jigsaw puzzle is difficult when one doesn't have the picture on the box, learning is difficult when students have no idea how the pieces fit together.

We are genetically programmed to make sense of complex situations, because much of our learning is survival oriented. The real world is complex, and information comes at us in integrated chunks delivered at breakneck speed. To survive, we have to perceive patterns quickly, weigh them, take action, and store the information for future use. Fortunately, the evolutionary process has made us good at this type of learning.

First Language Acquisition

Acquisition of a first language is a prime example of the brain's ability to thrive and make sense in complex environments. Learning to speak is a survival skill, and young children genetically are predisposed to learn a language. In fact, huge numbers of brain cells are designated solely for this purpose. During the learning process, children are bombarded with a variety of sounds that are rich, random, and for the most part, unorganized. Some of these sounds are in the form of language, but if we listen to the ways in which most adults communicate with young children or the ways in which children communicate with each other, we may realize that this is hardly a structured learning situation. From this complex stew of input, children eventually establish patterns and make sense. Contrast this with the way in which many teachers "teach" a second language by breaking it into logically sequenced bits. This seems contrary to the way in which the brain learns best. Have you ever wondered why all but the most severely mentally handicapped can acquire a first language, but many of us have great difficulty learning a second language . . . in school?

Many teachers think that the most successful language teaching takes place in immersion programs in which students are bathed in the language for significant periods of time during the day. Through a process of unconscious and conscious learning, they begin to perceive the patterns and structures on which the language is based. They then form responses based on these patterns, and within a relatively short period of time, they are able to communicate in the new language.

The brain has an enormous appetite for information, but it also has difficulty with information that is delivered at the slow, measured pace of the classroom. Many people seem to learn best when they are immersed in highly complex activities. For example, many students seem to thrive on sports, drama, field trips, concerts, and other multisensory, real-life learning experiences. In these types of activities, the information is not prepackaged, linear, or sequential, and students do these activities with their friends, which provides a social context for learning that makes the events more pleasurable and thus more appealing to the brain.

Learning Is a Function of Experience

Traditional theories of intelligence are based on the assumption that the level of intelligence and, hence, of learning potential is fixed at birth and is, for the most part, incapable of being changed for the remainder of life. Work by Marian Diamond (1988) at Berkeley and Howard Gardner (1991) at Harvard refutes this notion. They claimed that if we know and understand how the brain learns, then we can assist learners to capitalize on their brains' capabilities.

It has been postulated that although the genetic blueprint for a human being contains billions of pieces of coded information, in terms of brain development, there is only enough information to lay down the "hardware" and the "operating system" and load up the "applications." The hardware is the brain. The operating system includes reflex behaviors that are "hard-wired" into the brain and allow the organism to get up and running. The applications are neural networks that give us the potential to learn, just as applications give the computer its potential to do a wide variety of tasks, such as word processing, number crunching, and graphic design.

According to some theorists, notably Edelman (1992), the brain has all its capabilities in place at birth. However, it is the activation of the neural networks by "experiencing" the outside world that results in the process we call learning. Imagine your parents have given you a computer that has been loaded with software programs for every use imaginable. There is a problem, however. They don't know which programs are in place. Neither do you, until you use them. It is possible, therefore, to have a superb graphics program loaded and ready to use but to be unaware of it. The software, therefore, lies dormant until it is activated. Similarly, a rich and varied set of experiences activates the neural networks and allows them to flourish; an impoverished set of experiences results in limited development.

Learning, therefore, results from the powerful interaction between the neural networks with which an individual is genetically endowed and the experiences to which the individual is exposed over the course of a lifetime (Sylwester 1995). One person may be genetically endowed with a superior piece of equipment, but his or her potential may be stunted by a paucity of experience; another person may be born with inferior equipment but overcome the disadvantage by being exposed to rich and varied experiences. For example, two people may work with the same word-processing program. One person may write the great American novel, while the other person might produce a laundry list.

Learning and the Growth of Dendrites

Diamond's work (1988) illustrates what happens when the brain is stimulated by a variety of experiences and a sensory-rich environment. Electrochemical processes release enzymes that initiate the construction of synaptic connections between the dendrites of one neuron and the axon terminals of another. Synapses are the connections that join individual neurons and make networks of neurons possible.

The development of synaptic connections shows a rapid growth between infancy and approximately age ten. After age ten, right up to old age, the brain has the ability to form new connections and "rewire" itself as a result of learning. It is the profusion and complexity of these connections that give the brain its capacity to recognize and construct patterns and perceive subtle differences.

To demonstrate the number of possible connections that a human brain can form, we could take ten items and combine them in every possible way. There are 3,628,800 possible connections. If we were to take eleven items, the number would jump to 39,916,800. If we were to take the brain's 100 billion neurons, each of which has 20,000 dendrites, and combined them in every possible way, we would have an astronomically high number, which indicates the complexity of our neural network systems.

The brain remains remarkably plastic, or modifiable, throughout life. It is capable of making new connections at almost any time from birth to death. Independent studies carried out by neuroscientists Marian Diamond (1988) and William Greenough (Greenough and Anderson 1991) show how an enriched environment and a variety of stimulating activities seem to be the key to this plasticity. Their experiments were conducted on rats, some of which were exposed to environments in which they were able to socialize with other rats and engage in exciting activities, such as wheels and mazes. The rats in the control group were isolated in cages and deprived of stimulation. While the control group showed little or no brain growth, the rats in the enriched environment had much denser brains. In fact, Greenough found that he could increase the number of brain connections by up to 25 percent by exposing the rats to highly stimulating environments.

Although Diamond and Greenough's work was conducted on rats in various combinations of enriched and impoverished learning environments, the same concept seems to apply to humans, as can be seen from the work of neuroscientist Bob Jacobs and his associates (Jacobs, Schall, and Scheibel 1993). In studying the brains of graduate students and high school dropouts obtained through autopsies, he found that the graduate students' brains had 40 percent more dendritic connections than those of the high school dropouts. He also compared the brains of graduate students who participated in highly engaging activities such as music, sports, and drama with those of their more sedentary counterparts. Like Diamond and Greenough's study of rats, he found that those who had engaged in stimulating activities had 25 percent more brain connections than nonparticipants.

Dendrite Growth and Enriched Learning Environments

For those teachers and parents who crave a return to the "good old days" when children sat in straight rows and recited, copied, rote-learned, and regurgitated the information to the teacher at exam time, consider this: Jane Healy (1990) stated that the minds today's children bring to school are different from those of forty years ago. The difference is accounted for by the variety of real-life experiences that children bring with them to school. In many cases, students of the 1940s and

1950s tended to be more actively engaged with the community, its workings, and its infrastructures. Many children played and learned in the streets, woods, and fields without the looming, albeit well-meaning, presence of adults and coaches. Their experiences were real, varied, and enormously engaging.

These hands-on, or concrete, experiences with the real world prepared the brain for learning. What may have seemed to be unstructured play had a very serious purpose. It allowed students to discover the underlying rules and patterns that organize and make sense of the world. This kind of informal, discovery approach to learning equipped students to deal with the abstract world of the school curriculum. In effect, it may have set up a filing system for the storage and retrieval of information.

By contrast, many of today's students are starved for real-life experiences. For approximately six hours a day, five days a week, they function in the abstract, symbolic environment of the classroom, where experiences are often far removed from the real world. Then, they may spend an additional two to four hours glued to the television screen at home.

Television and Dendrite Growth

Television is a poor replacement for real hands-on experience and, in fact, may be contrary to the ways in which the brain is genetically disposed to learn. When children watch TV prior to age six, they are doing the opposite of what their brains are required by nature to be doing—that is, become actively engaged with the real world in a hands-on, interactive way. For most children, this problem is compounded by their lack of experience and knowledge to interpret what they see on the screen.

This can be compared to presenting a postgraduate-level video on quantum physics to a room full of adults, all of whom have different backgrounds and levels of education. Each person will derive meaning from the information based on prior experience and patterns of learning. But if there is no prior experience with which to interpret the program, the information has no place to go. The brain then has to learn a new vocabulary and set up a filing system for the new information. The more practice one has with a wide variety of learning experiences, the easier this becomes because there are more neural pathways available to begin constructing the new file. Learners with a wide range of experiences often have better problem-solving skills because they have more ways of recalling and connecting information to use in their search for solutions. In other words, they have learned how to learn.

For those without a wide range of experiences, the process of learning something new is hard work. The brain seems to learn best when it is allowed to use its potential for parallel processing. This means that information is taken in by all the senses simultaneously and processed by the brain to arrive at the most plausible meaning. Parallel processing tends to extend and strengthen neural networks, because each sensory input codes and stores information in different ways and in different parts of the brain. When these pieces of information communicate with each other, we experience a kind of synergy that amplifies our understanding.

Television, unlike interactive, concrete learning, provides input through only two senses—vision and hearing. This kind of information is processed in the posterior regions of the brain and may remain unconnected to other neural networks. In terms of brain development, the phrase "use it or lose it" is very applicable, and neural networks that are not used tend to shrivel up through a process called pruning. Thus, it appears that television may, in fact, stunt the neural basis for learning, especially in young children (Burns 1991). The passive reception of information, without discernment or thinking, requires no particular response and seriously undermines the ability to learn about and interact with the environment.

In comparison, television programs that provide interaction and encourage responses from young viewers promote thinking because responding to questions and paraphrasing the performers' comments require a certain level of comprehension. For example, the success of Fred Rogers (in *Mr. Rogers' Neighborhood*) most likely is because he elicited a response from his viewers: "Boys and girls, can you say the word accelerated particle? Ah, knew that you could."

When we combine the abstract, symbolic programs of many schools with the passive consumption of television in the home, we are creating an environment that is incompatible with how the brain learns best. In effect, a child's whole day may be lacking in the concrete experiences needed to provide hooks and connections for higher-order thinking and abstract learning. In teaching, we need to explore concrete examples before moving to abstract learning.

Growing Dendrites

The need for concrete examples is the reason a field trip to the Pioneer Museum might be useful before starting a teaching unit on pioneers. In this way, the students actually see, touch, and experience butter churns, apple peelers, and root cellars before dealing with them as abstractions in class. Similarly, in science, we might proceed from the concrete to the abstract by allowing the students to perform an experiment before discussing the related concepts. Talking about sublimation, precipitation, solids, and gases makes much more sense if the students have actually experienced the process and made their own observations. Hands-on, active learning facilitates the formation of neural connections much more readily than learning concepts from a purely abstract viewpoint. If the teacher actively conducts the experiment while the students passively watch, whose neural networks are getting a workout?

IN CLOSING

During recent years, many people have been reconceptualizing their understanding of the brain and how it engages in the process of learning. Recent interpretations suggest that the brain may be more like a jungle than a computer, or it may be like both. The brain is infinitely complex, somewhat disorganized, and definitely nonlinear. The whole-brain approach to learning is beginning to replace the older compartmentalized models in which certain functions were isolated in specific parts of the brain. Many people now believe that all parts of the brain are highly interconnected and involved in the process of learning.

As teachers, it is useful to understand the emotional component of all learning and the part it plays in creating classroom climates that support learning. We also need to be aware of the ways in which emotions focus our attention and the role they play in the formation, retention, and retrieval of memories.

The rich interconnection of our neural networks gives the brain its powers to recognize and construct patterns. Anything that we can do as teachers to promote this pattern-seeking ability constitutes a brain-compatible strategy. These strategies include making explicit connections between concepts or, better still, providing opportunities for the students to make their own connections by engaging in discussions and activities that promote concept formation and comprehension.

All learning is survival oriented. The brain attempts to make sense of the world by attaching meaning to whatever it encounters. At birth, the neural networks that give us the potential to survive as well as to perform complex tasks are already in place, but they seem to be activated only when we are exposed to experiences that bring them into play. Schools, therefore, need to provide a rich variety of experiences that activate students' brains. This is compatible with the brain's genetic disposition to thrive on complexity and to use a multisensory or parallel processing approach to derive meaning from complex situations. Therefore, the most favorable learning activities to activate neural networks are those that are complex, engage a variety of the senses, and are perceived by the learner as being novel, emotionally engaging, relevant, and useful.

Reflections

Take time alone or with a study group to consider the "Brain Bits" and discuss or write down ideas on supporting or implementing them into your classroom or school.

7 Brain Bits   **So in my classroom/school . . .**

Students need a safe environment

Relaxed alertness is a preferred state
- "High challenge and low threat"

Emotions have an impact on learning

Social relationships are important

The brain seeks patterns,
meaning, and relevance

Active learning and enriched environments
grow dendrites

We have many memory pathways

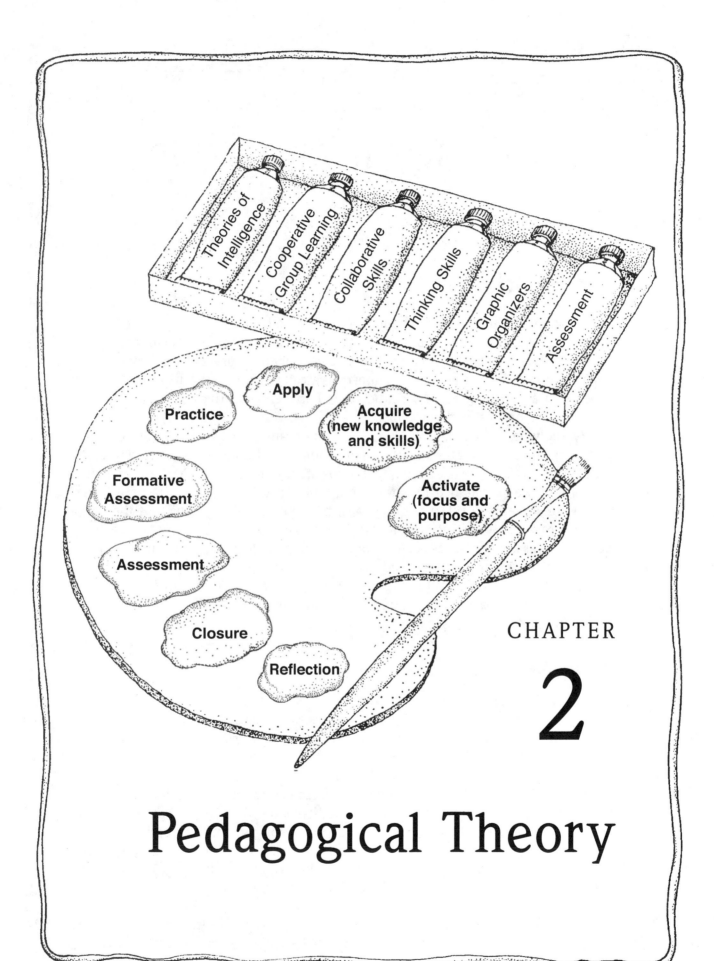

CHAPTER

2

Pedagogical Theory

CHAPTER 2

PEDAGOGICAL THEORY

WHAT IS IT?

During the past three decades, neuroscientists have begun to unravel the mysteries of how the brain captures, manipulates, stores, and retrieves information in the process we call learning. In response to this, cognitive psychologists working in partnership with teachers have begun to critically examine the teaching-learning process in an attempt to find connections between cognitive research and what actually goes on in the classroom.

By applying what is known about how the brain learns to classroom practice, pedagogical researchers and other educational professionals have identified a number of powerful instructional techniques that enhance learning, can be generalized across all areas of the curriculum, and can be applied at all grade levels. These are sometimes referred to as "best practices," which means that they have a sound research base and a proven track record in the classroom. Among these best practices are strategies such as cooperative group learning, concept formation, the direct teaching of critical and creative thinking, and graphic organizers. Jay McTighe (1990) has compiled these findings in *Better Thinking and Learning* for the Maryland Department of Education. Following are discussions of the most promising of these strategies.

Classroom Climate to Support Thinking

> **Finding:** *Teachers who establish classrooms characterized by an open, democratic climate promote learning because such a classroom climate correlates significantly with the development of critical and creative thinking abilities* (as cited in McTighe 1990, p. 6).

Classrooms that promote thinking are perceived to be safe, varied, and stimulating places, where a balance is maintained between the rights of all students to receive an education and the rights of individuals for personal expression. A learning environment should afford students opportunities to think creatively and critically, to deal with ambiguity and diverse opinions, and to develop interpersonal relationships that support and challenge their learning.

Both research and common sense lead us to believe that we learn best when the process is perceived as enjoyable. A well-constructed learning environment incorporates instructional practices based on cognitive psychology and pedagogical research to create an atmosphere of relaxed alertness where students are ready and eager to learn. A poorly constructed learning environment, on the other hand, may create tension and stress that prevent students from learning.

Activating Prior Knowledge

Finding: *Teachers who activate relevant prior knowledge promote learning by enhancing comprehension of text, especially when information in the text is compatible with prior knowledge* (as cited in McTighe 1990, 1).

Activating prior knowledge means calling to mind information that already is known about a topic before proceeding to new information. As early as 1938, educator John Dewey proposed that true learning develops from within as students connect what they already know to the new material to be learned.

Present-day researchers, such as Resnick (1987), also support the notion that learning occurs when students actively engage in experiences that connect their present knowledge with the structures needed for future learning. For this to happen, students often need to be prompted to bring information stored in long-term memory into short-term, or working, memory, where information is elaborated and connected to prior learning. Once the new learning has been elaborated and integrated, it is returned to long-term memory and stored for future use.

Two difficulties may arise: Students may be unaware of what they already know about a topic, or they may think they know more than they actually do, especially when their knowledge is based on a faulty premise or outdated information. Therefore, it helps to check the students' level and extent of prior knowledge before introducing new concepts, because what the students already know about a subject influences their ability to integrate new information and construct new and deeper meaning.

Advance Organizers

Finding: *Teachers who introduce new materials to students through the use of advance organizers promote learning because advance organizers help students to organize, integrate, and retain materials to be learned* (as cited in McTighe 1990, 3).

Advance organizers help students understand the general patterns or organization of information and assimilate the new material. They also provide a bridge from previous learning and context for new information. As an example of an advance organizer, newcomers to a town might understand its layout better if they first looked at the town from the top of a high building. From this vantage point, they would be able to see the overall pattern of how the streets and buildings relate to each other. Another example of an advance organizer is the picture on the cover of a jigsaw puzzle box. It provides a visual overview that aids the person assembling the puzzle to identify where each puzzle piece belongs.

In the instructional process, advance organizers are short sets of visual or verbal information that provide a conceptual, or organizing, framework prior to engaging with specific detail. The power of advance organizers as instructional strategies may be deduced from a meta-analysis of 112 studies conducted by researcher C. L. Stone (1983) that showed a high correlation between the use of advance organizers and increased learning and retention of material.

Cooperative Group Learning

Finding: *Teachers who employ cooperative learning methods promote learning because these collaborative experiences engage students in an interactive approach to processing information, resulting in greater retention of subject matter, improved attitudes toward learning, and enhanced interpersonal relations among group members* (as cited in McTighe 1990, 11).

Cooperative group learning is typified by heterogeneous groups of students working together for extended periods of time. Its basic premise is that students work together for the benefit of all as opposed to competing for the best individual score.

Research has shown that students in cooperative groups attain higher levels of achievement in all areas, but especially in the realms of higher-order processing of information, problem solving, and collaborative skills. This is particularly true for students at lower levels of ability. Students of higher ability typically improve their performance or at least do no worse than if they were working as individuals (Johnson, Johnson, and Holubec 1984; Lou et al. 1996).

Another advantage of working in cooperative groups is that students are more likely to accomplish goals and complete tasks that would prove difficult if they were working individually. Benefits also accrue in the areas of self-esteem, attitude toward school, interpersonal skills, and increased tolerance for the differences of others (Slavin 1981).

In recent years, many school districts have recognized the need for students to be able to think, solve problems, and work collaboratively and thus have placed a high priority on these skills in terms of exit outcomes or expectations. For this reason, cooperative group learning is one of the most important strategies in a teacher's repertoire, because once it is mastered, it opens the door to numerous other strategies that fall under the general heading of brain-compatible learning. Instruction in areas such as graphic organizers, inductive thinking, and collaborative skills is enhanced when students are allowed to exchange information and discuss ideas in cooperative learning groups.

Direct Teaching of Thinking

Finding: *Teachers who teach thinking skills and processes directly promote learning because such explicit instruction helps students to better understand and more effectively apply the types of thinking required by the curriculum* (as cited in McTighe 1990, 21).

To be effective, thinking skills should be taught explicitly, and the act of thinking should pervade the whole curriculum. Students of all ages and in all areas of the curriculum should receive direct instruction in creative thinking, critical thinking, and problem solving. Although most schools espouse the notion that thinking is important, it often receives only token coverage. All too often, thinking is delivered in one of two ways: as a separate program, usually attached to some type of "thinking workbook," or by being embedded in a commercially prepared or school district-developed curriculum. Neither of these approaches is particularly successful because thinking remains divorced from the rest of the curriculum and, for all intents and purposes, becomes an extracurricular activity. When thinking is reduced to a number of small discrete skills that are drilled and practiced out of context, the chance of their being transferred and applied to other situations is severely limited (Perkins and Salomon 1988).

If we wish to teach thinking successfully, it must become an integral part of instruction in all subject areas. Skills first should be taught explicitly and then applied to a particular problem or context that pertains to the subject. In addition, students should be made aware of the connections, adaptations, and possible uses of the skill in other subject areas and/or wider contexts.

Higher-Order Questioning

Finding: *Teachers who ask "higher order" questions promote learning because these types of questions require students to apply, analyze, synthesize, and evaluate information instead of simply recalling facts* (as cited in McTighe 1990, 38).

Higher-order questions are those that require students to think beyond mere recall of facts. A meta-analysis of eighteen experiments by Redfield and Rousseau (1981) concluded that when teachers use higher-order questions in the instructional phase of a lesson, there are positive gains on tests of recall and the application of thinking skills.

Andre (1979) reviewed research into the effects of higher-order questions inserted every few paragraphs in a text. At the end of these paragraphs, students were given an opportunity to work with the questions as a way of deepening their understanding of the content. He concluded that such procedures facilitate learning more effectively than fact-based questions.

Despite the demonstrated effectiveness of higher-order questioning, the majority of classroom questions are at the factual, recall level of Bloom's taxonomy of thinking skills (see chapter 7). Several researchers have reported the low frequency of classroom questions that require higher-level thinking such as analysis, synthesis, and evaluation. John Goodlad (1984) reported that only 1 percent of classroom discussions invited students to express their own opinions and reasoning.

Creative Problem Solving

Finding: *Teachers who teach creative problem-solving strategies improve learning by providing students with general purpose problem-solving tools appropriate for a variety of situations* (as cited in McTighe 1990, 15).

Many school districts in the United States and Canada have ranked the abilities to think creatively and solve problems as two of the most important exit outcomes or expectations for their students. Although people tend to agree that problem solving is a desirable skill, there is very little agreement about the best way to teach it. In fact, there is no best way, although some generalizations can be made about the characteristics of effective problem solvers. Among these is a willingness on the part of the person to suspend judgment and to avoid premature rejection of a potential solution. However, the tendency to stay with a potential solution should be balanced by the willingness to abandon unpromising methods and try new approaches.

Concept Development

Finding: *Teachers who teach concepts inductively through the use of examples and non-examples promote learning because this strategy actively involves students in constructing a personal understanding of a new concept* (as cited in McTighe 1990, 8).

Inductive reasoning involves the examination and piecing together of separate facts or cases to form a generalization. For instance, we might examine the general attributes of heroic figures in history. Next, we might take these and refine them into a list of critical attributes, from which we could then make a generalization of the concept hero.

Chunking facts, by linking them together to form generalizations or concepts, is a very efficient way to process information. It allows us to sort related ideas into files in much the same way as a librarian sorts books into categories such as mystery, romance, science fiction, and biography. In this way, if we want a particular book, we narrow the search by going to the shelf where all the books in that category are stored as opposed to scanning every book in the building.

Fortunately, we are genetically equipped to perform the function of forming concepts. The human brain continually looks for patterns and connections as it seeks to derive meaning and understanding from previously unconnected pieces of knowledge. We often construct these generalizations or concepts by a process of self-talk as we reflect on new experiences and reconcile them with what we already know. However, the understanding of concepts can be greatly enhanced through discussion. Students need to be given multiple opportunities to discuss, elaborate, and extend ideas with others. Good thinkers have always sought opportunities to put their heads together and discuss their ideas with others, in a process that some educators describe as "rubbing and polishing their brains."

Metacognition

> **Finding:** *Teachers who help students develop and internalize metacognitive strategies through direct instruction, modeling and practice promote learning because the effective use of such strategies is one of the primary differences between more and less able learners* (as cited in McTighe 1990, 48).

Metacognition refers to an awareness and control over one's own thinking processes. Effective thinkers constantly monitor their own thinking, frequently checking, reassessing, and setting goals. For example, good readers often check their understanding of a page of text by rereading it. Effective thinkers also engage in metacognition to know how and when to apply a variety of problem-solving strategies.

However, research shows that while students may be aware of certain metacognitive strategies, they may not understand when or how to use them. Art Costa (1995) commented on research done by Sternberg and Wagner with the following observation:

> We often find students following instructions or performing tasks without wondering why they are doing what they are doing. They seldom question themselves about their own learning strategies or evaluate the efficiency of their performance, some children virtually have no idea what to do when they confront a problem and are unable to explain their strategies for decision making. There is evidence, however, to demonstrate that those who perform well on complex cognitive tasks, who are flexible and persevering in problem solving, who consciously apply their intellectual skills, are those who possess well developed metacognitive abilities. (p. 75)

Graphic Organizers

Finding: *Teachers who utilize graphic organizers with their students promote learning because knowledge that is organized into holistic conceptual frameworks is more easily remembered and understood than unstructured bits of information* (as cited in McTighe 1990, 33).

Graphic organizers are visual representations that provide a means to organize and present information in an accessible way. Graphic organizers come in many forms; some are familiar to most people, such as flowcharts, wiring diagrams, and genealogical tables. Graphic organizers help learners to represent abstract concepts and ideas in a concrete form. They display the relationships among pieces of information, connect new learning to prior learning, and generally organize information into a more usable form.

WHY DO WE NEED IT?

The research on how the brain learns challenges many previous assumptions about education, and in recent years educators and cognitive researchers have begun to apply this knowledge to instructional practices.

As an example, we know that the emotional brain regulates our emotions. It also influences how the brain classifies and selects information to be stored in long-term memory (Thayer 1989). The emotions, therefore, play a critical role in the formation, retention, and recall of memories. In general terms, the greater the emotional impact, the greater the chance that the information will be recalled.

If we apply the research on emotion and memory to the classroom, it validates instructional strategies such as role plays and simulations. Both strategies provide an emotional context for learning and form a link between the information to be learned and the real-life context in which it will be recalled. Because role plays and simulations are acted out in visual, spatial, linguistic, and bodily terms, they not only tap into our emotions but often provide insights and understanding at much deeper levels than if the same information were transmitted by means of a lecture.

The findings from cognitive research challenge teachers to look beyond the traditional repertoire of instructional skills and try new and different techniques. In addition, the exit outcomes or expectations set by many school districts reveal the need for an expanded repertoire of instructional skills. These exit outcomes require students to think creatively, to understand and apply their knowledge, and to work collaboratively with their peers.

Many of these expectations are not well served by traditional classroom practice. If students are to think, they must first be taught the skills of thinking and then be placed in situations that cause them to apply their skills. If students are expected to work collaboratively, they need to be taught the skills of collaboration and then be provided opportunities to practice these skills by working on meaningful tasks in cooperative groups.

The findings in this chapter relate to a number of strategies that come under the general rubric of best practices. We now move on to some generalizations about how they should be implemented. More detailed information, with further examples, is provided in the specific chapters on thinking skills, graphic organizers, cooperative group learning, and collaborative skills.

HOW DO WE DO IT?

In writing this book, we have taken into account the work of numerous educators and researchers and culled practices that can be described as best practices for use in brain-compatible classrooms. Some are covered in more detail in later chapters. This chapter contains a digest of the major instructional strategies that should be in all teachers' repertoires. To be effective, these strategies should be implemented at a level where they can be applied at the right time and place, with wisdom and a degree of flexibility. This level is called mastery, or executive control (Joyce and Showers 1988).

To attain this level of mastery, teachers may wish to consider working with a learning partner who teaches in the same subject area or grade level. The statistics on the rate of transfer from theory into classroom practice when a learning partner is employed are very impressive. Joyce and Showers (1988) found that when teachers study the theory of an innovation, the chances of that innovation's being transferred into practice are not promising—about 3 to 5 percent in most cases. When teachers received a demonstration of the skill combined with practice and feedback on their performance, the rate of transfer increased to 5 to 10 percent. However, when the teachers took part in training with one or more partners and they were encouraged to help each other throughout the implementation process, the rate of transfer jumped to 90 percent. Although transfer of an innovation does not take place as a result of theory alone, implementation is enhanced when teachers understand the research behind the strategy and are able to explain the rationale for its use. When the theory is thoroughly understood, implementation proceeds with fewer problems, and attempts to adapt or modify the innovation are more likely to conform to the overall design as seen by the strategy's developers. Poor understanding, on the other hand, often leads to adaptations that are well outside the developers' specifications.

The ability to explain the rationale for an innovation with clarity and precision is an indicator of understanding. When teachers are able to explain a new strategy to students, parents, and the public at large, they tend to reinforce their own credibility and that of the innovation.

Creating Classroom Climates That Support Thinking

In order to create climates conducive to learning, teachers need to pay attention to how they establish agreements about behavior, how they interact with students, and how they set up the procedures that govern the day-to-day operation of the classroom. Author Jeanne Gibbs developed numerous strategies for establishing a positive classroom climate, building community spirit, and giving all students a sense of belonging. In her book *Tribes* (Gibbs 1995), she outlined norms such as attentive listening, appreciation, no put-downs, the right to pass, and mutual respect. The students are introduced to each of these skills and encouraged to develop a working definition of them. When they understand what a specific skill looks like and sounds like, they are encouraged to practice it until it becomes a part of their normal classroom behavior.

The teacher's behavior in the classroom is an important factor in creating a climate conducive to thinking, especially in the ways the teacher asks questions, responds to answers, and provides feedback. Educator and researcher Mary Budd Rowe (1987) reported that the time between a teacher's asking a question and then calling on a student for a response can often be measured in tenths of a second. It is obvious that more time is needed for a student to process the question and formulate a response.

A cooperative group strategy, called "think-pair-share," is useful for providing students both the necessary time and a process to extend thinking and formulate an answer. First, students are invited to think individually, then they pair with a partner and discuss their thoughts, and finally they share their findings with the rest of the group. This not only affords more time for thinking but also gives the students a chance to verbalize their thoughts and rehearse their answers with another person prior to sharing with a large group, thereby avoiding the downshifting phenomenon.

Activating Prior Knowledge

The logical place to activate prior knowledge is at the first part of any lesson, although activating prior knowledge may be used whenever a new topic or concept is introduced. The strategy may also be used to enhance comprehension prior to engaging with any topic. For example, the students in a math class might recall a variety of problem-solving strategies before selecting the most suitable strategy for the task at hand. In science, they might recall what they know about animals in general before studying the characteristics of a particular type of animal, such as mammals. In language arts or literature, they might recall movies or plays they have seen as a precursor to studying character and plot in dramatic presentations.

Students also may use graphic organizers, such as Venn diagrams and sequence charts, and advance organizers, such as graphs or video segments, in addition to general discussion and questioning to bring to mind relevant information. Another advantage of activating prior knowledge is that by assessing what students already know, teachers are able to modify or quickly adjust what they need to teach.

Using Advance Organizers

Advance organizers may be used at any point during a lesson when a new topic is introduced; however, they usually are used at the beginning of a lesson as a way of activating prior learning. They also may be used to set the context and expectations in the second phase of a lesson. For example, watching a video segment followed by a discussion about war and its effects on society may be a valuable precursor to a lesson on World War II. Videos, stories, maps, word webs, diagrams, and other graphic organizers all can be used to establish a context and allow students to gain insight into the objectives or expectations of a lesson.

Implementing Cooperative Group Learning

There are a number of approaches to cooperative group learning. We suggest teachers implement the conceptual approach developed by Johnson et al. (1984) and then supplement it with structures developed by Spencer Kagan (1990). The Johnson model is based on five elements that tend to increase the chances for successful implementation: positive interdependence, individual accountability, group processing, social skills, and face-to-face interaction. The Kagan structures include roundtable round robin, numbered heads together, and talking chips, each of which is described in detail in chapter 5, Cooperative Group Learning.

The teacher's role in cooperative group learning is to ensure that the students have a clear understanding of the elements and structures of cooperative group learning and then to redesign the classroom in such a way as to allow all the elements to be implemented successfully. This may entail moving the furniture, assigning students to groups, and relocating from the front of the room to a variety of other locations. In cooperative learning classrooms, the teacher moves from the traditional role of a dispenser of learning to the role of a resource provider who encourages students to learn for themselves. This shift is sometimes described as moving from "the sage on the stage to the guide on the side."

Direct Teaching of Thinking

Thinking requires more than incidental coverage in the classroom. Exposure to higher-order questions and problems alone is not enough. Students also need to learn about the basic structures of questions and ideas in order to acquire the understanding and necessary skills to deal with them. To be successful, the skills of thinking should be taught explicitly within the context of each subject area.

One of the traps to avoid is the "workbook" approach to skill development in which skills are broken down into small bits, then drilled and practiced out of context. Nor is thinking served well by programs that exclusively employ worksheets, end-of-chapter questions, or assorted brain teasers as an adjunct to teaching.

One of the keys to teaching thinking skills is to provide a context in which to apply the skills. Isolating thinking from its context is similar to teaching dribbling, shooting, and passing in basketball without giving the students a chance to practice their skills in a game situation. In other words, if one isn't going to use something, why learn it? As soon as the skill has been learned, it should be applied to a context and the students should be given a chance to practice it in some kind of meaningful and creative way. If thinking skills are to be generalized and transferred to a wider context, then the metacognitive discussion should center on questions such as how the skill might be used, modified, or adapted for transfer to other situations.

The direct teaching of thinking can be enhanced in a number of ways. Usually, higher-order thinking is facilitated when students work in small groups, where the risk-free environment encourages the interchange of ideas necessary for complete understanding. Graphic organizers are also helpful because they provide students with strategies to organize information and derive meaning from it. Therefore, if students are to apply thinking skills flexibly and appropriately in a variety of situations, the skills should be taught using the following process:

- Direct instruction and modeling of the skill
- Guided practice with immediate feedback
- Frequent checks for understanding
- Independent practice in a subject-specific context
- Metacognition, transfer, and generalization of the skill to wider contexts

Using Higher-Order Questioning

The purpose of higher-order questions is to extend the range of students' thinking. To facilitate this process, students not only need to be exposed to higher-order questions but also need to be taught to recognize the type of thinking required by a particular question. The ability to recognize levels of thinking increases the chance that students will be able to formulate appropriate responses.

The ability to ask good questions is another key to learning. This is where the ability to recognize different levels of thinking assumes even greater importance, for good questions, presumably, will be constructed around high levels of thinking. It appears, then, that students should be encouraged to formulate higher-order questions as well as to answer them, and as in all brain-compatible learning situations, this is facilitated by opportunities for guided practice and metacognition.

Promoting Creative Problem Solving

Good problem solvers have a number of characteristics in common. Among these are flexible thinking, perseverance, precision, and the ability to continually monitor one's own performance. Problem-solving skills will only develop with exposure to a variety of problem-solving situations combined with opportunities for guided practice over time. The first role of the teacher is to develop a classroom climate that supports open-mindedness and the willingness to take risks and experiment with new ideas. The second role is to build a variety of problem-solving situations into the curriculum. The third is to teach the students explicit information-processing strategies, such as graphic organizers, concept formation, and concept attainment.

Problem solving also requires fluency, flexibility, and the ability to generate multiple solutions. Teaching creative thinking strategies such as SCAMPER (Eberle 1982), Synectics (Gordon 1961), and brainstorming promotes the development of these skills. (These strategies are discussed in depth in chapter 7, Thinking Skills.) Finally, the students should be encouraged to engage in metacognitive reflection as a way of consolidating and transferring knowledge and skills.

Advancing Concept Development

The ability to classify, sort, and categorize information into concepts is one of the primary methods by which people make sense of the world. Two very powerful inductive strategies for engaging students with concepts are concept attainment (Bruner, Goodnow, and Austin 1967) and concept formation (Taba 1967). Concept attainment and concept formation are both inductive thinking strategies in which students organize information and construct meaning for themselves by examining particular instances or cases and then developing a generalization or concept that fits the facts.

In the concept attainment strategy, students are presented with a series of examples of a particular concept, some of which have the necessary characteristics attributed to the concept. These are called "Yes" examples. They are contrasted with examples that do not have the necessary characteristics; these are called "No" examples. The students arrive at an understanding of the concept by differentiating between the Yes and No examples.

In the concept formation strategy, students are given a set of data in the form of facts or cases. They then work in small groups to sort and classify the information into groups or categories. Once the information is sorted, they draw inferences, make a generalization, and develop concepts from it.

It is possible to engage in either of these strategies as an individual. However, they are much more powerful when the students discuss and exchange ideas in small groups as they recognize and isolate attributes, make connections between the facts, and construct meaning from the data.

Teaching Metacognition

Metacognitive strategies provide students with the tools to monitor their performance before, during, and after a learning activity. In effect, metacognition is a form of self-regulation or feedback. Feedback is an essential element in all learning because it helps us assess our performance and it reveals what we need to do to improve.

Teachers are usually the persons most likely to assess student performance. However, many teachers are unable to assess as effectively as they would like. In a class of thirty students, it is difficult to gather frequent assessment data and provide frequent feedback, to say the least. Students, therefore, must be encouraged to provide their own assessment data through metacognition.

Providing feedback or assessment data can take many forms, from general-purpose questions such as *Why am I doing this?* to specific questions for problem solving such as *What is the nature of this problem?* and *What are the criteria for a successful solution?*

Other methods of self-assessment include journal writing, rubrics, self-assessment checklists, and strategies such as the PMI (covered in chapter 7, Thinking Skills). The teacher's role is to teach the metacognitive strategies explicitly and then to allow time during the lesson for the students to reflect on their performances as a means to improvement.

The importance of metacognition cannot be overstressed. If students do not reflect on their use of a skill, few gains are made. Teachers who help students to acquire the skills and an understanding of how and when to use them enable their students to build a strong foundation for growth as thinkers.

Using Graphic Organizers

Graphic organizers are metacognition in a visible form. They allow students to organize information either into more usable forms or as a way of deriving meaning or making sense of it. Graphic organizers also enhance the direct teaching of thinking because they provide frameworks, or templates, that help students to process and organize information. When graphic organizers are used in conjunction with cooperative group learning, their power is enhanced because of the synergy created when students bounce ideas off each other, piggyback on others' ideas, and receive immediate feedback on their own solutions.

Classroom Strategies That Work

McREL documented overwhelming research on the instructional strategies that increase student achievement (Marzano et al. 2001). Nine instructional techniques from their research are described here.

1. **Comparing, contrasting, classifying, analogies, and metaphor**
   Teachers can facilitate the examination of information for similarities and differences between and among things or ideas. The ability to classify in groups based on like attributes or the same theme or patterns can be explicitly demonstrated, supported, and encouraged. Venn diagrams, cross-classification charts, synectics, and metaphors are helpful for students to connect new learning and ideas to past learning.

2. **Summarizing and note taking**
   The ability to summarize, delete, distill, and analyze information in order to be able to select what is important or relevant for learning is a skill all learners need. Strategies include a variety of summary frames that help students accomplish this task.

3. **Reinforcing effort and providing recognition**
   Students are often unaware of the importance of effort in achieving success. Teachers can facilitate this awareness by using strategies such as recognition, rewards and praise, and metacognition as ways of demonstrating to students how extra effort can lead to achieving growth.

4. **Assigning homework and practice**
   Homework should be different from what students do in the classroom, not "just more of the same." Parents shouldn't be involved other than providing a place for homework and supporting the process. The purpose for homework, as well as the policies, outcomes, and feedback, should be clear to all who are involved. Homework should serve as further rehearsal as well as assessment data for teachers relating to knowledge or skills.

5. **Generating nonlinguistic representations**
   A variety of methods, such as graphics, models, mental pictures, drawing, and movement, should be used to elaborate and rehearse new learning.

6. **Using cooperative learning**
   One of the most effective and well-documented instructional strategies is the formation of heterogeneous groups to accomplish academic tasks. This strategy uses higher-order thinking skills as well as focusing on the development of social skills.

7. **Setting objectives and providing feedback**
   Clear instructional goals help students focus when the goals are stated in general terms and personalized by the individual learner. Continuous feedback from the student, teachers, and peers is important.

8. **Generating and testing hypotheses**
   This can be done through the inductive or deductive process. Students should be able to articulate their hypothesis and, ultimately, the conclusions that they draw.

9. **Providing questions, cues, and advance organizers**
   They help students open "mental files" to access prior knowledge before new learning takes place. This helps in pre-assessing the knowledge and skills (related to standards) that a student possesses and gives a context for the learning experience to come.

Figure 2.1 (page 48) relates the general strategies from the McREL (2000) study to brain research and to specific tactics for the classroom.

In the left-hand column is the McREL/Marzano study; next is the percentile gain attributed to its use. A percentile gain shows what a particular student would gain from using the strategy. For example, imagine a student is at the 50th percentile, precisely in the middle of achievement in a group of 100 students. If we find in the study that cooperative group learning will result in a percentile gain of 27, a student at the 50th percentile may improve to the 77th percentile.

Best Practices, Brain Research, and Classroom Tactics

Strategy	Percentile Gain	How the Brain Works	Strategies
Comparing, contrasting, classifying, analogies, and metaphors	45	The brain seeks patterns, connections, and relationships between and among prior and new learning.	• Classifying • Compare, contrast • Venn diagrams • Synectics • Concept attainment • Concept formation
Summarizing and note taking	34	The brain pays attention to meaningful information and deletes that which is not relevant.	• Mind maps • Word webs • Jigsaw • Reciprocal
Reinforcing effort and providing recognition	29	The brain responds to challenge and not threat. Emotions enhance learning.	• Stories of determination • Celebrate successes
Assigning homework and practice	28	If you don't use it, you lose it. Practice and rehearsal make learning "stick."	• Create challenges in a variety of ways
Generating nonlinguistic representations	27	The brain is a parallel processor. Visual stimuli are recalled with 90% accuracy.	• Mind maps • Graphic organizers • Models
Using cooperative learning	27	The brain is social. Collaboration facilitates understanding and higher-order thinking.	• Think-Pair-Share • Jigsaw • P.I.G.S.F.
Setting objectives and providing feedback	23	The brain responds to high challenge and continues to strive based on feedback.	• Helpful feedback • Rubrics • Criteria • Expectations
Generating and testing hypotheses	23	The brain is curious and has an innate need to make meaning through patterns.	• Problem-based inquiry • Portfolios • Case studies
Providing questions, cues, and advance organizers	22	The brain responds to wholes and parts. All learners need to open "mental files" into which new learning can be "hooked."	• Wait time • Questioning techniques • Agenda maps • Advance organizers • Diagrams and charts

Figure 2.1

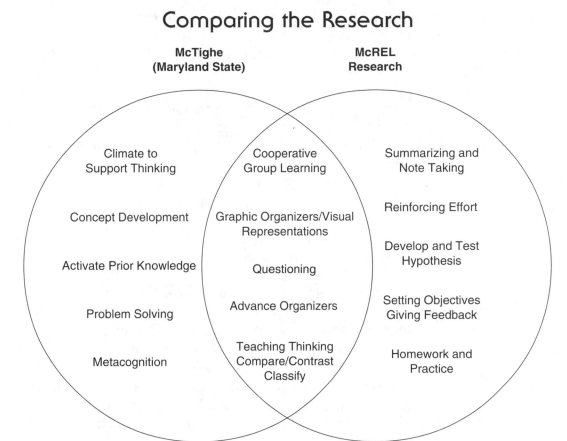

Comparing the Research

**McTighe
(Maryland State)**   **McREL
Research**

Climate to Support Thinking

Concept Development

Activate Prior Knowledge

Problem Solving

Metacognition

Cooperative Group Learning

Graphic Organizers/Visual Representations

Questioning

Advance Organizers

Teaching Thinking Compare/Contrast Classify

Summarizing and Note Taking

Reinforcing Effort

Develop and Test Hypothesis

Setting Objectives Giving Feedback

Homework and Practice

Figure 2.2

The large percentile gains in student achievement are not surprising when we consider how well they align with the research on how the brain learns. Figure 2.2 compares the strategies from Maryland State and the Marzano study with the similarities in the center and the unique strategies on each side. It's clear that we should pay attention to these best practices and include them in our classrooms.

IN CLOSING

Strategies' Relationship to Constructivism

Many of the educational theories presented here are closely related to constructivism, an educational theory based on the work of Piaget. It says, in effect, that we learn by constructing personal meaning from the information that is presented to us. Learning may be seen as the brain's attempt to derive meaning from and make sense of the external world. The brain learns by connecting new information to concepts and ideas that it already understands. Thus, old learning becomes the foundation on which new learning is constructed.

Jacqueline Brooks and Martin Brooks (1993) proposed the following set of principles for constructivist teaching:

- Engage the students with questions of emerging relevance so that they are encouraged to search more deeply for answers
- Structure learning around major concepts and ideas to provide a relevant context for learning
- Seek out and value the students' points of view
- Challenge the students' thinking by provoking them to examine and confront their suppositions and premises
- Assess student learning using authentic strategies that are an extension of the teaching-learning process

A constructivist classroom, for all intents and purposes, is synonymous with a brain-compatible classroom. In both the constructivist and brain-compatible classroom, the day-to-day learning experiences are rooted in the theories related to cooperative group learning, classrooms that support thinking, metacognition, and graphic organizers. Cognitive research and educational theory form the foundation on which both constructivism and brain-compatible learning stand, while instructional skills and strategies form the bridge that links them to the classroom.

Figure 2.3 shows the links between constructivist principles, brain-compatible elements, and classroom applications.

Strategies' Relationship to Cognitive Research

The strategies outlined in this chapter were selected for their relationship to the research discussed in the previous chapter on cognitive research. They are also important because they are a foundation for the range of instructional skills that teachers need to move their students in the directions indicated by the exit outcomes or expectations established by school districts everywhere.

The cognitive research covered in the previous chapter is built around four main concepts that relate to classroom practice: emotions, patterns, experience, and multiple intelligences. The first relates to the emotional component involved in all learning and the role it plays in building a classroom climate that supports learning. The related strategy here is cooperative group learning, which, when used appropriately, can create the conditions that favor the implementation of all the other brain-compatible strategies. We believe that cooperative group learning is foundational for the brain compatible and differentiated classroom.

The second concept is concerned with the brain's ability to recognize and construct patterns. This ability not only allows us to make sense of the world but also allows us to connect information and recall it. The ability to link information and organize it in ways that make sense is predicated in part on being able to use

Brain-Compatible Constructivist Classrooms

Constructivist Principles (Brooks & Brooks 1993)	Brain-Compatible Elements	Classroom Applications
Pose problems of emerging relevance	Tap into the brain's natural tendencies to seek meaning and make sense of the world. Stimulate the brain's natural curiosity to seek novelty and variety.	Present problems in such a way that students are invited to develop questions and pursue answers that have personal meaning.
Structure learning around primary concepts	Use the brain's ability to recognize and construct patterns and to make connections between and among ideas.	Present the "big picture" or context so that students see how the parts relate. Isolate skills and teach them separately when necessary, but put skills back into context as soon as they are mastered.
Seek out and value students' points of view	Foster an emotionally safe environment where learners are able to take risks and engage in creative thinking. Strengthen the neural connections through articulation of ideas.	Encourage students to express their own ideas related to major concepts. Value their points of view and foster an open interchange of ideas.
Adapt curriculum to address students' suppositions	Provide a variety of concrete experiences as a way of developing neural connections. Provide opportunities to clarify concepts through discussion.	Challenge the students' thinking by provoking them to examine their suppositions, premises, and beliefs.
Assess student learning in the context of teaching	Practice the new learning in context through elaboration and rehearsal, enabling the brain to establish connections between the context and the learning, thus making it easier to recall and apply in the future.	Be sure that the assessment strategies are an integral part of the teaching-learning process. Apply assessment strategies that relate closely to ways in which they are used in the real world.

Figure 2.3

higher-order thinking skills such as analysis, synthesis, and evaluation. These, in turn, are facilitated by direct teaching enhanced by the use of inductive reasoning strategies and graphic organizers.

The third aspect of cognitive research is based on the theory that we all learn best from experience, especially when the brain is actively engaged in the process. Active involvement and learning by experience are two of the defining characteristics of brain-compatible learning strategies and the reason why all the instructional tools in this book encourage hands-on, concrete, active experiences. It seems that when students actively construct and organize meaning for themselves, they understand the information at much deeper levels than when the teacher provides the information.

The final concept related to cognitive research is that of multiple intelligences, which says in effect we can increase our students' learning and problem-solving abilities if we increase their repertoires of problem-solving tools by actively encouraging them to use all facets of intelligence. The strategies in this book are designed to harness the power of multiple intelligences and to apply it to all areas of instruction and assessment.

Constructivism is a key concept when we consider differentiating instructional strategies. "One size doesn't fit all" . . . thus using a variety of ways for students to develop or construct meaning is essential when we know that every brain has been nurtured and wired differently. We also know that it takes many forms of elaborative rehearsal to develop enduring understanding and construct meaning.

Reflections

You can respond personally to the following prompts or discuss them in a study group.

What?
What did you learn about pedagogy from this chapter?

So What?
What difference does this make to your thinking?

Now What?
What can you use in your classroom/school?

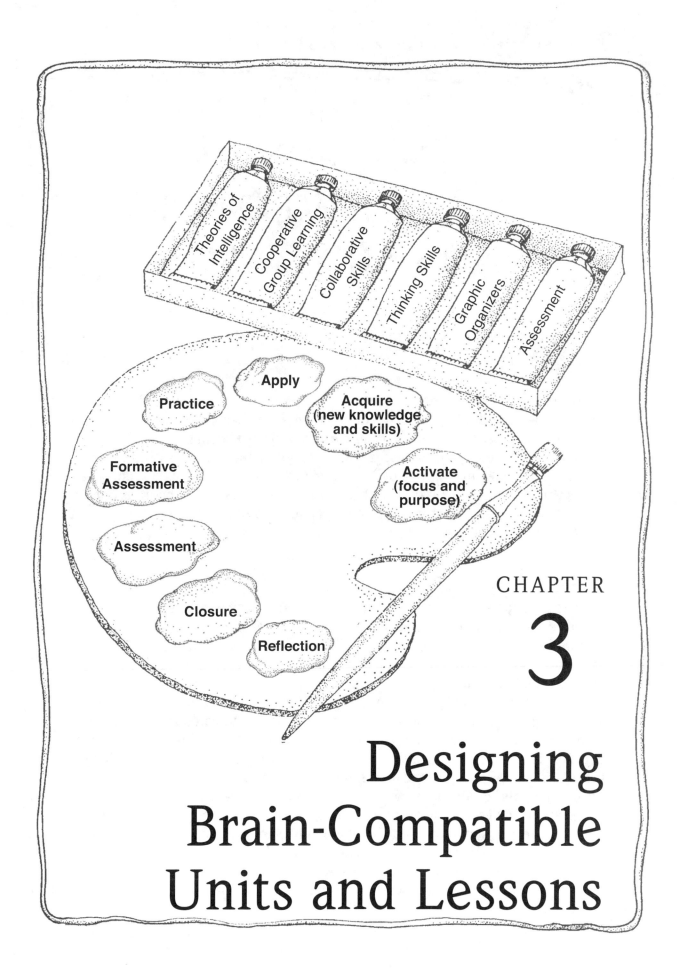

Theories of Intelligence

Cooperative Group Learning

Collaborative Skills

Thinking Skills

Graphic Organizers

Assessment

Apply

Practice

Acquire (new knowledge and skills)

Formative Assessment

Activate (focus and purpose)

Assessment

Closure

Reflection

CHAPTER

3

Designing Brain-Compatible Units and Lessons

CHAPTER 3

DESIGNING BRAIN-COMPATIBLE UNITS AND LESSONS

WHAT IS IT?

In this chapter, we present two methods for designing brain-compatible learning. The first deals with planning large units of work, the second deals with planning individual lessons. Unit plans usually cover a span of teaching time from two or three days to more extensive pieces that cover a number of weeks. A unit plan can be within a single subject area or it can integrate concepts and skills from several subject areas. Lesson plans are usually cover a period measured in hours as opposed to weeks. This is the point in the planning cycle where instructional strategies and assessment strategies are built in.

Unit Planning

The plan for a large unit of work provides an overview of the knowledge and skills we want students to achieve on completion of the unit and also describes the standard that students are expected to achieve. Unit plans should be based on the expectations for student achievement as laid out in the curriculum documents provided by the local school district or state department of education. Whether or not district curriculum guides and sequences are available, all unit plans should start with standards and grade-level expectations. Many jurisdictions use different names to describe the end point of learning. In Colorado they are called standards and benchmarks, and in other states they are learning expectations. In Ontario, Canada, they are called expectations and indicators. In this book we will use the term *standards* for the large overriding or long-term goals, and *benchmarks* or expectations to describe subject area or course requirements. The teacher's task is to subdivide the standards into the "big chunks" of learning for each discipline (such as math, language arts, or science) for more manageable units of study tailored to the needs, interests, and aptitude of the students. When the big chunks are developed into units of study, they become the road maps for planning individual lessons.

Phases of Lesson Planning

Planning individual lessons brings into play the instructional strategies described in chapters 4 through 9. The individual lesson is the basic structure for building learning experiences. It is the point where many of the brain-compatible elements such as thinking skills, graphic organizers, collaborative skills, and ongoing or formative assessment come together and are linked. It is our contention that by focusing on a limited but powerful set of instructional strategies (best practices) and combining them in many different ways, teachers can design learning experiences that conform more closely to the ways in which the brain learns best.

To be useful, unit and lesson plans should conform to the following criteria:

- *Flexible*—Controlled by the teacher and amenable to modification and adaptation
- *Brain compatible*—Consistent with what is known about how the brain learns
- *Differentiated*—Capable of accommodating a variety of instructional strategies, such as cooperative group learning, direct instruction, thinking skills, multiple intelligences, graphic organizers, and authentic assessments

Lesson planning as described in this book is divided into a number of phases or elements, each designed to ensure that lessons are laid out in a logical way that progresses smoothly and concludes satisfactorily. These elements have been around in one form or another since Madeline Hunter first described them in the 1970s and 1980s (M. Hunter, 1982; R. Hunter, 2004). Because they conform to many attributes of brain compatibility and curriculum mapping, we continue to honor Madeline's original idea, but we have added a few bell and whistles of our own. We focus on seven phases of lesson planning:

1. *Selecting benchmarks:* What will the students know and be able to do?

2. *Forming essential questions:* What questions should students be able to answer at the end of the lesson?

3. *Identifying content:* What specific knowledge and skill will students acquire or practice in this lesson?

4. *Activation:* Focus students' attention and assess their prior knowledge?

5. *Acquisition:* Students acquire knowledge and skill by engaging with instructional strategies as planned by the teacher.

6. *Application:* Provide opportunities to practice and apply the new learning. Monitor student performance through self, peer, and teacher assessment.

7. *Assessment:* Apply a summative assessment of knowledge, skill, and mastery of the essential questions.

8. *Closure:* Bring the lesson to a close through personal, group, and teacher reflection on what has been learned and what might come next.

Emotions are critical to learning, and ideally, the affective component of student enjoyment, preferences, satisfactions, or frustrations should be considered at the end of every lesson and unit. We will cover each of the seven phases of lesson design in more detail in the "How Do We Do It" section of this chapter.

Our organizing metaphor for lesson design is the painter's palette, which appears on the title page of each chapter of the book. Our use of the painter's palette is a metaphor for flexibility, the key to lesson design. The palette or mixing board represents the process for designing lessons, and the different tubes of paint are the groups of instructional strategies or tools to be used in each lesson to differentiate the instructional process.

Artists seldom use paint straight from the tube; similarly, teachers seldom plan lessons according to a rigid lockstep formula. Lesson design is similar to painting in that it is a process of mixing and matching. The basic "colors" are selected and then combined to provide a variety of shades, hews, and tints. The resulting paint is then thoughtfully applied to the canvass of the classroom. Sometimes we apply a wash of one color with a broad brush as in a whole-class experience such as a field trip or the exploration phase of examining a topic. Other times, we may use a fine brush and apply painstaking attention to detail. In other cases, a few bold strokes may get the message across. By keeping the palette metaphor in mind, we can see how a relatively small but wisely selected set of colors can be mixed and applied in a variety of ways. Integrating and using layers of best practice better ensure a greater impact on student achievement and meet more of the learning styles and preferences of the diverse learners in classrooms today.

WHY DO WE NEED IT?

As we begin to understand and use instructional and brain research, we realize that the information is interesting but not particularly useful unless it can be translated into classroom practice. The planning processes described in this chapter are an attempt to bring the best practices in instructional strategies together with what we know about how the brain learns and the diversity of learning profiles in the class. Without an organizing philosophy and framework, both long-term planning and lesson design can devolve into a series of unconnected activities that may be interesting but that result in significant gaps in comprehension and achievement.

HOW DO WE DO IT?

How Do We Plan a Unit of Study?

After examining curriculum guidelines thoughtfully as part of phases one through three on benchmarks, essential questions, and content, we can begin to develop a list of topics, skills, and areas of study. This is a useful exercise in convergent or critical thinking because it narrows our focus and allows us to concentrate on a shorter and more defined set of expectations. Once we have narrowed our focus, we can begin to expand it again by thinking divergently and creatively about possibilities for instruction that will cover the topics and help students meet knowledge and skill expectations.

We now have a list of topics and skills, and we are ready to plan a unit of study. The next step is to consider one simple but powerful idea: START WITH THE END IN MIND. This advice is deceptively simple but it is a step that is often missed. In practice, teachers will often obtain a topic from a state or district curriculum guideline and immediately begin by thinking of activities, which will engage the children's interest and motivate them to learn. This would seem to be sensible, since very few teachers start out with the intention of being boring. But if we do not keep the overall purpose, standard, or benchmark firmly in mind, individual lessons can become a series of engaging but disconnected activities. This means that although the activities may be enjoyable for the students, they may not lead them toward the desired standards and benchmarks.

When we jump into planning based only on "activities" without some kind of organizing framework, the whole area of student assessment is often pushed to the side and left until instruction has been completed. This may lead to a situation in which the curriculum appears to have been covered through a set of activities, but in reality, significant gaps in student understanding and skill development may still exist. Another result of this kind of planning is that student evaluation is tailored to what the teacher has covered as opposed to what the students are expected to know or be able to do.

There is, however, an alternate process that alleviates some of these difficulties. It is not easy; it is sometimes painful and requires a great deal of thinking and soul searching and, for many teachers, it is a departure from traditional practice. It is called "reverse planning" or backward design (Wiggins and McTighe 2005).

Why Do We Use Reverse Planning?

In reverse planning, we focus on our expectations for students' knowledge and skill development, as opposed to focusing on what the teacher intends to do. The following statements provide an example of the difference:

Teacher intent statement: "This semester we will cover World War II and the Vietnam War."

When we state our intentions in this way, we do not address the question of what students are supposed to learn.

Reverse planning statements: "By the end of this semester, students will
* understand the causes and effects of World War II and the Vietnam War,
* identify the pivotal event or turning points in both conflicts, and

- compare and contrast the role of public attitudes and values in determining the outcomes of both wars."

When we use reverse planning, it creates a different mind-set in both teachers and students and increases the chance that our instruction will be more focused on the knowledge and skills the students are supposed to acquire.

However, there is an overarching set of ideas to consider even before we get to the level of student expectations. It concerns the higher purpose of teaching that cuts across all areas of the curriculum and should be applied to all our planning. For example, in our unit on World War II and the Vietnam War, is our purpose to expose students to a wealth of information about war, or should we be more concerned that they become competent critical thinkers with a firm set of ideals related to social issues?

Few people would disagree with the concept of teaching students to become critical and creative thinkers or decisive problem solvers. But keep in mind that any decisions that deal with values, morals, or ideals are best considered in conjunction with other staff members, parents, and the local school district.

Once we have this higher purpose firmly in mind, we have a destination or a goal for both students and teachers. It should inform and guide all our decisions about instruction *and* assessment. When teachers use the reverse-planning method, it increases the chance that instruction and assessment become an integrated whole as opposed to separate functions. As described throughout this book, we have a firm belief that assessment is an integral part of the teaching-learning process. Assessments and instruction should be planned together as opposed to creating assessments as add-ons that are planned only when the teaching is complete. When planning a unit of work, teachers should ask themselves the following question: What is the STANDARD and what are the BENCHMARKS?

When we plan units of study, we should make sure that they are firmly grounded on the standards and benchmarks. There is a good reason for starting with the desired end in mind, because when we and the students know where we are going, there is a higher probability that all of us will get there.

Key Concepts

Key concepts describe what the students are expected to know be able to do. It is important to clarify the student expectations for the unit of study before beginning to teach. Knowing the expectations gives both teachers and students a clear picture of what the end point of the journey will look like. Apart from the key concepts spelled out in a particular benchmark, you may also wish to develop a further set of concepts, depending on the particular needs of your students.

How will the students demonstrate competence in achievement of the key concepts?

- Students demonstrate competence by engaging in some form of culminating activity or performance.
- Students demonstrate competence by delivering written reports or essays, projects, performances, or products such as models or other types of artifact.
- Students demonstrate competence by taking quizzes, short constructed-response tests, and multiple-choice tests.

What are the critical attributes of excellent work, and what are the indicators of successful completion? Determining the essential elements of excellent work explicitly before beginning to teach and sharing this information with the students clarify the expectations for both students and teachers. We deal with essential elements of excellent work in greater detail as we begin to examine an example of unit planning. When we engage students in this way, not only does it allow them to see the big picture, but it also shows them how the individual parts are related to the whole. This satisfies the brain's basic need to make sense of the parts and connect to the big picture. This also begins to address the question of relevance and helps students to understand why they are doing what they are doing.

Example of a Unit Plan

To see how this might work in practice, we will examine one of the U.S. National standards for math.

We have already established the notion that standards and benchmarks answer the question, *What must students know and be able to do?*

For example, in math, for the national standard on *data analysis and probability,* the expectations for students are as follows (see Fig. 3.1, page 62).

These benchmarks in Figure 3.1 are designed to cover grades prekindergarten to Grade 12. A cursory examination of what is expected of students might lead you to think that these concepts are impossible for kindergarten students and extremely difficult for twelfth graders. However, there are two key factors to consider: the first is the ingenuity of teachers, and the second is a phenomenon called *concept range.*

Concept Range

Concept range, as the name implies, allows us to engage with a concept at different levels of understanding. To a young child, the concept "justice" may be understood in the simple terms of an eye for an eye and a tooth for a tooth. A more mature student begins to realize that justice is hardly ever spelled out in black or white terms. In fact, justice is fraught with many shades of meaning and is open to a range of interpretations. Concepts, therefore, can be understood at many different levels.

Good teachers have always had the ability to engage students at a point where they can achieve a level of understanding that is commensurate with their age and abilities. When teachers are presented with a seemingly impossible task, they click into creative thinking mode and begin to generate a wealth of instructional strategies. They might consider representing data with a bar graph or visual representation and asking predictive questions such as, "Who can guess (predict) what kinds of things most students have in their lunch boxes?" They might also begin to engage students with verification of data by asking, "What kind of questions can we ask to find out if our predictions are correct?" All these good ideas should be saved until the next two phases of planning are complete.

U.S. National Standards and Benchmarks for Math

Standard 1: Instructional programs from pre-kindergarten through grade 12 should enable all students to *formulate questions* that can be addressed with data and collect, organize, and display relevant data to answer them.

Expectations for grades 3-5:

- Design investigations to address questions and understand how data-collection methods affect the nature of the data set;
- Collect data using observations, surveys, and experiments;
- Represent data using tables and graphs such as line plots, bar graphs, and line graphs;
- Recognize the difference in representing categories and numerical data.

Standard 2: Instructional programs from pre-kindergarten through grade 12 should enable all students to *select and use* appropriate statistical methods to analyze data.

Expectations for grades 3-5:

- Describe the shape and important features of a set of data and compare related data sets, with an emphasis on how the data are distributed;
- Use measures of center, focusing on the median, and understand what each does and does not indicate about the data set;
- Compare different representations of the same data to evaluate how well each representation shows important aspects of the data.

Standard 3: Instructional programs from pre-kindergarten through grade 12 should enable all students to *develop and evaluate* inferences and predictions that are based on data.

Expectations for grades 3-5:

- Propose and justify conclusions and predictions that are based on data and design studies to further investigate the conclusions or predictions.

Standard 4: Instructional programs from pre-kindergarten through grade 12 should enable all students to *understand and apply* basic concepts of probability.

Expectations for grades 3-5:

- Describe events as likely or unlikely and discuss the degree of likelihood using such words as certain, equally likely, and impossible;
- Predict the probability of outcomes of simple experiments and test the predictions;
- Understand that the measure of the likelihood of an event can be represented by a number from 0 to 1.

Figure 3.1

Determining Key Concepts

The next step is to determine the key concepts on which to base the demonstrations of learning. These concepts are the big ideas stated or implied in the standards and benchmarks. Some jurisdictions spell out the key concepts in great detail and with specific directions as to selection. Others allow teachers far more latitude in both designing and selecting concept.

Choosing a Theme or Topic

As you can see from Figure 3.2, there are far more possible concepts than we can realistically deal with in one unit. Our next step, therefore, is to decide on a theme or topic on which to base a unit. This will allow us to design learning experiences and assessment strategies that involve some, but not all, of the concepts. Our sample lesson (see Fig. 3.3) shows key concepts and unit skills for a data analysis and probability unit called "The Survey Says" for Grades 3 through 5.

A Partial List of Possible Concepts

Standard 1	Standard 2	Standard 3	Standard 4
Data collection	Data shape	Predict	Certain
*Data	Data features	Infer	Equally likely
Relevant	Statistical methods	Conclude	Impossible
Experiment	*Analyze	Study	Test
Survey	Measure	*Investigate	*Probability
*Tables	Center	*Justify	*Predict
*Graphs	*Median		
Line Plot	*Compare		
Bar Graph	Importance of data		
Line Graph			
Category			

Figure 3.2

A List of Possible Unit KEY CONCEPTS:
What must students remember and be able to use, even after this unit?

Standard 1	Standard 2	Standard 3	Standard 4
*Data	*Analyze	*Investigate	*Probability
*Tables	*Median	*Justify	*Predict
*Graphs	*Compare		
Line Plot			
Bar Graph			
Line Graph			

Figure 3.3

Designing Tasks

When we have finished establishing our key concepts and unit skills according to the standards and benchmarks of what students must know and be able to do, we reach the point where we must decide how the students will demonstrate mastery of the required learning. We then begin to design tasks that spell out exactly what we expect students to do (Fig. 3.4).

Standard/Benchmark 1:	Standard/Benchmark 2:
1. Students will design investigations to address a question. 2. Students will decide which data methods will give them the needed information.	3. Students will represent data in two or more ways to help others understand and compare the data. 4. Students will demonstrate the use of median and mean to understand and analyze data.
Standard/Benchmark 3:	**Standard/Benchmark 4:**
5. Students will propose and justify a prediction based on data collection and interpretation.	6. Students will predict the probability of a result and test the accuracy of that prediction.

Figure 3.4

Creating the Final Unit Assessment Description

The next step in unit planning is to create a simple, clear, and concise description of the final assessment for your plan. This will guide and focus your work no matter which method of performance assessment you choose. The final unit description has three parts, although you might wish to consider a fourth, which is the presentation of exemplars and a model of excellent work.

1. The unit description (Figure 3.5)

2. An assessment prompt (Figure 3.6, page 67)

3. A rubric (Figure 3.7, page 68)

Final assessment descriptions should include a clear and succinct prompt. A prompt, as the name implies, details the student's responsibilities. The rubric describes what the student is actually doing in terms of the concept. A rubric should always describe observable behaviors, artifacts, or phenomena as a way of differentiating advanced performance from proficient or partly proficient learning (Fig. 3.7).

Figure 3.8 (page 69) presents a template to facilitate thinking for a unit plan.

Unit Plan for: Survey Says . . .	Subject: Math	Grade: 3-5

Standards/Benchmarks: *What should students know and be able to do?*

Standard 1: Instructional programs from pre-kindergarten through grade 12 should enable all students to *formulate questions* that can be addressed with data and collect, organize, and display relevant data to answer them.

Standard 2: Instructional programs from pre-kindergarten through grade 12 should enable all students to *select and use* appropriate statistical methods to analyze data.

Standard 3: Instructional programs from pre-kindergarten through grade 12 should enable all students to *develop and evaluate* inferences and predictions that are based on data.

Standard 4: Instructional programs from pre-kindergarten through grade 12 should enable all students to *understand and apply* basic concepts of probability.

Key Concepts: *What must students remember and be able to use, even after this unit?*

Standard1	Standard 2	Standard 3	Standard 4
*Data	Analyze	Investigate	Probability
*Tables	Median	Justify	Predict
*Graphs	Compare		
Line Plot			
Bar Graph			
Line Graph			

Skills: *How will students demonstrate they can utilize what they learned in a meaningful way?*
Standard/Benchmark 1:

1. Students will design investigations to address a question.
2. Students will decide which data methods will give them the needed information.

Standard/Benchmark 2:

3. Students will represent data in two or more ways to help others understand and compare the data.
4. Students will demonstrate the use of median and mean to understand and analyze data.

Standard/Benchmark 3:

5. Students will propose and justify a prediction based on data collection and interpretation.

Standard/Benchmark 4:

6. Students will predict the probability of a result and test the accuracy of that prediction.

Relevance: *Why must students learn this and what need is there for this learning across time and applications?* Students may understand the relevance by having to review data representations from various sections of the newspaper and from magazines. A few graphs off the Internet from a television station on viewership may also provide relevancy. It is important that students see the everyday application of what they are about to learn. This review of graphs could provide an engaging small-group introduction to the unit.

Final Assessment Description: *What does the demonstration of learning for this unit look like?* Students will investigate the entertainment preferences of peers and staff. During this process students will analyze and report the results of an investigation that is supported with data and select a method

Figure 3.5 (Continued)

Figure 3.5 (Continued)

of reporting that demonstrates their use of data, prediction, and analysis. A rubric and set of directions will support student learning and assessment. *See rubric and directions for final assessments.*

Critical Unit Questions: *The students will answer what questions, if they are successful on the final assessment?*

1. How can we use data to predict how people think about and choose preferences?

2. How does the collection and analysis of data increase the accuracy of our predictions?

Preassessment Design: *What do we already know about our math students? What do we need to know to get student growth from where they are to the final assessment?*

Students will be given a table and graph that represent the same data. Partners will discuss the data and decide what conclusions they can draw from the information. Teacher will listen for:

1. Understanding of the visual representations of data

2. Logical conclusions given the data

Students will "Quick Write" about their conclusions. (Quick Write in Math: topic sentence is the big understanding, next two to three sentences are the supporting detail for the big understanding, and last sentence is the rationale or why the conclusion makes sense)
   Teachers will not grade these paragraphs; instead they will note whether the writing:

1. Is logical given the prompt and supports the conclusion

2. Demonstrates the ability to express analysis through writing about math

Teachers will be able to teach the concepts as expressed, but adjust their coaching, time, order, difficulty level, and supporting resources to address these results.

Chunking or Outlining the Unit: *How will teachers break up the unit into chunks of learning that represent various degrees of growing skill and thinking?*

1. Activating learning for the total unit and developing a survey question

2. Learning about visual representations of data

3. Summarizing using median and mean

4. Predicting with data

5. Analyzing data results and sharing

Next steps to finish unit planning:

1. Create the final Assessment Prompt and Rubric. Collect or create models.

2. Create student self-assessment tool or checklist

SOURCE: *Data-Driven Differentiation in the Standards-Based Classroom* (Gregory & Kuzmich, 2004, Corwin Press).

FINAL UNIT ASSESSMENT Prompt

Unit Title: The Survey Says . . . We are going to investigate what forms of entertainment students and staff prefer during their free time. You can choose to survey people's preferences for any form of entertainment.

Please follow these steps:

1. Create a question that you will ask to gather information about preferences.
2. You will need to survey at least 25 students from several grades.
3. Then you will need to create a table and a graph to show your results.
4. Summarize your results using median and mean to help your audience understand the results and these mathematical terms.
5. Create a prediction about how the next 25 students may answer (use the same number of students from each grade as in your first survey).
6. Create another set of data displays.
7. Now compare the results from both surveys and decide how accurate your prediction was from step 5.
8. Choose a method of sharing your data displays, prediction, and analysis. Be certain to make certain you use data to support your conclusions.
9. Use the rubric to help you plan and think about your work.

Remember:

- Use of correct grammar, usage, punctuation, and spelling is required in all parts of your work.
- You can use the computer to create your tables and graphs or you can neatly write and draw them.

Figure 3.6

Chunking for Student Success

After the unit plan has been completed, teachers will then want to decide scope and sequence for chunks of learning that will build toward the final assessment. Dividing the learning into appropriate "chunks" that will be used to design lessons or series of lessons brings the unit to the day-to-day learning for students. Chunks will include the concepts and skills that build knowledge and understanding in a way that makes sense to learners, using a variety of the best practices available for student learning. Chunks will help students progress successfully toward the targeted standards and final assessment.

The chart on page 70 (Fig. 3.9) identifies the chunks for the math unit on data and probability.

From these chunks lesson planning can commence.

Preassessment for Targeted Learning

There once was a teacher who spent whole summers planning all manner of neat, nifty, and entertaining lessons for his students only to find that in September they sent entirely the wrong learners. We will not fall into that trap. We have invested a lot of time in planning units of study. We now need to find out what our students already know, as well as what they don't know, before proceeding.

RUBRIC FOR: The Survey Says . . .

Key Concepts	Advanced	Proficient	Partially Proficient
1. Data in Graphs and Tables	Tables and graphs are easy to interpret and contain labels and data that clearly answer the question.	Tables and graphs are accurate, labeled, and clearly display important data.	Tables and graphs have a title, are easy to read, and are accurate.
2. Median and Mean	Students use the median and mean to help them draw conclusions and make predictions.	Students explain the median and mean result in their data interpretation.	Students report the median and mean.
3. Investigation Process and Questions	Students can explain the process they used and develop interview questions that helped them to create the analysis.	Steps were followed and the interview questions developed helped students collect data.	Steps were followed and the interview questions make sense given the assignment.
4. Predict and Justify	Students make predictions based on data and can justify their prediction using the first data collection step.	Predictions make sense given the first data collection step.	Predictions include elements (words) from the first set of data.
5. Analysis and Sharing	Students describe why the data sets are similar or dissimilar and what may have caused that result. Students share their conclusions such that peers could use the mean and median to draw similar conclusions.	Students compare the two sets of data collect and describe the accuracy of their prediction. Students share this information such that peers draw a similar conclusion.	Students describe the final data collection and whether or not it matched the prediction. Students share this information clearly. Students share tables and graphs such that peers can check the accuracy of the data.

Figure 3.7

Unit Plan Template

Unit Plan for:	**Subject:**	**Grade:**

Standards/Benchmarks: *What should students know and be able to do?*

Key Concepts: *What must students remember and be able to use, even after this unit?*

Skills: *How will students demonstrate they can utilize what they learned in a meaningful way?*

Relevance: *Why must students learn this and what need is there for this learning across time and applications?*

Final Assessment Description: *What does the demonstration of learning for this unit look like?*

Critical Unit Questions: *The students will answer what questions, if they are successful on the final assessment?*

Preassessment Design: *What do we already know about our _____ students? What do we need to know to get student growth from where they are to the final assessment?*

Chunking or Outlining the Unit: *How will teachers break up the unit into chunks of learning that represent various degrees of growing skill and thinking?*

Next steps to finish unit planning:

1. **Create the final Assessment Prompt and Rubric. Collect or create models.**

2. **Create Student self-assessment tool or checklist**

Figure 3.8

SOURCE: Adapted from *Data-Driven Differentiation in the Standards-Based Classroom* (Gregory & Kuzmich, 2004 Corwin Press).

Chunking

Chunking or Outlining the Unit for the Math unit on *Data Analysis and Probability, Grades 3-5*: How will teachers break up the unit into chunks of learning that represent various degrees of growing skill and thinking?

1. Activating learning for the total unit and developing a survey question
2. Learning about visual representations of data
3. Summarizing using median and mean
4. Predicting with data
5. Analyzing data results and sharing

Figure 3.9

Here is an example of a preassessment plan from our math unit (Fig. 3.10):

Our thinking is complete when . . .

We know where our students are now and where they should be at the end of the unit.

We know what the key concepts and skills are.

We have developed essential questions.

We know what the final assessment will look like.

We will share this information with the students.

We are now ready to begin planning lessons.

The term *lesson plan* is often used to denote the work of one or two periods in the school day. Some of these concepts are complex in nature and may take more than one or two periods to accomplish. We should plan accordingly.

The Elements of Lesson Design

These elements were listed briefly at the beginning of the chapter and identified with the palette in the painting metaphor. In practice, the framework for designing brain-compatible learning is much more stylized than a painter's palette. A lesson is composed of phases, or elements, each of which is designed to enhance learning. These phases are illustrated in Figure 3.11 (page 72) and a short description for each follows. If you reflect on the ideas related to memory in the cognitive research chapter, you will realize that the phases of lesson design conform closely to the way in which the brain learns.

In most cases, the phases are completed sequentially, from focusing students' attention through closure and extension. But it is common to repeat a phase if instructional goals aren't reached. For example, if a check for understanding in the

Preassessment Design for the Math unit on *Data Analysis and Probability, Grades 3-5*:

Part One—
What do we already know about our math students?

We will have information about their written reflection in math, calculation accuracy, ability to estimate, and some idea of their ability to create simple graphs or tables.

Part Two—
What do we need to know to get student growth from where they are to the final assessment?

We need to know: student understanding and interpretation of data and student ability to communicate at an analysis level using the language of math accurately.

A Way to Preassess the Gap

Students will be given a table and graph that represent the same data. Partners will discuss the data and decide what conclusions they can draw from the information. Teacher will listen for:

1. Understanding of the visual representations of data
2. Logical conclusions given the data

Students will "Quick Write" about their conclusions. (Quick Write in Math: topic sentence is the big understanding, next two to three sentences are the supporting detail for the big understanding, and last sentence is the rationale or why the conclusion makes sense)

Teachers will not grade these paragraphs; instead they will note whether the writing:

1. Is logical given the prompt and supports the conclusion
2. Demonstrates the ability to express analysis through writing about math

Teachers will be able to teach the concepts as expressed, but adjust their coaching, time, order, difficulty level, and supporting resources to address these results.

Figure 3.10

apply-and-adjust phase isn't successful, the instruction in the acquire phase may be repeated or reviewed in another way before moving on. The same might be true if the assess phase reveals that student are having difficulty with the essential questions, which means we may have to reteach parts of the lesson.

Phases of Lesson Design in Detail

We will now examine the phases of lesson design in more detail to see how they relate to the notion of brain-compatible learning.

Benchmark

Lay out in fairly succinct terms what the students should know and be able to do.

Essential Questions

Decide on two to four questions that students should be able to answer by the end of the lesson.

Instructional Phases

ACTIVATE (Creating focus and purpose, open mental files)	Students begin to engage with the business of learning in three ways, presented in the order the teacher prefers or that would make the most sense to the learners. • Activating prior knowledge or skill • Stating the expectations • Providing an overview
ACQUIRE (Getting new knowledge and skills)	Teachers may use two methods: • Didactic (lecture)—Stand and deliver • Active learning—"Guide on the side"—where the teacher plans and facilitates the acquisition of information and skills and orchestrates the learning.
APPLY, PRACTICE, FORMATIVE ASSESSMENT (Demonstrating the learning)	Students consolidate new skills and content through practice. This practice and application includes a wide variety of strategies and is synonymous with how the brain makes meaning and stores information through multiple pathways and rehearsals. Ongoing assessment of student learning and program quality is done through observation, conversation, questioning, and feedback.
ASSESSMENT, CLOSURE, AND REFLECTION	Summarizes the main points of the lesson through a group debriefing, or teacher direction. Reconnect to purpose and standards, essential questions, etc. Foreshadow next steps and transfer their learning to life situations. Summative assessment will influence planning of subsequent lessons.

Figure 3.11

Content

What are the specific knowledge, concepts, and skills that students will acquire or practice in this lesson?

Activate

Activating prior learning. From what we know about how the brain stores and retrieves memories, we realize that all the information in long-term memory is not available to us at all times. Particular pieces of information have to be activated, or called to mind, and then transferred from long-term memory into our short-term, or working, memory before new learning can begin. Students often need to be prompted to reactivate what they already know so that they can connect it to new learning. Activating prior learning also means checking how much the students actually know about a topic before proceeding with a lesson.

Stating the expectations and purpose. The brain likes to know where it is going and why it should make the trip. When students know why they are engaging with a topic and understand what is expected of them, it increases relevance. When students perceive learning as useful, they are more likely to pay attention. In brain terms, whatever grabs a student's attention gets learned. In some cases, the purpose of a lesson may be for students to discover for themselves why an idea or a concept is important. However, in these cases, an explanation of the expectations and purpose may be left until the end and included as a part of bringing the lesson to a close.

Provide an overview and make connections. The brain learns by making connections between what it already knows and any new information. This process is facilitated when a teacher makes an overt effort to demonstrate how the new information connects to old information and how it will in turn connect to information in the future. In other words, it helps students to know where they are at present with regard to a topic, where they are going next, and possibly the ultimate destination. An analogy for this could be the map in a shopping mall that has the location of every store. This may be good information, but it is rendered much more useful by the addition of one piece—an arrow and the words YOU ARE HERE. Teachers should always point out where students are now as well as where they are headed.

Acquire

Students acquire knowledge and skill by engaging with instructional strategies as planned by the teacher. Although there are a number of instructional models, they can be grouped into two basic types: the lecture method and active learning. In the lecture method, information is transmitted from the teacher to the student without any other kind of intervention. In active learning, the teacher provides opportunities for an exchange of ideas through student interaction. Although lecturing is the primary method of instruction in many schools, it is not particularly effective for achieving comprehension of material or long-term retention. Active learning, on the other hand, allows students to make connections between new and old learning so that the information is not only understood but also retained in long-term memory. Active learning methods are detailed in all chapters on instructional strategies (chapters 4–9). Active learning does not necessarily mean that students get up from their desks and move around. It can involve didactic teaching as long as the teacher pauses from his or her lecture every five to ten minutes to allow students to engage in small-group discussion and metacognitive activity or to take notes.

To sum up the difference between the two modes of teaching:

- In lecture method, the teacher is the "sage on the stage."
- In active learning, the teacher becomes the "guide on the side," and the active brain of the learner makes connections and forms new dendritic growth.

Apply, Practice, Formative Assessment

The acquisition of knowledge and skill is not an end in itself. Knowledge and skill become useful only when they are used to acquire higher levels of information or to solve more complex problems. The apply-and-practice phase of a lesson should afford the students an opportunity to consolidate new skills through a series of thoughtfully designed practice activities that are graduated from easy to difficult. Practice may be independent or guided by the teacher. In some cases, the guide might also be a peer or learning partner.

When students have mastered the new work, they should begin to apply it to new and different situations or use it to solve practical problems. This phase of a lesson should encourage and promote higher-order thinking such as analysis, synthesis, and evaluation. Practice exercises designed to promote rote memorization and little else are not particularly useful. An exception to this might be the acquisition of certain key facts, such as multiplication tables or the rules of spelling. This practice and application includes a wide variety of strategies and is synonymous with how the brain makes meaning and stores information through multiple pathways and rehearsals. Ongoing assessment of student learning and program quality is done through observation, conversation, questioning, and feedback. Feedback is the "breakfast of champions," and without it, students don't know what to stop, start, or continue in the learning process.

Summative Assessment, Closure, and Reflection

As the name suggests, this is the part of the lesson where the teacher conducts summative assessment of student learning. This information may be gathered by means of question-and-answer activities, a pop quiz, or merely monitoring the level of metacognitive discussion between students as they work in small groups. The final part of the lesson should be devoted to summarizing the main points. The teacher may do this, but it is usually more effective when the students are given the task as part of a group debriefing. The closing phase of a lesson should also be used to revisit the essential questions. This is especially important in cases where students were expected to discover a generalization or concept for themselves and were not given the expectation and purpose up front. We need to be more explicit in this phase of the lessons. Perkins and Salomon (1990) suggest that we often teach by the "Bo Peep" method, leaving them alone to figure it out. However, good shepherds help guide and direct their "sheep" to the desired destination. So teachers should be clear about the big learnings and connections for students so that they grasp the ideas, concepts, and skills being taught and reinforced.

Summative assessment of knowledge, skills, and mastery of the essential questions also may be done at this time. Although teachers may grade the work, feedback is still much more useful than grades for student learning (Black et al. 2004). It points to successes and makes suggestions for growth and improvement, whereas a grade only ranks the student in terms of others. A grade alone is not sufficiently useful data to adjust, refocus, or improve.

The students may also be given the task of finding ways to extend the use of the new learning to other practical situations. In addition, the closing phase of a lesson might be used to foreshadow whatever is to come next. Or better yet, allow the students to predict what comes next.

Types of Instructional Strategies

Lesson phases may be accomplished using a wide variety of instructional strategies. Skilled teachers select strategies that fit their own teaching styles and preferences, but more important, they select strategies that fit their students' readiness, interests, and learning profiles, and they change and modify strategies according to their effectiveness. Skilled teachers are "instructionally intelligent." That is to say, they have a repertoire of instructional strategies (research-based best practices) from which they select appropriately. Knowing their curriculum and their students, they plan strategically so that all students have the opportunity to reach the targeted standards and benchmarks.

As we have examined research-based best practices in chapter 2, we can now use them selectively to teach to the chunks identified in the unit plan.

The six groups are listed on the "paint tubes" in Figure 3.12 (page 76). These strategies would be used as a painter mixes his or her colors to create a "masterful learning experience" for students. The strategies provide variety in the learning process and allow teachers to differentiate instruction based on student needs, interests, and multiple intelligence and learning styles.

The key to the lesson design framework is its flexibility. As stated previously, many of the strategies or tools can be used at several phases of the lesson. For example, the graphic organizer strategy *concept formation* can be used at the beginning of a lesson to activate prior learning, during the instructional phase, or as a way of applying and practicing a new skill. The chart (Fig. 3.13, page 77) provides some examples of ways in which you might employ a variety of types of strategies and individual activities as you plan your lessons. The lesson phases are listed in the left-hand column and represent the palette where colors are mixed. Some examples of the strategies and skills available in the tubes of color are listed on the right.

Although each activity appears as a stand-alone item, in practice, they are often used in combinations. For example, you might combine a cooperative group learning structure such as numbered heads with a graphic organizer like a mind map, or a three-step interview with a role play.

By combining the strategies in whatever combinations work best for you and your students and using the phases of lesson design, you can create a truly brain-compatible classroom in which each student can maximize his or her learning potential. As you continue through the book, you can start planning how to customize these strategies to make the most of them for your students.

Figure 3.14 (page 78) shows an example lesson plan that focuses on one chunk in "The Survey Says" unit in math. Notice that the teacher has selected the best

Cooperative Group Learning

5 Elements

Positive independence
Individual accountability
Group processing
Social skills
Face-to-face interaction

Simple Structures

Think-pair-share
3-step interview
Numbered heads
4 corners
Jigsaw
Paraphrase passport
Roundtable
Gallery walk
Graffiti
Talking chips

Collaborative Skills

Behaving responsibly
Consensus building
Clarifying
Extending ideas
Equal participation
Group maintenance
Summarizing
Assertiveness
Accepting differences
Resolving conflict
Paraphrasing
Disagreeing agreeably
Encouraging
I have, who has

Theories of Intelligence

Verbal/linguistic
Logical/mathematical
Visual/spatial
Bodily/kinesthetic
Musical/rhythmic
Intrapersonal
Interpersonal
Naturalist
Emotional intelligence
Persistence
Decreasing impulsivity
Flexible thinking
Accuracy and precision
Posing questions and
  problems
Using all the senses

Thinking Skills

Inductive thinking
Divergent thinking
Analyzing
Evaluating
Sequencing
Inferring
Cause & effect thinking
Deductive thinking
Recalling
Synthesizing
Prioritizing
Generalizing
Comparing
Convergent thinking
Comprehending
Applying
Classifying
Defining
Contrasting
Brainstorming
Metacognition

Graphic Organizers

Concept formation
Venn diagrams
Fishbones
Pie charts
Concept attainment
Mind maps
Flowcharts
Word webs
Classification grids
Right angles
Sequence charts
T-charts

Assessment

Portfolios
Logs/journals
Rubrics
Checklists
Observation guides
Performances
Demonstrations
Products
Exhibitions
Contracts
Interviews
Graphic organizers
Selected response tests
Projects
Constructed response
  tests

Figure 3.12

Lesson Planning Template

Unit Title:		Grade level:
STANDARDS: What should students know and be able to do for this portion of the unit (chunk)?	**Preassessment lesson strategy:** Such as journals, ticket out, quick writes, quizzes	
CRITICAL QUESTION FOR THIS PORTION OF THE UNIT:	**Personal Question(s):**	
CONTENT (Concepts)	**SKILLS (What will students do?)**	

Instructional Phases:

ACTIVATE (Creating focus and purpose, sharing standards and essential questions, and opening mental files)	Think-pair-share Field trip Video clip Short reading KWL People search Four corners	Jigsaw Three-step interview Mind map Carousel brainstorm Graffiti Give one, take one Fishbone
ACQUIRE (Getting new knowledge and skills)	Direct teaching Mini lecture Socratic dialogue Guest speaker Video clip Jigsaw Simple square	Learning contract Concept attainment Concept formation Simulation Case study Text reading Problem-based learning
APPLY, PRACTICE, FORMATIVE ASSESSMENT (Demonstrating the learning)	Venn diagram Fishbone Projects Experiments Metacognition Generalizations Note taking	Pop quiz Right angle Presentation Word web Hypothesizing Interview Problems
SUMMATIVE ASSESSMENT, CLOSURE, AND REFLECTION	Presentations Demonstration Revisit KWL 3-2-1 Give one, take one Journal entry Gallery walk	Carousel brainstorm Ticket out Goal setting Mind map Word web Model Debate

Figure 3.13

Math Lesson Plan

Unit Title: Survey Says . . .	Grade level: 3-5

STANDARDS: What should students know and be able to do for this portion of the unit (chunk)? Activating learning for the total unit and developing a survey question	Preassessment lesson strategy: Use the data from the adjustable grid designed from unit preassessment tool to start the unit and data from formative assessments throughout the unit such as journals, ticket out, quick writes, quizzes.
CRITICAL QUESTION FOR THIS PORTION OF THE UNIT: How can we use data to predict how people think about and choose preferences?	Personal Question(s): Student question written in math journal
CONTENT (Concepts) Data Investigate Predict	SKILLS: (What will students do?) Benchmark 1: Students will design investigations to address a question.

Instructional Phases:

ACTIVATE (Creating focus and purpose)
Class will engage in the mock game based on television show Family Feud
Students will work in **triads** and be given a survey questions to ask of other students. They will collect the answers from students in the classroom and display the responses. Then they will rank the top three responses. The teacher will set up the game that will use these survey results. Two teams of students will compete. All students will get a chance to be on a team.
    The **whole class** develops three criteria for good survey questions.
    Teacher shares critical question for this unit and asks students to **personalize** it in their math journal.

ACQUIRE (Getting the information and grouping choices)
Total group: Rationale for need to analyze data and survey. Real world examples of how surveys are used. **Direct instruction** on how to design a survey, ways to collect data, tally, and present a variety of ways to organize data **(pie chart, vertical bar graph, etc.).** Independent application or representation of simple data presented (differentiating product).

APPLY, PRACTICE, FORMATIVE ASSESSMENT (Demonstrating the learning)
Alone: Write a survey question (differentiating by interest and choice). Consider the options for displaying his/her data once collected.

SUMMATIVE ASSESSMENT, CLOSURE, AND REFLECTION
Partner work: Structured by teacher to peer edit their survey questions based on criteria identified.

Figure 3.14

practices to be used in the lesson. This, of course, is only one way. There are many pathways to achieve mastery. That is the art and science of teaching—using best practices in a creative way to help students reach standards. This plan uses cooperative group learning, thinking skills, and graphic representations and has embedded literacy skills of communication, writing, speaking, and representing. The teacher has provided brain compatibility in the following ways:

Providing for student movement

Chunking of activities to help focus attention

Tapping into emotions and relevancy

Providing variety and novelty

Facilitating social interaction

Designing active learning for optimum dendritic growth

The teacher has also tried to honor students' interests and preferences by giving them choices for data presentation and survey topics.

The following lesson plans (Figures 3.15–3.19, pages 80–84) are examples of different subject disciplines and grade levels to show the variety and integration of strategies that may be used. The power of best-practice strategies comes through the planning and layering to produce greater impact on learning and meet more learning styles and preferences for learning in our classrooms. The strategies may be selected from the "paint tubes" in Figure 3.12 (page 76) or using the lesson planning template in Figure 3.13 (page 77) to help you get started and think of the possibilities at each phase of the lesson. All the strategies are explained fully in chapters 4–9 in this book.

Elementary Science Lesson Plan

Unit Title: The Weather Reporter	Grade level: K-2

STANDARDS: What should students know and be able to do for this portion of the unit (chunk)? Students know and understand interrelationships among science, technology, and human activity and how they can affect the world. The seasons in our area and the weather	**Preassessment lesson strategy:** Use the data from the adjustable grid designed from unit preassessment tool to start the unit and data from formative assessments throughout the unit such as journals, ticket out, quick writes, quizzes

CRITICAL QUESTION FOR THIS PORTION OF THE UNIT: Can you tell what the weather will be like during the winter, spring, summer, and fall?	**Personal Question(s):** Students post a personal question

CONTENT (Concepts) Temperatures Season	**SKILLS: (What will students do?)** Students describe the type of weather characteristics for each season.

Instructional Phases:

ACTIVATE: (Creating focus and purpose)

Students work in **pairs** to engage in a **concept formation.** Students organize the materials in categories based on like attributes (i.e., seasons, weather, clothing or activities) The data set should include examples of seasonal clothing, sports, etc.
    Students report their categories and rationale with another **pair.**

ACQUIRE: (Getting the information and grouping choices)

Large group discussion: What do people wear when it is cold? What are things that we do in hot weather?
    What does winter look like? What happens in the spring? Which season do you like best and why? Invite students to go to **four corners** each labeled with one of the seasons. They will discuss with the other students who have selected that season why they chose that one and what they like about it.
    The students form **small heterogeneous groups to** create a poster showing why their season is best.

APPLY, PRACTICE, FORMATIVE ASSESSMENT: (Demonstrating the learning)

Using large chart paper divided in **four quadrants** labeled with the four seasons, students are given a bank of vocabulary words (such as warm, hot, sunny, shady, heat, chilly, sticky, swimming, hiking, skating) as well as pictures from their envelope and place them in the appropriate quadrant. (Use tables or floor for working space.)

SUMMATIVE ASSESSMENT, CLOSURE, AND REFLECTION

In your season construction paper book, one season per page, draw and write the following in each of three sections. (Differentiating by interest)

I am dressed for _____ wearing my _____

I like to _____ in _____ because _____

My house looks like this in _____ . It has _____

Students will resource vocabulary and pictures from previous activities. Learners who are at a more proficient level of verbal ability may write without sentence stems. Less able writers may use inventive spelling and correct it for the final product.

Figure 3.15

Social Studies Lesson Plan

Unit Title: Do you know your rights?	Grade level: 7-8

STANDARDS: What should students know and be able to do for this portion of the unit (chunk)? Developing a sense of historical background and context, including the concepts of freedom and citizenship. What were some of the influences that led to the Preamble and the first 10 rights?	Preassessment lesson strategy: Use the data from the adjustable grid designed from unit preassessment tool to start the unit and data from formative assessments throughout the unit such as journals, ticket out, quick writes, quizzes.
CRITICAL QUESTION FOR THIS PORTION OF THE UNIT: 1. How will you compare the reasons the Bill of Rights was drafted and the reasons it is still a powerful and influential document today?	Personal Question(s): Generated by students after activating the learning.
CONTENT (Concepts) Bill of Rights Constitution Historical context	SKILLS: (What will students do?) Benchmark a: (as in curriculum unit plan) Students will explain the reasons for the Bill of Rights and how this critical document has changed over time.

Instructional Phases:

ACTIVATE: (Creating focus and purpose)
One way for a teacher to set the stage for this unit is to bring in the following:

> ➤ A school district job application or college application with a nondiscrimination clause
> ➤ A copy of the "Miranda Rights" (from the local police)
> ➤ A copy of a blank tax form
> ➤ A newspaper
> ➤ A ballot
> ➤ A church bulletin or notice

Students are given a summary copy of the Bill of Rights and organized into **small heterogeneous groups.** Ask students from each group to explain to the whole group which right corresponds to a particular document. In addition, ask if they can think of any other examples.

ACQUIRE (Getting the information and grouping choices) Total group: Before viewing: Divide into groups of 5. Give each group a five-section puzzle or star with five questions on it. Each student will use a puzzle piece or point of a star to record his or her question and answer. The Bill of Rights is the central idea.

1. Why were the amendments written?
2. Listen some of the issues that leak to the Bill of Rights
3. Did everyone agree? Why or why not?
4. What else was going on in the colonies at that time?
5. What were some of the influences that led to the Preamble?

Students will take notes on their questions during the video. **(Jigsaw strategy)** (Special needs or English as a second language learners may work with a partner)
Total group: View video clip from PBS on **Creation of the Bill of Rights** and answer questions

APPLY, PRACTICE, FORMATIVE ASSESSMENT (Demonstrating the learning)
Small groups: In a group of 5, share answers to their question with the others and take **notes on a summarizing star sheet.**
   Total group: Discussion to summarize historical context of Bill of Rights.
   Given the reasons for certain rights, are they still applicable today?
   Which one is most important to you and why? **Think, Pair, Share**

SUMMATIVE ASSESSMENT, CLOSURE, AND REFLECTION
Using a T chart. In the film, list some issues we still deal with today. On the right side, what are some issues that may be different today?
   Resources: *Film Notes* and current newspaper or news magazine. Could be assigned as homework.

Figure 3.16

Language Arts Lesson Plan

Unit Title: American Literature	Grade level: 8
STANDARDS: What should students know and be able to do for this portion of the unit (chunk)?	**Preassessment lesson strategy:** Use the data from the adjustable grid designed from unit preassessment tool to start the unit and data from formative assessments throughout the unit such as journals, ticket out, quick writes, quizzes.
CRITICAL QUESTION FOR THIS PORTION OF THE UNIT: What is the importance of making good choices in life?	**Personal Question(s):** Students create their own question
CONTENT: (Concepts) Writing styles of poets Literary devices used in poetry Tone used to maintain attitude in poetry	**SKILLS: (What will students do?)** Distinguish author's purpose for writing Analyze conflict and resolution in author's message Compare and contrast

Instructional Phases:

ACTIVATE: (Creating focus and purpose)
Using a Three-Step interview. Think about a time when you had a difficult choice to make. How did you decide? What would you do differently?
   As a large group read Robert Frost's poem "The Road Not Taken" and "The Choice" by Dorothy Parker

ACQUIRE: (Getting the information and grouping choices)
In **roundtable discussion** have students discuss the following:

Roles for group: A. Facilitator, B. Recorder, C. Reader. These roles rotate through the group as each question is considered. The social skill will be **Attentive Listening.** A reporter will be chosen when the task if finished.

Questions: What is the importance of making good choices?

Explain what happens when you make a choice.

Why do poets think it is important for readers to understand their tone in poems?

What were the choices in the two poems read?

Should people be held responsible for their choices?

APPLY, PRACTICE, FORMATIVE ASSESSMENT: (Demonstrating the learning)
In their small groups, students will create a **Venn diagram and compare and contrast the two poems** as to poetic devices used, theme, structure, etc.
   Students will create a **poster on the theme, What If?** Use poetic devices in the poster.

SUMMATIVE ASSESSMENT, CLOSURE, AND REFLECTION
On a **3-2-1 students will reflect on**
3 things to consider when making a choice
2 things that intrigued them in the poems
1 thing they learned about choices

QUIZ
Students will find other poetry dealing with choices and share with classmates.

Figure 3.17

Science Lesson Design Plan

Unit Title: Reptiles	Grade level:

STANDARDS: What should students know and be able to do for this portion of the unit (chunk)? Classify living things by their characteristics Describe the basic needs of living things Describe the relationship of an organism to its environment	**Preassessment lesson strategy:** Use the data from the adjustable grid designed from unit preassessment tool to start the unit and data from formative assessments throughout the unit such as journals, ticket out, quick writes, quizzes.

CRITICAL QUESTION FOR THIS PORTION OF THE UNIT: What is a reptile? Where do reptiles fit in the food chain?	**Personal Question(s):** Students will identify a question they would like to answer.

CONTENT: (Concepts) Characteristics of reptiles Needs of reptiles Relationship of reptile to its environment	**SKILLS: (What will students do?)** Use research skills to investigate reptiles Express finding orally and in writing

Instructional Phases:

ACTIVATE: (Creating focus and purpose)
Students will work in small groups to fill a KWL chart.

ACQUIRE: (Getting the information and grouping choices)
Class will view a video about reptiles
   With a **partner,** students will examine trade books and search engine sites to garner information about reptiles
   An **advance organizer** will help them record their information.

APPLY, PRACTICE, FORMATIVE ASSESSMENT: (Demonstrating the learning)
Students will create a note-taking activity using a **fishbone** to note characteristics of a reptile. Using the information they have gathered, students will **write and illustrate** a story about reptiles.

SUMMATIVE ASSESSMENT, CLOSURE, AND REFLECTION
Students will peer edit their stories and check for accuracy about characteristics of reptiles. They will revisit **KWL** charts.

Figure 3.18

Science Lesson Design Plan

Unit Title: This Planet Rocks	Grade level:

STANDARDS: What should students know and be able to do for this portion of the unit (chunk)? Design and conduct simple scientific investigations in which observations are made, data are gathered and organized, and reasonable conclusions are drawn. Investigate, describe, and compare properties of earth's basic materials (water, air, rock).	Preassessment lesson strategy: Use the data from the adjustable grid designed from unit preassessment tool to start the unit and data from formative assessments throughout the unit such as journals, ticket out, quick writes, quizzes.
CRITICAL QUESTION FOR THIS PORTION OF THE UNIT: How are the different types of rocks formed?	Personal Question(s): Students create their own question and post on chart.
CONTENT (Concepts) The characteristics of four Illinois minerals Rock and mineral scientific vocabulary	SKILLS: (What will students do?) Identify and describe properties of minerals Compare and contrast minerals using scientific criteria

Instructional Phases:

ACTIVATE (Creating focus and purpose, open mental files)
To reconnect from last day's lesson:
   Roundtable, Round Robin: In small groups of four, each student will hold one mineral and share one item of information about it, then pass the minerals to the right and take another turn sharing additional information.
   Review **KWL** chart ready to find answers for **L**
   Students will receive **a chart/graphic organizer** to complete during the lesson.Scientific vocabulary will be reviewed: luster, Mohs' hardness scale, texture, fluorite, calcite, gypsum, quartz, scratch test.

ACQUIRE: (Getting the information and grouping choices)
Teacher will model the use of the **chart/graphic organizer** through **role play,** observing a mineral sample to demonstrate the process of completing the organizer.
   Vocabulary will be reviewed and used in the context of the activity.

APPLY, PRACTICE, FORMATIVE ASSESSMENT: (Demonstrating the learning)
Working in **cooperative groups** students will list properties of each mineral using scientific vocabulary.
   Individually, student will look for **similarities and differences** between 2,3, or 4 minerals.
   Geology Online web site may be used to research for more information.
   Discuss/debate similarities/differences with their cooperative group members.

SUMMATIVE ASSESSMENT, CLOSURE, AND REFLECTION
Using **Give one, Take one,** group members share their findings.
   Revisit **KWL** and report one fact about minerals
   Extension Check out Web site This Planet Really Rocks

Figure 3.19

Reflections

You can use these stems as catalysts for reflection or dialogue with colleagues.

SUMMING UP

Consider????
What strategies are you already using?

Questions???
Which strategies do you wish to know more about?

Actions???
How could you become more proficient?

Study groups?

Attend a workshop?

Read a book?

Work with a coaching/planning partner?

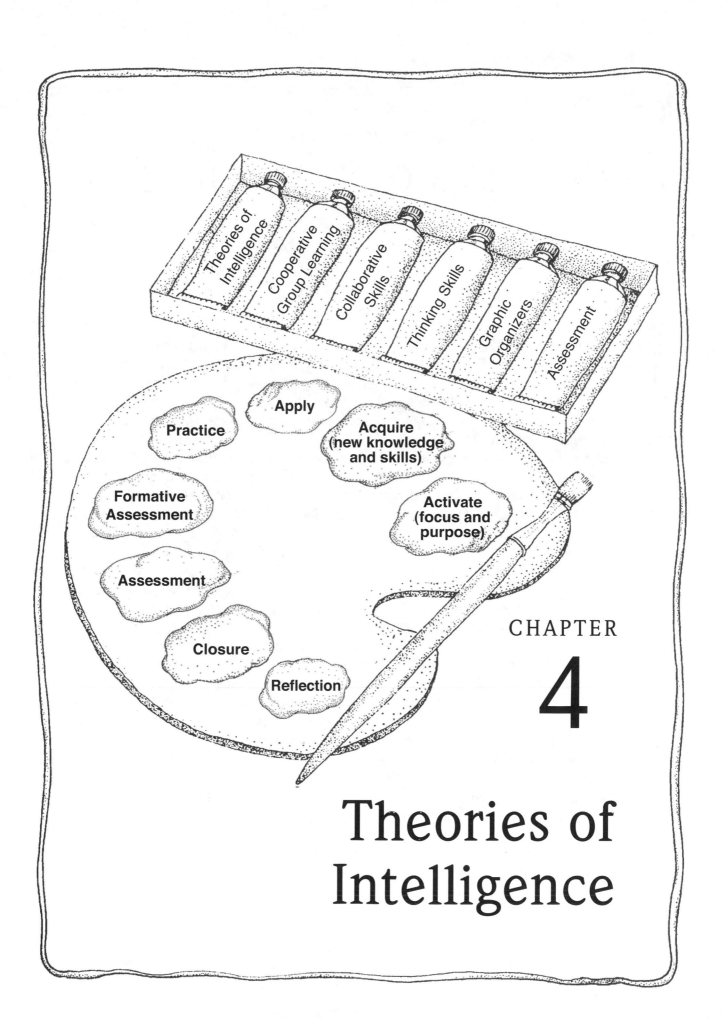

CHAPTER

4

Theories of
Intelligence

CHAPTER 4

THEORIES OF INTELLIGENCE

WHAT ARE THEY?

For the first part of the twentieth century, intelligence was measured by one of the many forms of intelligence tests. These usually were based on logical, mathematical, and verbal abilities and yielded an intelligence quotient (IQ). Intelligence was perceived as a quantity, fixed at birth, and for the most part, unchangeable thereafter. In the past two decades, cognitive psychologists and educational researchers have developed theories of intelligence that are beginning to replace some of the older ideas. In 1983, psychologist Howard Gardner postulated a theory of multiple intelligences, which described and defined seven distinct types of intelligence: verbal/linguistic, logical/mathematical, musical/rhythmic, bodily/kinesthetic, visual/spatial, interpersonal, and intrapersonal. In 1995, he added an eighth intelligence, naturalist.

Author Daniel Goleman (1995) described the theory of emotional intelligence in his book *Emotional Intelligence.* Emotional intelligence includes a set of competencies that allows one person to flourish while another person, of seemingly higher intelligence, flounders. These competencies include self-awareness, managing emotions, self-motivation, empathy, and social arts.

In the same year, Art Costa (1995), a world-renowned educator, developed a set of intelligent behaviors, which he described in his book *Teaching for Intelligent Behavior.* He defined these as the traits or attributes that distinguish excellent thinkers and problem solvers. Costa's set of intelligent behaviors includes many of Coleman's items but also lists persistence, flexibility in thinking, checking for accuracy and precision, using all the senses, and a sense of efficacy as a thinker.

The main ideas that link the alternate theories are that all people can learn and that intelligence can be improved through instruction. This is what sets them apart from more traditional intelligence theories, which maintain that people are born bright or dull and nothing can be done to change one's intelligence.

Traditional views of intelligence are usually restricted to a narrow range of abilities. The nontraditional, or alternate, theories of intelligence are much broader in scope. They encompass a wide range of human abilities and have major implications for the classroom. There are many ways of looking at intelligence. In this book, we restrict the discussion to the three theories of intelligence that have the greatest relevance to education: multiple intelligences, emotional intelligence, and intelligent behavior.

Multiple Intelligences

When students take an IQ test, their intelligence is usually measured in terms of their verbal and mathematical abilities. Howard Gardner (1983), who outlined his theory of multiple intelligences in *Frames of Mind: The Theory of Multiple Intelligences,* acknowledged these abilities but proposed that there are additional distinct types of intelligence. Following are brief descriptions of each of the intelligences identified by Gardner.

Verbal/Linguistic

Verbal/linguistic intelligence is the most commonly shared and crucial competence of the human species. At its highest level of functioning, it allows us to comprehend the meanings of words in spoken and written form. It also allows us to follow the rules of syntax and grammar and appreciate the sounds, rhythms, and inflections of language.

Logical/Mathematical

Logical/mathematical intelligence is in the domain of math and science. This intelligence allows us to assess, weigh, measure, and compute. It allows us to work with numerical symbols and to sequence and align information as a way of solving problems.

Visual/Spatial

Visual/spatial intelligence forms the basis for our abilities in the visual arts, including drawing, painting, and sculpture. It gives us the ability to work in three-dimensional space as in architectural or industrial design. It allows us to form mental images and manipulate them so that we can see them from other viewpoints. The ability to draw and interpret maps and to navigate and find our way around in the world is also mediated by our visual/spatial intelligence.

Bodily/Kinesthetic

The main characteristic of bodily/kinesthetic intelligence is our ability to use the body in highly differentiated ways for expressive, recreational, or goal-directed purposes. Dancers, athletes, and high-steel construction workers all possess a high degree of bodily/kinesthetic ability. When we involve the body in learning, the generated neural activity helps to provide the cognitive structures that allow us to understand and recall the information at a later date. As an example, our learning of concepts such as space and volume is greatly enhanced when we play with and manipulate wooden blocks, cylinders, and pyramids.

Musical/Rhythmic

Musical/rhythmic intelligence deals with rhythm, melody, tone, pitch, and pattern. Of all the intelligences, the musical/rhythmic intelligence has the greatest consciousness-altering effect on the brain. Music can calm, excite, or inspire us. It can make us move faster or slower, buy more products at the supermarket, or relax in elevators. Music can help us maintain a steady rhythm when exercising, marching, or typing. Music also helps us to recall information. For example, many of us can remember learning the alphabet by singing the ABC song. When asked, "How many days in August?" most of us recall the rhythmic verse that begins "Thirty days hath September, April, June, and November."

Intrapersonal

Intrapersonal intelligence involves the internal knowledge of oneself, such as the range of feelings and emotional responses we are likely to display in any given situation. It monitors our thinking and reflecting processes as well as our thoughts about self-image and personal identity. Intrapersonal intelligence gives us the capacity to see wholeness and unity and to be cognizant of higher states of consciousness.

Interpersonal

Interpersonal intelligence allows us to work in groups effectively and to communicate verbally and nonverbally with other people. It provides us with the capacity to perceive emotions, moods, motivations, and intentions in others. It also allows us to empathize with another person's feelings, fears, and beliefs.

Naturalist

Naturalist intelligence provides us with the ability to recognize the critical attributes of flora and fauna, weather patterns, and other phenomena in the natural world. Historically, people with these abilities were those in the community perceived as possessing wisdom. They were the ones who could read signs and portents in nature. They knew when to plant and when to harvest, what plants could be eaten and what plants could be used for medicinal purposes. Modern-day applications of this intelligence include hunting, farming, and the biological sciences. In an urban setting, young people may be using an adaptive variation of naturalist intelligence when they decide which streets are safe and which are dangerous or make the fine distinctions between brands of running shoes, sweatshirts, or hairstyles.

Gardner theorized that each intelligence is relatively independent, with its own schedule for growth and development. Because of the different cultural influences each of us experiences, some intelligences develop strongly, others slightly, and some not at all. Each person's intelligence profile is a jagged line, or a series of peaks and valleys, unique to that person.

Much of the research on multiple intelligences is predicated on pathological conditions or the results of brain injury. The existence of prodigies or mentally handicapped individuals with savant abilities tends to prove the existence of a particular intelligence. Dustin Hoffman portrayed a fictional character with savant abilities in the movie *Rain Man* (1988), a seemingly dysfunctional person who had an extraordinary, or savant, ability with numbers. Brain trauma can result in whole areas of intelligence being wiped out or seriously damaged. For example, the abilities to speak, recognize patterns, or respond emotionally can be impaired by injury to the brain, depending on which part of the brain is damaged.

Each intelligence has a distinct developmental history and a definable set of criteria by which to judge expert performance. For example, one aspect of visual/spatial intelligence is the ability to draw. If we examine the ability of children to draw a human figure, we find that most children follow a sequence of definable stages. At first they draw large heads with small sticks for arms and legs. This is followed by stick figures with increased attention to proportion and detail. Finally, they begin to render more realistic representations. If they have ability and are encouraged to persevere, many children can draw a reasonable facsimile of the human figure; however, very few people will attain the level of expertise of an acknowledged master of the human form such as Michelangelo.

Emotional Intelligence

Most of us know of exceptionally bright people who are socially inept and have difficulty maintaining a relationship or keeping a job. Although very bright, as measured by an intelligence test, they seem to lack common sense and the ability to get along with others. We also may know of people of more modest ability who seem to thrive and make achievements in life far greater than would have been predicted by their IQ scores. What is it that allows these people to thrive while the very bright person fails? The answer is emotional intelligence, the ability to get along with others.

The concept of emotional intelligence was originally formulated by psychologist Peter Salovey of Yale University and his collaborator, John Mayer, of New Hampshire University (Goleman 1995). They defined emotional intelligence as having three domains: the ability to understand and express emotions in one's self and in others, the ability to regulate emotions, and the ability to use emotions in creative thinking, reasoning, and problem solving.

In *Emotional Intelligence,* Daniel Goleman drew on research from both the cognitive and behavioral sciences to demonstrate the factors at work when people of seemingly high IQ struggle, while others with more modest ability thrive. Goleman called these factors emotional intelligence and identified five domains of emotional intelligence—self-awareness, managing emotions, self-motivation, empathy, and social arts. These domains include competencies such as impulse control, persistence, hopefulness, delaying gratification, and handling relationships (see Fig. 4.1, page 92).

According to Goleman, emotional intelligence is an aptitude that allows us to mobilize the forces of enthusiasm, confidence, and energy and bring them to bear on a situation. Although emotions are an important factor in this equation, they can get in the way. Most of us have been in situations that were so stressful that we were unable to generate enough energy to think clearly and act appropriately.

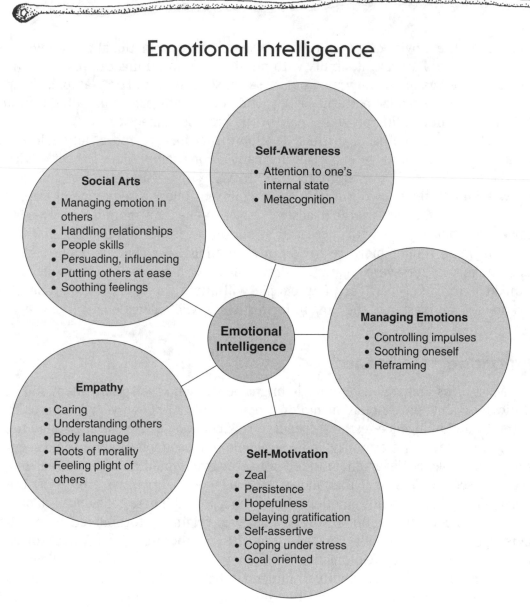

Emotional Intelligence

Self-Awareness
- Attention to one's internal state
- Metacognition

Social Arts
- Managing emotion in others
- Handling relationships
- People skills
- Persuading, influencing
- Putting others at ease
- Soothing feelings

Emotional Intelligence

Managing Emotions
- Controlling impulses
- Soothing oneself
- Reframing

Empathy
- Caring
- Understanding others
- Body language
- Roots of morality
- Feeling plight of others

Self-Motivation
- Zeal
- Persistence
- Hopefulness
- Delaying gratification
- Self-assertive
- Coping under stress
- Goal oriented

Figure 4.1

The extent to which emotional upset can interfere with learning is obvious to anyone who has spent time in a classroom. Many students who are in the grips of emotion have difficulty learning and concentrating. Their working memories are overloaded with negative information that interferes with the learning process.

Emotional stress often results in people's working memories being overloaded, their capacity for information being overtaxed, and their ability to think rationally being hampered. The opposite of this is the state of relaxed alertness, which is engendered by a feeling of energy, enthusiasm, and confidence. In the latter case, the mind is ready, willing, and able to engage in learning.

Self-Awareness

Goleman proposed that emotional intelligence is the sum of a number of parts, one of which is self-awareness. Self-awareness closely parallels Howard Gardner's (1983) concept of intrapersonal intelligence and Art Costa's (1991) concept of metacognition. Self-awareness is the ability to be in touch with internal states of mind so that emotions can be identified and labeled as a first step to assuming control over them.

To understand the factors that triggered a specific mood, it is first necessary to identify the mood. Consciously analyzing an emotion while in the midst of it can help keep a person from becoming swept away by it. This is the first step in being able to control the emotion. If we recognize that we are "down in the dumps," we can look for reasons for this feeling and make changes in our mood. The theory here is that behavior often is intertwined with emotion and that by modifying one, we can change the other.

The ability to make appropriate decisions and wise choices is a major factor in attaining a well-balanced emotional life. Our emotional lives are affected to a large extent by the decisions we make. Similarly, the decisions we make are affected by our emotional lives.

Emotions are survival oriented and play an important role in our ability to make wise choices. Contrary to popular belief, decisions that are made purely on the basis of what is rational and logical are not necessarily the best ones. Neurologist Antonio Damasio (1994) stated that the brain, mind, body, and emotions form a linked system, and although uncontrolled emotion can cause irrational behavior, decisions devoid of an emotional component may be equally disastrous.

The emotional brain regulates our emotional lives by controlling the flow of neurotransmitters and the related hormones that result from emotional experiences. Traditionally, many of us have been encouraged to put emotion aside and make all decisions based on logic alone. What we really need is to strike a balance between logic and emotion.

Managing Emotions

A sense of self-mastery and the ability to negotiate the emotional peaks and valleys of life are praised as virtues in most cultures. Many schools respond to this by suppressing emotion in an attempt to provide a quiet and calm atmosphere. This may lead to an unbalanced emotional climate that appears tranquil at the surface but is, in reality, a seething mass of suppressed emotion. The goal of all schools should be to attain a climate that is emotionally balanced, where all feelings and emotions are recognized as having value and significance.

To balance the emotional climate in classrooms, it is necessary to manage negative emotions, such as anger and fear, while encouraging those that have a more positive effect, such as joy and delight. This is not to say that students should be "happy all the live-long day" because that is unbalanced and unrealistic; a variety of emotions keeps life interesting. But for people who frequently experience predominately negative feelings, the lack of positive feelings can lead to depression. Prolonged bouts of negative emotion can seriously impair a student's ability to focus on tasks and to learn.

Of all the negative emotions, anger seems to be the most difficult to control. Indeed, many people seem to enjoy an emotional rush as they engage in self-righteous inner dialogue directed against the objects of their ire.

Self-Motivation

According to both Goleman and Costa, impulse control is perhaps the most fundamental psychological skill. Research indicates that the ability to control one's impulses and emotional reactions correlates very highly with achievement both in school and in life.

An experiment known as the Marshmallow Study (Shoda, Mischel, and Peake 1990) shows the importance of impulse control and delaying gratification. The study was carried out at Stanford by Walter Mischel in the 1960s. In the experiment, four-year-old children were presented with one marshmallow each. They were told that if they waited a while without eating the marshmallow, they would be given two marshmallows. The researcher then left the children alone and observed them through a one-way glass. Some children immediately gobbled up the marshmallow, others held out for a while, and still others lasted until the researcher returned with their rewards.

The predictive power of this experiment was remarkable. When the candidates were tracked down twelve years later, the emotional and social differences between the impulsive students and those who resisted temptation were dramatic. Those who had controlled their impulses were more socially adept, self-confident, and generally well adjusted. When the students were evaluated again, prior to graduation, the students who had controlled their impulses the longest did better academically and had significantly higher SAT scores. It appears, then, that impulse control at age four may be a powerful predictor of academic and social competence.

According to Goleman, the ability to control impulses in pursuit of a goal is the key to the self-regulation of all our emotions. Indeed, the degree to which our emotions enhance or inhibit our capacity to learn, think, plan, and pursue far-off goals may define the limits of all other mental capacities. In other words, a high IQ in the absence of emotional intelligence may limit our ability to succeed in life. Those who can delay immediate gratification and persevere toward a planned goal generally are more successful in life and more able to cope under stress. They tend to remain hopeful when faced with opposition or setbacks and stay motivated and optimistic. A sense of efficacy combined with a strong work ethic allows one to have a sense of personal control and self-motivation, which in turn helps in goal achievement.

Empathy

Empathy is the ability to see things from another person's point of view and, to some extent, to know how that person feels. The ability to understand another person's point of view often arises out of the ability to decipher one's own feelings. This corresponds with Howard Gardner's notions of intrapersonal and interpersonal intelligences. People who lack an awareness of or are confused about their own feelings often are unable to interpret or even acknowledge the feelings of others.

The roots of empathy appear in early childhood, when children begin to imitate the distress of others. For example, a child might see someone in pain, caused by a bump on the head, and respond by feeling his or her own head. The theory is that by imitating the distress of others, we begin to evoke similar feelings in ourselves. The ways in which children are disciplined can also reinforce their growing sense of empathy. Instead of being scolded, children should be made aware of the distress they have caused someone else. The development of empathy also is shaped by seeing how others react when someone else is distressed. It is by precept and example, then, that children gradually build a repertoire of empathic responses.

Researcher Martin Hoffman (1984) believes that morality lies within empathy. It is the ability to feel for others, read verbal and nonverbal clues, and share their distress that encourages people to help rather than hurt others.

Social Arts

Social competencies are built on the ability to manage one's self and to be empathic. Being able to develop rapport with others is an important trait of a socially adept person. The old adage "People need to know you care before they care about what you know" still holds true.

People who are adept at social and people skills and in handling relationships are able to connect easily with others because they show a caring, empathic nature. Using cooperative group learning in classrooms helps this development because it enables students to work with others and to develop social skills in a safe environment in which they receive feedback.

The first step in developing social arts is being able to express feelings well. Displays of emotion are ways in which we reach out to others. Having the ability to read the reactions of others quickly and accurately and being able to effectively deal with others is a social art. This ability is helpful when assuming interpersonal roles such as inspiring, motivating, managing, and mediating. People with this ability are often referred to as having polish or finesse. This ability can be used in a sensitive, caring way, with integrity and respect for others, as well as in a Machiavellian way to achieve certain ends.

Intelligent Behavior

Many theorists postulate what they think intelligence is. Art Costa (1995), for example, proposes that being intelligent is being able to handle the unexpected or unknown with confidence and strategies to problem solve. Art Costa (1996) defined intelligent behavior as "knowing what to do when you don't know what to do." Costa (1995) proposed a set of intelligent behaviors, which includes many of the emotional competencies described by Goleman (1995):

Dr. Costa proposed twelve intelligent behaviors that help us with our thinking. These evolved into sixteen "habits of mind":

- *Persistence:* to persist in spite of obstacles or challenges to find solutions to dilemmas or problems
- *Decreasing impulsivity:* to control physical and emotional responses so that successful thinking can take place
- *Empathic listening:* to feel for another by putting oneself in another's place, taking on the other's persona and experiencing the thoughts and feelings he or she might be having
- *Flexibility in thinking:* to be able to adjust to and try to explore other points of view
- *Metacognition:* to be aware of one's own thinking and reflect on situations, challenges, or problems
- *Checking for accuracy and precision:* to focus on what quality looks like and to work toward quality, including correctness and clarity
- *Posing questions and problems:* to continue to be inquisitive and question new information to extend one's learning
- *Drawing on past experience and applying it to new situations:* to reflect on past situations so that prior experiences are helpful in new situations
- *Using precise and accurate language:* to use specific descriptive language that accurately conveys meaning
- *Using all senses:* to fully understand new things and information by exploring one's environment using all the senses
- *Creativity:* to create something new by taking one's knowledge and skills and exploring solutions to problems
- *Being excited and awed about our world:* being intrigued and wonder struck about the world around us
- *Risking appropriately:* stretching one's competencies to continue to grow
- *Using humor:* laughing and being whimsical and appreciating the unexpected
- *Collaborative interdependence:* using reciprocal learning to grow and develop
- *Being open to new learning:* being humble and inquisitive and avoid complacency

Intelligent behavior is intelligent thought transposed into action. In other words, it is the external application of an internal process. In schools, however, we often come across students who appear to be bright but have no repertoire of skills with which to apply their intelligence. Teaching for intelligent behavior is based on the proposition that all students can be taught a repertoire of skills that will allow them to behave in more intelligent ways.

WHY DO WE NEED THEM?

In the first half of the twentieth century, students routinely were consigned to a particular type of schooling and, hence, a particular occupation based solely on an IQ score. Today, schools are moving away from this way of viewing intelligence and are expanding opportunities for students to use and increase their abilities in areas formerly not recognized or valued in school settings.

Developing all forms of intelligence is important because achievement in multiple areas, including but not limited to academic success, is what marks people who excel in life. Typically, people who excel are emotionally balanced, flexible thinkers, and creative problem solvers. These are the people whose relationships flourish, who succeed in the careers of their choice, and who maintain balanced and healthy lifestyles. In short, they possess the qualities and attributes most teachers would describe as being desirable goals for all students.

If we want students to attain these goals, we need to look to nontraditional theories of intelligence for insight.

Multiple Intelligences

One of the major implications of Gardner's theory is that intelligence can be taught—that people can learn to behave in more intelligent ways if multiple forms of intelligence are nurtured and valued. This is a significant departure from traditional concepts of IQ, which are based on the premise that intelligence is fixed at birth and immutable thereafter.

This fundamental premise, or cornerstone, to how intelligence has traditionally been viewed has had a major impact on how the learning process has been structured. In the past, many schools have typically concentrated their efforts on verbal and mathematical abilities. Some schools still do. Doing so may be likened to using a tool kit that contains only a hammer and a screwdriver. Certainly, there are problems that can be solved with a hammer and a screwdriver, just as there are problems that can be solved with logic and words. However, if the kit is extended to include a variety of tools, then presumably we can solve a whole range of other problems. Extending the tool kit to provide students with more than a hammer and screwdriver, or logic and words, therefore, is a fundamental premise of the multiple intelligences theory.

Emotional Intelligence

The basic premise of the theory of emotional intelligence is that emotional intelligence is at least as important as IQ. In fact, the ability to recognize, monitor, and regulate our emotional lives may be the key to maximizing the potential of all other aspects of intelligence.

Many of society's problems appear to be linked to a lack of emotional intelligence. Violence may stem from individuals' inabilities to delay impulsiveness or gratification.

Family violence can result from family members' lack of ability to manage their emotions. Problems in the workplace are often the result of employees who cannot empathize or who do not have the social skills to work with others. Many people are not able to be optimistic and self-motivated in the management of goals or projects.

If we want to help students become better able to function in classrooms, families, and society, we need to build in opportunities for them to practice collaborative/ social skills and to develop strategies to manage emotions such as anger.

Intelligent Behavior

As teachers, we should be more interested in how students produce and apply knowledge than in how much information they recall. An intelligent person not only possesses information but knows how to use it. It is impossible to predict exactly what information one will need to know in the future. Likewise, life in the future promises to be more complex than we know it today. The information explosion will cause us to shift our emphasis from content and memorizing facts to accessing and managing information, critical thinking, and verifying accuracy. To meet these challenges, individuals will need to be problem solvers, critical and creative thinkers, and team players who can feel deeply and act wisely.

For years, we have continually added to the curriculum without ever "selectively abandoning" (Costa 1991) items that are no longer essential or worthy of classroom time. As our curriculum is overloaded, we need a way of integrating the multiple intelligences, emotional intelligence, and intelligent behavior into classroom practice. Figure 4.2 shows an overview of all three theories.

HOW DO WE TEACH THEM?

The following pages deal with each of the theories of intelligence in greater detail while providing practical suggestions for classroom implementation. Integrating multiple intelligences, emotional intelligence, and intelligent behavior into the day-to-day process for instruction is one of the most effective ways of implementing these skills.

Multiple Intelligences

As teachers, we can engage students in developing their multiple intelligences by expanding their opportunities to use a broad range of intelligence in nontraditional ways. Teaching for multiple intelligences includes processing and demonstrating learning through all the intelligences; for example, musical/rhythmic, visual/ spatial, or bodily/kinesthetic intelligence as opposed to the more traditional verbal/ linguistic or logical/mathematical intelligence. Songs, raps, model making, and role

Three Theories of Intelligence

Gardner's Multiple Intelligences

- Verbal/Linguistic
- Logical/Mathematical
- Visual/Spatial
- Bodily/Kinesthetic
- Musical/Rhythmic
- Intrapersonal
- Interpersonal
- Naturalist

Costa's Intelligent Behavior

- Persistence
- Decreasing Impulsivity
- Empathic Listening
- Flexibility in Thinking
- Metacognition
- Checking for Accuracy and Precision
- Posing Questions & Problems
- Drawing on Past Experience and Applying it to New Situations
- Using Precise and Accurate Language
- Using All Senses
- Creativity
- Being Excited and Awed About Our World
- Risking Appropriately
- Using Humor
- Collaborative Interdependence
- Being Open to New Learning

Goleman's Emotional Intelligence

- Self-Awareness
- Managing Emotions
- Self-Motivation
- Empathy
- Social Arts

Figure 4.2

plays all may be used in place of traditional paper-and-pencil activities. In the assessment and evaluation phase of learning, students might submit work in forms other than those traditionally used to demonstrate learning. For example, a video-tape might be substituted for a written essay, or a report might be delivered in the form of a dramatic presentation.

Figure 4.3 (pages 100 through 102) presents suggestions of ways to implement each of the multiple intelligences. Because it is useful to provide a link between the real world and the theory of multiple intelligences, we begin each section with the names of people who exhibit a high degree of ability in a particular area. For example, for the musical/rhythmic intelligence, we list Mozart, Paul Simon, and Madonna. Students can take note of these examples and generate a list of their own examples as a way of linking multiple intelligences to their own experiences.

The Multiple Intelligences

Verbal/Linguistic
Exemplified by John F. Kennedy, William F. Buckley

To stimulate verbal/linguistic:
- Generate a list of people who exhibit this intelligence, historical or contemporary, or literary characters, family, friends
- Rewrite the ending of a book or novel or add an epilogue
- Write a response to a newspaper editorial
- Summarize an article or annotate a book
- Make an oral presentation to a group
- Keep a diary

Classroom activities:
- Think-pair-share
- Oral reports/speeches
- Choral readings
- Dramatizations and role plays
- Speeches and debates
- Three-step interviews
- Logs and journals
- Socratic seminars/debates
- Reciprocal teaching

Musical/Rhythmic
Exemplified by Mozart, Paul Simon, Madonna

To stimulate musical/rhythmic:
- Tell a story in song
- Use a familiar tune and create a song about your pet, hobby, vacation, etc.
- Listen to different kinds of music and see how you react or adjust your mood
- Add appropriate music as you tell a story or dramatize an event

Classroom activities:
- Rap/songs
- Rhythms and rhymes
- Movement and exploration
- Mood music and instrumental
- Echo clapping
- Choral reading
- Mnemonics
- Sounds in nature

Logical/Mathematical
Exemplified by Albert Einstein, Carl Sagan

To stimulate logical/mathematical:
- Outline the procedures for a task in a linear, sequential manner
- Create an argument defending an idea that some people might find controversial
- Keep track of your day by logging your time on productive tasks, level of energy or fatigue, and things that stimulate or cause frustration
- Sequence and dovetail tasks to organize your activities to be more efficient

Classroom activities:
- Advance organizers
- Graphic organizers
- Logic puzzles/games
- Timelines
- Mental math
- Experimentation/problem solving
- Debates
- Critical thinking
- Interpret charts, graphs, and grids
- Data and statistics

Figure 4.3

The Multiple Intelligences

Visual/Spatial
Exemplified by Leonardo da Vinci, Frank Lloyd Wright

To stimulate visual/spatial:
- Picture the setting and the characteristics in detail in your mind's eye as you read
- Use photography to express yourself
- Visualize an experience or event—how it will unfold, what it will look like if you are successful, and/or what it will look like if you achieve your goals
- Sketch your ideas rather than write them

Classroom activities:
- Mind maps and graphics
- Video, CD-ROM, DVD
- Geometry
- Overheads
- Art activities
- Bulletin boards, charts, and posters
- Murals and storyboarding
- Models

Bodily/Kinesthetic
Exemplified by Marcel Marceau, Michael Jordan

To stimulate bodily/kinesthetic:
- Use body movement or physical motion to learn concepts or ideas
- Observe yourself on video—note your body language
- Try a new sport, dance, or exercise program
- Use your body to depict your thoughts

Classroom activities:
- Role play/drama
- Dance/movement
- Lip sync, skits, charades, mime
- Construct and build models
- Math manipulatives and experiments
- Gestures and body language
- Physical activity and sports
- Activity centers

Naturalist
Exemplified by Charles Darwin, David Suzuki

To stimulate naturalist:
- Take nature walks and spend time in the outdoors
- Go camping, canoeing, and backpacking
- Spend time at the zoo or the aquarium
- Observe the passing seasons and note the behavior of birds and animals

Classroom activities:
- Growing plants/gardening/nature study
- Collecting and classifying
- Creating charts and graphs
- Maintaining terrariums and aquariums
- Constructing ecosystems
- Creating displays
- Recording observations and experiments
- Logging weather and related elements

Figure 4.3 (Continued)

The Multiple Intelligences

Intrapersonal
Exemplified by Buddha, Steven Covey

To stimulate intrapersonal:
- Stand outside yourself and listen, observe, and feel you
- Become aware of your moods—what makes you happy, sad, angry, or frustrated
- Reflect on how you solve problems and deal with crises
- Keep a log or journal

Classroom activities:
- Metacognition/diaries
- Poetry/reflection
- Logs/journals
- Goal setting
- Positive affirmations/self-expression
- Autobiographies
- Independent study/choice

Interpersonal
Exemplified by Princess Diana, Oprah Winfrey

To stimulate interpersonal:
- Try different situations in which interdependence with other people is required for success; for example, working in cooperative groups or collaborating with others on a project
- Practice different ways to communicate with someone else; for example, use facial expressions, body posture, gestures, and sounds
- Test your assumptions about body language, both your own and other people's

Classroom activities:
- Think-pair-share
- Interviews
- Cooperative/interactive structures
- Shared dialog and debates
- Class meetings
- Reciprocal teaching
- Peer tutoring
- Study buddies
- Use e-mail

Figure 4.3 (Continued)

Suggestions for stimulating or awakening intelligences for those students for whom a particular intelligence may be dormant, as well as suggestions for classroom activities, are included. Many of the suggested activities pertain to more than one type of intelligence. For example, a role play may be listed under bodily/kinesthetic, but it also may involve visual/spatial dimensions. In fact, it is difficult to find an activity that contains only one aspect of intelligence. The suggested activities, however, provide an excellent opportunity for students to demonstrate ability in a particular intelligence.

Target the Multiple Intelligences

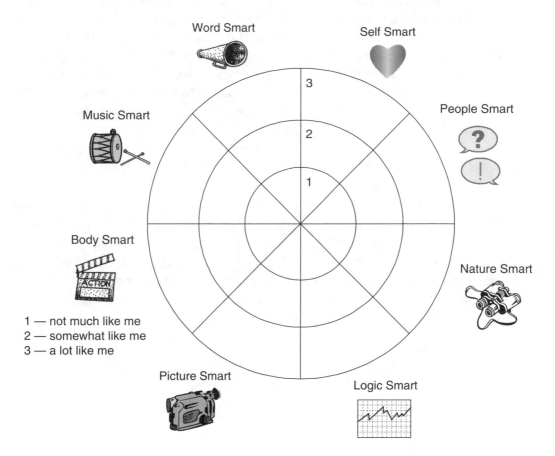

Figure 4.4

Targeting the Multiple Intelligences

It is our contention that by focusing on a limited set of teaching strategies and combining them in many different ways, teachers can design learning experiences that conform more closely with the ways in which the brain learns best.

You can encourage student self-assessment and self-knowledge by using the Multiple Intelligences Target shown in Figure 4.4. After the eight areas have been identified, explored, and stimulated, have students fill in the target based on their self-perceptions in each of the different "smarts."

Emotional Intelligence

Many of the intelligence theories overlap. When we examine the specific attributes related to the five domains described by Goleman, we see many skills and competencies that need to be practiced in order to improve the ability to manage one's self and others. As with other skills, the skills needed for emotional intelligence should be diagnosed and identified through observation of students' behavior so that they can be practiced in lessons or units of study designed by the teacher.

For example, when a teacher targets the need for a skill, such as showing empathy, the first step is to help the students understand what the intended behavior is. This may occur as a "teachable moment," or one in which the teacher sees that empathy is needed in a particular instance, or when a teacher notices that students are not very skilled in showing empathy to others. This may be done by defining the skill or reading a book or watching a video where the skill is evident. A story such as Mildred Taylor's (1976) *Roll of Thunder, Hear My Cry* gives students clear examples of empathic behavior.

The next step is to make the behavior explicit. A strategy such as a Y-chart (Hill and Hancock 1993) can be used for students to generate a list of what empathy looks like, sounds like, and feels like (see Fig. 4.5).

Role-playing a situation in which empathy is displayed also helps students to understand this concept. Role-playing is a powerful strategy, because when one is playing a role, the emotions often take over, thus allowing the role player to feel the emotions of the assumed character.

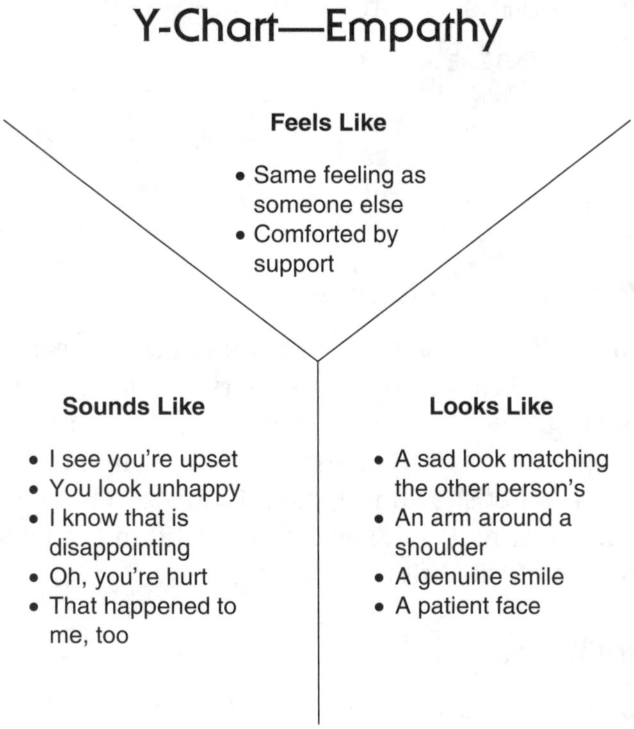

Y-Chart—Empathy

Feels Like

- Same feeling as someone else
- Comforted by support

Sounds Like

- I see you're upset
- You look unhappy
- I know that is disappointing
- Oh, you're hurt
- That happened to me, too

Looks Like

- A sad look matching the other person's
- An arm around a shoulder
- A genuine smile
- A patient face

Figure 4.5

Learning experiences can be integrated into the curriculum so that students can continue to understand and to use the skill. The writing process is another way that students can use this skill. For example, in a middle school language arts–social studies unit dealing with World War II and the Holocaust, students can demonstrate their writing skills and understanding of historic events, as well as the concept of empathy, by writing journal entries as if they were children in hiding or children evacuated during the war.

When the students understand the reason for learning the skill and have developed a working definition of the targeted behavior, they should practice the skill in a variety of situations. Practice should always be followed by metacognitive reflection as a way of deepening understanding and improving performance. Finally, students should persevere with the skill until it becomes the natural way of doing things.

Focusing on the need for a specific skill helps to develop self-awareness. By learning about specific emotions, behaviors, and concepts, such as empathy, students gain an awareness of not only what these concepts are but what their own feelings and thoughts about them are. Self-awareness is an integral part of all skill development related to emotional intelligence.

Practicing the skills in a variety of situations enables students to interact with others and practice their social arts. Role playing is especially helpful because it presents nonthreatening and hypothetical situations. By acting out how they could, or would, respond to different situations, students gain not only practice in demonstrating a behavior but also the opportunity to consider multiple options and think before they act.

The ability to control one's impulses is another emotional intelligence competency. Having multiple opportunities to practice different skills and behaviors gives students a repertoire of skills they can call on in stressful situations, thus giving them the ability to respond less impulsively. Learning different ways to respond to different behaviors helps students to feel more self-confident and self-motivated in new and different situations.

Another emotional intelligence competency is the ability to manage emotions. Teachers can help students to manage feelings, such as anger and hostility, by first getting them to recognize the feelings and understand what causes them (self-awareness). Next, students need to develop procedures that help them to regain composure and to be able to rationally process an anger- or hostility-laden situation. Techniques such as deep breathing, taking a time-out, and using soothing self-talk are useful in gaining time to move to conscious consideration of the situation that has caused the anger or hostility. Under stressful situations, the amygdala "hijacks" the brain before the stimuli reach the cerebral cortex and, therefore, rational thought doesn't enter into the process. The brain downshifts to the limbic system where there is no language or rational problem solving.

Simple strategies, such as slowly counting to ten and taking deep breaths, help students get through the fight-or-flight response and allow time for the heart rate to slow and oxygen to reach the brain. Having a corner of the room where students can sit quietly, calm down, and reflect on the situation may be helpful. These strategies help students calm themselves and soothe their angry feelings until they can again fully use the cerebral cortex where problem solving can occur. One needs to be able to think rationally and not react emotionally to deal successfully with anger and hostility. Although emotions are natural and benefit us in many ways, they also can result in negative consequences. Part of emotional intelligence is learning how to manage all kinds of emotions.

Intelligent Behavior

When we reflect on the skills students will need to succeed in a rapidly changing world, we realize that people will need to be "intelligent" in order to face and deal with complex problems and challenging dilemmas and to produce things that will be needed by their cultures. Many of the habits of mind identified by Arthur Costa relate closely to Gardner's multiple intelligences and Goleman's emotional intelligence. We need to examine these behaviors and explore ways to monitor their acquisition by students in our schools.

Following are suggestions for how to incorporate intelligent behaviors in the classroom.

Persistence

Persistence means to persevere in a search for alternate or creative solutions. Students should be encouraged to persist in their search for solutions. To do this, they need a systematic method for analyzing problems. The steps should include the following:

- Scanning their repertoires of problem-solving strategies to see if a previous solution can be applied
- Developing a plan that includes gathering or generating data
- Applying a strategy
- Monitoring progress
- Trying alternate strategies when necessary

This process typifies persistence. However, Sternberg (1996) suggested that we also need to recognize when persistence is not the best course and, in some cases, when we should cut our losses and move on.

Decreasing Impulsivity

Decreasing impulsivity is the ability to control impulses in order to find a successful solution to a situation, problem, or conflict. It includes counting to ten, taking a time-out, and soothing self-talk. The ability to control impulses is a major factor in the ability to learn and solve problems. Students should be encouraged to take the time to understand the nature of a problem, clarify a task, and decide on a set of criteria for a successful solution as opposed to impulsively engaging in a series of trial-and-error activities. Teachers need to encourage students to verbalize rationales for problem-solving strategies. Students should use logs and journals to reflect on solutions, to note similarities to past problem-solving situations, and to predict situations that may require similar strategies in the future.

Empathic Listening

Many people consider the ability to listen to and to understand another person's point of view one of the highest forms of intelligent behavior. Teachers can encourage listening skills through a variety of strategies. For example, teachers can encourage students to paraphrase another person's words to ensure that they accurately heard and understood what the other person said. T-charting can be used to identify what "checking for understanding" looks like and sounds like by charting phrases such as Do you mean . . ., Are you saying . . ., and It sounds to me that. . . .

It also is useful to teach students how to read and interpret body language, including facial expressions, postures, and body stances, as well as how to use one's own body language to express ideas. Giving students an opportunity to role-play and to analyze expressions in drama, stories, and films helps them recognize and analyze others' emotions, problems, and reactions.

Flexibility in Thinking

Some students seem to have an attitude that says "My mind is made up; do not confuse me with facts." They often have difficulty acknowledging different points of view, become confused by ambiguous information, and tend to avoid considering multiple solutions. These students often have a limited range of problem-solving strategies and therefore seek simplistic solutions. Very often, because they do not consider multiple viewpoints, they become inflexible and limited in their thinking and problem-solving skills.

Flexible thinking is characterized by the willingness to consider other people's points of view. In group situations, flexible thinkers paraphrase, clarify, and probe other people's thought processes, generalizations, and rationales. They often have expanded repertoires of problem-solving skills and are confident in their ability to back up and start over when a particular solution does not work out. To encourage flexible thinking, students should engage in active listening, consensus building, and checking the validity of their conclusions.

Metacognition

Teachers can promote metacognition by providing students multiple opportunities to engage in metacognitive thinking. Examples of metacognitive thinking include writing a journal entry after completing a project and setting a goal after receiving feedback on a task. Activities in which students should have opportunities for meta-cognitive reflection include learning a new computer skill and practicing a behavior such as listening attentively in a cooperative learning group.

Teachers can encourage students to use metacognition in problem solving by asking them to think of previous experiences with a similar type of problem, to apply alternate solutions when necessary, to monitor progress, and to reflect on their performances.

Checking for Accuracy and Precision

Many students hurry through tasks, with a goal of completing the work rather than creating quality work. When students monitor their own performances by checking work for precision, clarity, and excellence, there is often an increase in quality and student growth. Students need to develop skills for reviewing the performance criteria and the rules for successful completion prior to doing an assignment. They need clear standards and criteria, or models of quality, and rules or processes for their work. Students should be directed to review and to check their work against these standards to monitor the accuracy of their efforts. They should be encouraged to verify sources and to double-check information for accuracy so that they become self-monitors of quality in their work.

Posing Questions and Problems

Asking good questions leads students to inquire about topics and issues that interest them and engage them in thinking. In many classrooms, the teachers do most of the talking and ask most of the questions. Thus, the teachers, instead of the students, are growing more dendrites. When students are active participants in their learning, through discussion and asking questions, they grow dendrites, make connections, and engage in new learning opportunities. Using strategies such as KWL—What do I know? What do I want to know? and What have I learned?—helps generate student questions. Using inquiry in the classroom, where students come up with the questions that interest them, is more engaging for students than responding to teacher-generated questions and allows them to use a multitude of skills that facilitate thinking.

Drawing on Past Knowledge and Applying It to New Situations

Teachers can help students to develop the ability to transfer processes and strategies from one situation to another by teaching a skill in one situation and then asking students to reflect on where else it might be useful. Before beginning a task or solving a problem, teachers can help students recall their previous experiences to elicit possible methods of solving a problem or tackling a task. Students are often able to apply their learning to similar situations but need to develop their skills in applying learning to new and different situations.

Using Precise and Accurate Language and Thought: Clarity of Communication

Students often use language that is vague and imprecise. They need to be encouraged to refer to things using their correct names and to employ precise and descriptive words to define concepts and ideas. They also need the ability to supply supporting evidence or criteria to back up their evaluations and judgments. In other words, they need to be able to communicate both orally and in writing using concise, descriptive, and coherent language.

Without precise language, misconceptions easily can be formed. Precision is needed in description and directions for accuracy of action. Teachers need to model precise language and encourage students to do so as well. Probing for precision when vague language or generalization is used can be done by using questions such as *Which people? Never? Always? Everyone?* to allow the speaker to respond with more precise and descriptive speech.

Using All the Senses

The human body receives information through all of its senses: sight, hearing, touch, smell, and taste. Schools typically focus on visual and auditory information, thereby losing many avenues or pathways to learning. Students whose sensory pathways are open and alert are able to absorb more information than those whose pathways have fallen into disuse.

One of the chief failings of formal education is that it begins with language and abstractions instead of starting with the real and concrete and then moving to the theoretical. Arnold Scheibel (1995), professor of neurology at UCLA, stated that

> the number of synaptic connections rises rapidly in the first seven to ten years. Plateaus and downswings begin as the brain becomes more specialized, focused and efficient during adolescence. The process continues largely genetically driven but strongly influenced by the environment/experience up to ten, twelve, fourteen years. From that point on, nature, in a sense, steps aside and says a lot more is up to you. It is at this point that the increasing enrichment of school and life experience plays its role in producing and increasing dendritic growth.

The primary grades generally have emphasized concrete, hands-on learning. Perhaps reintroducing these types of activities into classrooms at all grade levels would enhance brain compatibility and would enable more learners to understand and internalize concepts and new learning.

Creativity

In the past, it was commonly assumed that people were born creative (or uncreative) in much the same way as they were born intelligent (or unintelligent). We now know that all persons have the capacity to generate original or ingenious products, solutions, and techniques as long as that capacity is developed. Encouraging students to take risks and to think "outside the box" by looking at problems from many different angles before deciding on a solution promotes creativity and originality. Teachers who encourage diversity as opposed to conformity and who provide helpful feedback and questioning rather than critical responses help to foster growth in this area.

Being Excited and Awed About Our World

Without wonderment, inquisitiveness, and curiosity, we are complacent and accepting of the status quo. All advancements or creative ventures have come from individuals and groups who had a quest for something more. Thus, teachers who can increase their students' sense of efficacy as thinkers increase their chances of being creative and of taking the risks to be so. Encouraging students to seek out problems and conundrums and to solve them independently of parents and teachers promotes this sense of efficacy. One of the best ways to achieve this goal is by modeling. Thus, in the day-to-day events of the school, the students should observe teachers not only employing intelligent behavior but obviously enjoying it. As teachers, we want to help students move from the attitude of "I can" to one of "I enjoy thinking and problem solving of all kinds."

Risking Appropriately: Stretching One's Competencies to Continue to Grow

Flexible people are sometimes willing to take extra risks that may not be necessary because they are so compelled to succeed in all situations. Intelligent people are willing to take only "educated risks" and are not reckless. They weigh the consequences and act accordingly. Past experiences are considered, and calculating the risk factors makes decisions more acceptable. Teachers can foster this intelligence by having students consider the options when difficult situations present themselves, brainstorm actions possible, and weigh the consequences of selecting each option. They can do this when reading stories in language arts using empathic thinking to consider the character's risk management and predicting outcomes based on a variety of choices. This can also be used in social studies looking at historic situations and in hindsight considering if the risk people took in a particular situation was appropriate or worth taking.

Using Humor

Humor is a powerful tool that intelligent people use to diffuse a tense situation. Laughter actually raises the level of endorphins in the body, lowers the stress hormone cortisol that is released during anxious scenarios, and lowers the heart rate. All this breaks the tension and allows people to remain attentive and focused and creative in a troublesome situation. We need to foster laughter in the classroom and laugh at ourselves as teachers and encourage students to do so as well. Establishing a climate where it's acceptable to risk ideas and answers and laugh at whimsical ideas will foster creativity and collaborative thinking.

Collaborative Interdependence

Together we're better. Collaboration generally brings out more thinking as people bounce ideas off each other and think more deeply about the concept. A key is being able to cooperate with others to come up with new and creative ideas and solve problems. Cooperative group learning is so important that we have dedicated two chapters to helping teachers implement successful collaborative groups in their classroom.

Being Open to New Learning

We want our students to be continuous lifelong learners who don't shy away from challenges and problems but who seek solutions and persevere to accomplish what needs to be done. Throughout life, new concepts and innovations need to be created and understood. We want to help students face new learning armed with tools that will aid their quest. We need to teach them problem-solving processes, note taking and summarizing skills, and how to access resources. Increasing their repertoire of ways to continue to learn and grow by empowering them with intelligent behaviors will make the journey more hopeful and promising

Intelligent behavior is intelligent thought transposed into action. In other words, it is the external application of an internal process. In schools, however, we often come across students who appear to be bright but have no repertoire of skills with which to apply their intelligence. Teaching for intelligent behavior is based on the proposition that all students can be taught a repertoire of skills that will allow them to behave in more intelligent ways.

Figure 4.6 (page 112) shows the relationship between Goleman's emotional intelligence, Costa's intelligent behaviors, and classroom strategies that support their development.

IN CLOSING

In conclusion, the alternate theories of intelligence are powerful, generalizable theories that have a practical application in the classroom. These theories and their attendant strategies can be integrated into all areas of the teaching-learning process in the following ways:

- Provide opportunities for students not only to learn but also to show what they know by using the full range of multiple intelligences

Developing Emotional Competencies

Goleman's Emotional Intelligences	Costa's Habits of Mind	Classroom Strategies
Self-awareness	Metacognition Being excited and awed about our world Uses all senses Drawing on past experiences	Logs, journals, metacognitive time Reflection, alone or in pairs
Managing emotions	Decreasing impulsivity Using precise and accurate language Risking appropriately Using humor Posing questions and problems	Count to 10 Case studies Deep breathing
Self-motivation	Flexibility Checking for accuracy and precision Using all the senses Persistence Creativity	Goal setting and planning Time management Optimism and hope Problem solving
Empathy	Empathic listening Flexibilty of thinking Using humor	Literature, historical figures Cooperative group learning
Social skills	Creativity Empathic listening Precision language & thought Collaborative interdependence Using humor	T-charts Y-charts Role play Cooperative group learning

Figure 4.6

- Teach students to reflect on their internal states of mind and apply that knowledge to learning and internalizing the collaborative skills necessary to use the power of emotional intelligence
- Demonstrate intelligent behaviors and ensure that students understand the behaviors by providing opportunities to apply them on a regular basis

Reflections

3 Things I learned

2 Connections I made

1 Thing I intend to do!

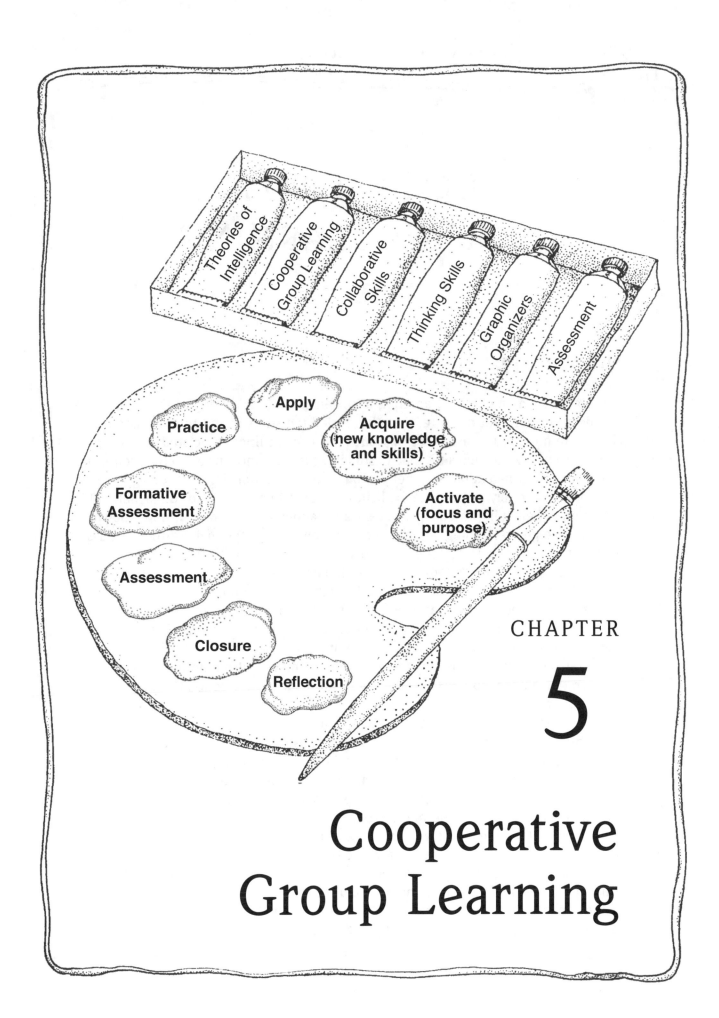

Theories of
Intelligence

Cooperative
Group Learning

Collaborative
Skills

Thinking Skills

Graphic
Organizers

Assessment

Apply

Practice

Acquire
(new knowledge
and skills)

Formative
Assessment

Activate
(focus and
purpose)

Assessment

Closure

Reflection

CHAPTER

5

Cooperative
Group Learning

CHAPTER 5

COOPERATIVE GROUP LEARNING

WHAT IS IT?

Group work, in one form or another, has been around for as long as there has been public education, but many teachers have tried the strategy and then abandoned it. There are numerous reasons for this, such as the difficulties associated with keeping students on task, making sure that all students make a contribution to the group, and class discipline in general. Another reason is that the rationale for students working in groups has rarely been made explicit, nor was it fully explained to teachers. This situation is beginning to change. Recent adaptations of the strategy, now known as cooperative group learning, are based on an awareness of the major difficulties associated with group work and incorporate structures to deal with them.

The capacity to work cooperatively has been a major contributor to the survival of the human race. This is as true of collaborating in the hunt or building basic shelter as it is in modern medical research or space exploration. The use of cooperative learning is not new in the field of education in North America. Colonel Francis Parker, the superintendent of schools in Quincy, Massachusetts, from 1875 to 1880, was a strong advocate for cooperative group learning, and his notion of promoting cooperation among students was the dominant mode of instruction through the turn of the twentieth century.

Following Colonel Parker, American philosopher and educator John Dewey promoted the use of cooperative learning groups as part of his project method in instruction. In the late 1930s, however, schools began to emphasize interpersonal competition as the organizing philosophy that informed public education, and the use of cooperative groups declined. This philosophy of intense competition was the dominant mode up until the mid-1980s.

In the 1980s, there was a resurgence of interest in cooperative group learning principles as a way of combating a perceived lack of social skills and cooperation among socially deprived and alienated students. One of the beneficial side effects of this type of instruction was that not only did social skills improve, but so did academic achievement. Students also improved their self-esteem, became more self-motivated, developed more positive attitudes toward school, and had higher achievement for higher-level tasks such as concept attainment and problem solving (Bellanca and Fogarty 1991).

Educators and researchers such as David Johnson, Roger Johnson, and Edyth Johnson Holubec (1984), Robert Slavin (1981), Shlomo Sharan and Yael Sharan (1976), and Spencer Kagan (1992) have been instrumental in establishing the rationale, philosophy, and organizing structures for cooperative group learning. Authors James Bellanca and Robin Fogarty described the cooperative group models proposed by these researchers in *Blueprints for Thinking in the Cooperative Classroom* (1991) and presented a synthesized model that builds on the Johnson and Johnson (Johnson et al. 1984) model.

The Johnsons and their associates examined the similarities and differences of group work and cooperative group learning and determined that in many cases teachers who had put students together to work in small groups were disappointed that the students did not naturally succeed at the collaboration or the task. This failure often resulted from the students' lack of appropriate collaborative/social skills and tasks that were not structured to ensure success.

The Johnsons and their associates developed a model for implementing cooperative group learning based on five elements that increase the likelihood that students will work effectively and interdependently in cooperative learning groups, thus promoting their success:

- Positive interdependence
- Individual accountability
- Face-to-face interaction
- Collaborative/social skills
- Group processing

The Johnson and Johnson cooperative group model is based on the belief that students need to have a clear understanding of the goal or task before they begin to work in cooperative groups. The concept of interdependence means that students need one another to succeed at the task or to accomplish the desired goal. The structuring of positive interdependence is one of the major tasks of teachers who engage in cooperative group learning. An underlying premise of the model is that not all students come to school with a full set of collaborative or social skills, and thus, many of these skills need to be taught and practiced.

WHY DO WE NEED IT?

The brain learns by building on past experience. In effect, it "hooks" new information to that which one already knows, clarifying concepts through discussion and questioning (Brooks and Brooks 1993).

Our brain's ability to relate, reshape, transform, and perceive parts and wholes supports the constructivist premise that the growth of knowledge is the result of the personal, unique constructions made by the learner. This construction of knowledge is generally accomplished with the help of others through dialogue and questioning. Thus, using cooperative group learning to make meaning or sense out of the world, to find relevance, and to grapple with issues and problems supports what we know about how the brain learns.

In the cooperative learning classroom, teachers act as resource providers and brokers of information rather than as dispensers of knowledge. When constructivism and cooperative group learning are combined, they facilitate the acquisition of meaning through the interactive process of collaborative tasks.

A study conducted by Ekwall and Shanker revealed some interesting findings in terms of how people learn. They discovered that the more actively engaged people are in their learning, the more they learn. Following are the results of their study:

How People Learn

People learn . . .
10 percent of what they read
20 percent of what they hear
30 percent of what they see
50 percent of what they both see and hear
70 percent of what they say as they talk
90 percent of what they say as they do a thing.
(Ekwall and Shanker 1988, 370)

To this, William Glasser (1990) added that people retain 95 percent of what they teach to someone else.

Thus, it appears that students learn best by discussing, elaborating, and explaining to others. If we provide students opportunities to discuss, elaborate, and explain ideas with others, we can promote the development of skills such as higher-order thinking, problem solving, and constructing meaning. Cooperative group learning provides students with these opportunities.

In 1981, Roger Johnson, David Johnson, and their associates undertook a meta-analysis of 122 studies on this subject in response to various negative reviews of the effects of cooperative group learning on student achievement. They reported their results in *Circles of Learning*.

The results indicate that cooperative group learning experiences tend to promote higher achievement than do competitive and individualistic learning experiences. The results hold for all age levels, for all subject areas, and for tasks involving concept attainment, verbal problem solving, categorization, spatial problem solving, retention and memory, motor performance, guessing, judging and predicting. (Johnson et al. 1984, 15)

Cooperative group learning is a megastrategy that is among the more powerful and flexible instructional tools for learning. Once the basic framework is in place, it becomes an effective way of implementing many brain-compatible strategies, such as direct teaching of thinking skills, concept formation, and teaching to multiple intelligences. When used skillfully, cooperative group learning enables students to increase their communication, interpersonal, and problem-solving skills.

HOW DO WE DO IT?

For students to work together successfully, they must be taught the skills and strategies that will increase their chances for success. The five elements of the cooperative group learning model—positive interdependence, individual account-ability, face-to-face interaction, collaborative/social skills, and group processing—are designed to eliminate the problems that arise from establishing cooperative groups and implementing cooperative group learning.

The Johnson and Johnson model of cooperative is built on five elements. We use "Pigs' Face" (PIGSF) to remember the five.

5 Elements of Cooperative Learning

P Positive interdependence
I Individual accountability
G Group processing
S Social skill focus
F Face-to-face interaction

Following are explanations of how to implement each element in the classroom.

Elements of Cooperative Group Learning

Positive Interdependence

The term *positive interdependence* refers to nine ways to structure learning so that students are obliged to work together. Its basic premise is that all of us together are smarter than one of us alone. From this we can draw the conclusion that we will be more successful as a group than we would be as individuals.

Teachers do not need to use all nine types of positive interdependence in a lesson. Two, three, or four types may be used to ensure that students are more likely to work together to achieve the group's goal.

The nine ways in which positive interdependence can be structured are as follows:

- *Goal interdependence:* The group has a common goal, and every member of the team is expected to achieve it.
- *Incentive interdependence:* Everyone receives the same reward but only if every member of the team succeeds.

- *Resource interdependence:* Resources, information, and material are limited so that students are obliged to work together and cooperate in sharing available resources.
- *Sequence interdependence:* The overall task is divided into a sequence of subtasks. Individual group members perform their particular tasks as part of a predetermined order.
- *Role interdependence:* Each group member is assigned a role with specific responsibilities. Each role contributes to and supports the task's completion.
- *Identity interdependence:* The group establishes a mutual identity through a name, flag, logo, or symbol. These can be augmented by a group song or cheer.
- *Outside force interdependence:* The group, as a whole, competes against other groups.
- *Simulation interdependence:* The group members imagine that they are in a situation or role where they must collaborate to be successful.
- *Environmental interdependence:* The group members work together within a specified physical space, such as a section of the classroom.

Individual Accountability

By structuring learning so that each student contributes to the group effort and is responsible for his or her own learning, one allows for individual accountability. In a group, some students may sit back and let others do all the work. This is unfair to other group members and fosters disharmony. The following strategies can be used to promote individual accountability and to increase the likelihood that all students will engage in learning and contribute to the group's effort:

- *Numbered heads:* Each student is assigned a number. Then a question is asked or a progress report is requested from the entire group. After a reasonable period of time for discussion, a student is called on by a random number to provide the answer. In this way, nobody in the group knows who will be called on, so each individual needs to be prepared to answer and, hence, be accountable.
- *Shared task/individual assessment:* Cooperative group learning is a very effective method of learning, but it may not be the best way to evaluate that learning. One way around this dilemma is to allow students to learn together but to assess students individually through an individual test or individual culminating activity.
- *Conferencing:* At some time during the completion of a project or other group work, the teacher may hold short conferences with individual students to help keep them on track.

Collaborative/Social Skills

Collaborative skills, sometimes called social skills, are those skills that enable individuals to work effectively within a group. They include skills such as team building, communication, leadership, and conflict resolution. (See chapter 6, "Collaborative

Skills," for a detailed discussion of these skills.) If students do not have a firm grasp of these skills, it is difficult for them to engage in many of the learning opportunities embedded in cooperative group work. Some students come to school with many of these skills in place, but for others, the teacher needs to provide direct instruction.

The general pattern for teaching collaborative/social skills is as follows: Diagnose the skill that students need most and make sure that they know what the skill looks like and sounds like. Allow the students to practice the skill and take time to process or debrief the skill after every practice.

Group Processing

Debriefing, or processing a group's performance, is a necessary element of cooperative group learning. Without a review of the group's performance, there is only limited improvement. Group processing allows the students to identify areas for growth in the use of a particular skill. It is a metacognitive process in which the group examines its performance by answering questions such as the following:

- How well did we practice the collaborative/social skill?
- How could we use this skill more effectively in the future?
- Where else in our lives would this skill be useful?
- What should we focus on next time?

Face-to-Face Interaction

Face-to-face interaction literally means that students are seated nose to nose and toes to toes as a way of facilitating eye contact, communication, and active listening. Children learn best when they are given an opportunity to discuss ideas with their peers. Face-to-face interaction sets up the conditions for this to happen. The teacher's role is to arrange for the placement of desks and chairs, to provide the information to be learned, and to move aside and let the students go to it. Cooperative groups learning should be used when necessary and preferable to have students brainstorm, problem solve, teach each other, or reach consensus. Thus fostering higher order thinking through collective dialogue.

Types of Cooperative Groups

One of a teacher's first tasks when beginning to use cooperative groups is to decide how groups will be structured. There are several ways to group students, but they fall into two broad categories—heterogeneous and homogeneous groups.

Heterogeneous Groups

Heterogeneous groups are formed by selecting a mixture of individuals with different genders, ethnicities, socioeconomic backgrounds, and levels of ability. One aim of cooperative group learning is to combat negative attitudes based on tension

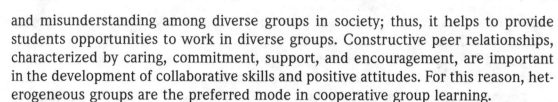

and misunderstanding among diverse groups in society; thus, it helps to provide students opportunities to work in diverse groups. Constructive peer relationships, characterized by caring, commitment, support, and encouragement, are important in the development of collaborative skills and positive attitudes. For this reason, heterogeneous groups are the preferred mode in cooperative group learning.

Heterogeneous groups that stay together for a lengthy period of time sometimes are referred to as home or base groups. These groups usually stay together for the duration of a course, a semester, or the school year in order to allow the students to bond and build relationships.

In heterogeneous groups, all students benefit by interacting with people with a wide range of opinions and abilities. High-achieving students benefit by explaining and restating their points of view while helping others. All students benefit by having opportunities to verbalize their thoughts and share them with others.

Homogeneous Groups

Homogeneous groups are those in which the students have a number of characteristics in common. Cases in which a teacher may choose to use homogeneous grouping include the following:

- Special-difficulty groups
  - Organized around a specific area of need
  - Short term until skill is mastered

- Interest groups
  - Organized according to interest in the topic
  - Short term until project is completed

- Single-gender groups
  - Organized around a specific topic in which one sex may dominate or inhibit if the genders are mixed
  - Short term until topic is discussed

- Cognitive development groups
  - Organized according to cognitive levels (regardless of age)
  - Short term until skill is mastered

- Sociometric groups
  - Organized around existing patterns of friendships
  - Short-term fun project

Familiarizing Students With Cooperative Group Learning

Students who are not familiar with working in small groups may need to begin working with one or two other students on simple, uncomplicated tasks or activities before working in larger groups.

A simple strategy, such as think-pair-share, may be a good place to start. For example, a teacher may say, "Think to yourself—what might happen if global warming continues to rise?" The students think for approximately thirty seconds. Then, the teacher says, "Now, turn to a partner and share your answer." Pairs discuss for sixty seconds and then are asked, "Now, who would like to share their answer with the whole group?"

The think-pair-share is an excellent strategy to introduce students to the concept of cooperative group learning. Having time to think about a question and then discuss it with another person is less stressful than being called on to answer without having time to prepare. In addition, many students initially may find it easier to share ideas with one person than with several, as in cooperative learning groups. With think-pair-share, students get a chance to express their thoughts in a non-threatening situation, which alleviates some of the problems associated with an emotional reaction to stress. Discussion with a partner clarifies and broadens their answers. When used in conjunction with complex, higher-order, open-ended questions, think-pair-share increases the chance for full and complete responses.

When starting with cooperative learning groups, small groups generally work better than larger groups. In general, the smaller the group the greater the chance that a student will have an opportunity to talk. It is easy to get lost in a group of six, but it is hard to get left out of a pair. For this reason, groups of two and three provide students the best opportunity to acclimate themselves to working in a group.

Establishing Base/Home Groups

After about two weeks of working in small flexible groups, students may be ready for more permanent base groups. The selection of base groups is too important to be left to chance and should be done by the teacher. Following are tips to keep in mind when establishing base groups:

- Assign four persons—the largest number—to each group.
- Arrange a mix of abilities and personalities.
- Discourage student requests for a change of group. One of the significant things learned from cooperative groups is that, in real life, we often have no control over who works with whom; therefore, we have to learn to get along with all types of people.
- Encourage students to persevere with the group unless the situation becomes extremely dysfunctional or dangerous.

Team Building

The chances for students to withdraw from the group and allow others to do the work are greatly decreased when individuals feel a sense of loyalty or belonging to the group. This bonding does not happen overnight. Nor does it occur spontaneously.

The process of team building is an important step in establishing effective groups. Using getting-acquainted strategies helps to foster group bonding.

Getting-Acquainted Strategies

Catch

Students throw and catch a paper ball. As the ball is thrown, the thrower says his or her name and the name of the person who is to catch it.

Group Identifiers

Groups choose a group name, cheer, and/or handshake.

Venn Diagram

Team members compare personal characteristics using a Venn diagram.

Three-Step Interview

A three-step interview is both an active listening strategy and a getting-to-know-you activity. Students, working in groups of four, interview their partners and then introduce their partner to the other pair.

- *Step 1*—Form groups of four students and assign a letter (A, B, C, or D) to each participant. The students interview each other based on the following pattern: A interviews B, and C interviews D.
- *Step 2*—The students reverse roles: B interviews A, and D interviews C.
- *Step 3*—Students share what they have learned. A tells about B, then B tells about A. When this pair has finished, C tells about D and then D tells about C.

What's in a Name?

"What's in a name?" is an interviewing strategy that can be combined with the three-step interview. The interviewer asks questions such as *How did you get your name? Where does the name come from? Is there another name that you would prefer?* and *Do you have a nickname?* This strategy promotes active listening because the participants are responsible for relating what they learned from their partner to another pair. It also provides opportunities for students to practice paraphrasing.

People Search

People search is based on a strategy devised by Laurie Robertson called Find Someone Who (Kagan 1990), which was adapted by Fogarty and Bellanca (1993). People search can be conducted as a getting-acquainted or team-building activity, or it can be used to diagnose prior knowledge, introduce a new topic, or review material prior to a test. It values people as knowledgeable resources in the classroom and increases motivation through focus and discussion.

People search is an interactive strategy that energizes students by giving them an opportunity to move around the room and use their verbal/linguistic, bodily/kinesthetic, interpersonal, and intrapersonal intelligences. It gives students the opportunity to practice their collaborative/social skills and to deepen their understanding of content through dialogue and interaction with others.

To conduct a people search, students are given a list or grid of items for which they need to find a person who matches the description of each item. Figure 5.1 is a people search that focuses on multiple intelligence activities and helps find out who in the group has an interest or expertise in one area or another.

People Search

Find someone who . . .

• Read the same book as you _____

• Spends leisure time outdoors _____

• Plays or sings alone or with a group _____

• Loves to design, paint, or create _____

• Is intrigued with solving problems and developing solutions _____

• Keeps a diary or journal _____

• Plays a sport _____

• Likes working in groups _____

Figure 5.1

People search can be used with subject content in a similar way as a prelearning strategy or to review for a test. Students may also make up a people search to challenge other students in a review process.

Figure 5.2 (page 126) is an example of a review for a chapter in *Charlotte's Web.* This allows students to share their understanding and develop expressive language, as well as practice active listening.

Students walk around the room and approach others, offering help with one of the items. As one person gives information relating to the item, the other person actively listens so he or she can recall the information later.

Find Someone Who . . .

Can describe Charlotte	Knows why Wilbur is afraid	Thinks that a pet pig would be fun to have
Can list several chores on a farm	Can name three words that Charlotte uses to describe Wilbur	Can describe Templeton
Thinks that all animals should be useful	Has a pet that they love	Can predict what might happen next

Topic: _____

Introduction/preassessment: _____

Rehearsal strategies: _____

Review/test preparation: _____

Figure 5.2

Students practice paraphrasing and asking questions to make sure they understand and can remember the information. After the activity, the students meet as a large group and share information, ask questions, and clarify answers. The discussion and articulation of ideas help clarify meaning, deepen understanding, and improve retention of information.

Another teacher may use a people search to recall body systems and their functions. Students are asked to find someone who can:

- Explain the steps of digestion
- Name the organs involved in respiration
- Name foods essential for healthy teeth and bones
- List foods essential for healthy skin and gums
- Name three foods that provide lots of energy
- Name foods that build muscles

Find Someone Who . . .

Topic: _____

Introduction/preassessment: _____

Rehearsal strategies: _____

Review/test preparation: _____

Figure 5.3

Working With Simple Structures

Once students are familiar with working in small cooperative learning groups, they will be ready for working in small groups using more complex strategies. Kagan (1990) developed a number of simple structures that facilitate getting students to think, interact, and process information. They are easy to use and can be used in a variety of situations. Examples are roundtable round robin, paraphrase passport, numbered heads together, talking chips, and four corners.

Roundtable Round Robin

Roundtable round robin is a simple structure that can be used to generate as many answers as possible to a particular question or request; for example, "Name as many of the planets as you can." The first student writes a response on a sheet of paper and then passes it on to the next student and so on around the group. The paper continues to circulate until there are no more responses.

Roundtable round robin may be varied as follows:

- Students take turns answering questions without recording them.
- You can circulate two, three, or four sheets at once. For example, distribute one sheet for each of the four food groups; then ask students to generate lists of the foods that belong to a particular group.
- Students create a group poem, story, or other compilation by writing ideas one at a time. For example, a student writes one line of a poem or limerick and then passes the paper to another student for the next line, and so on.

Its advantages include the following:

- Builds team participation
- Allows everyone in the group a chance to participate
- May be used at the beginning of a lesson to activate prior learning

Paraphrase Passport

Paraphrase passport is similar to roundtable round robin except that the participants paraphrase what the person to their right has said before adding their own contributions.

Its advantages include the following:

- Promotes active listening
- Increases retention of information by expressing another's ideas in one's own words

Numbered Heads Together

Numbered heads together is a method of processing information and fostering individual accountability. It has four steps. First, the teacher assigns students within each group a number—1, 2, 3, or 4. Then, the teacher poses a higher-order, complex question. The students put their heads together and develop an answer. The teacher then calls a number at random. The students in each group with that number answer the question.

Numbered heads together may be varied as follows:

- Assign letters instead of numbers.
- Have the students spin a wheel or roll a dice to select a number. When a number is called, all students with that number provide a solution.

Its advantages include the following:

- Promotes discussion and honors a variety of answers
- Ensures group accountability because the team must make sure that all members can answer the question
- Increases individual accountability because students do not know when they will be called on to answer

Talking Chips

Talking chips is a way of ensuring equal participation by all members of the group. Each participant is given four chips or counters. Whenever a person speaks, he or she places one chip in a bowl or a central location. When all of a person's chips have been used, that person remains silent until all members have used their chips, at which time the chips are redistributed.

Its advantages include the following:

- Prevents one or more students from dominating the group
- Promotes equal participation
- Encourages reticent individuals to participate

Four Corners

Four corners is a simple structure used to explore issues, develop rationales, and support opinions. Four corners of the room are designated to represent varying degrees of a particular viewpoint, such as strongly agree, agree, disagree, and strongly disagree. (Teachers may wish to substitute hot, warm, cold, and freezing or walkers, joggers, runners, and sprinters as designations.) The students are given a topic to debate or an opinion to express. For example, students may be presented with the statement "All learning takes place in the classroom." They decide how they personally feel about the statement and go to the corner designated for that viewpoint. Once there, they discuss the rationale for their agreement or disagreement.

Its advantages include the following:

- Allows students to develop richer rationales through articulation and collaboration
- Provides a way of energizing a class by moving and regrouping the students

"I have . . . Who has?"

"I have . . . Who has?" (adapted from *Inclusion: A Fresh Look,* 1996, by Linda Tilton) is another cooperative strategy for reviewing and rehearsing information and engaging students orally rather than using worksheet practice. It is adaptable at any grade level. The reinforcement is through auditory interaction, and students are really "studying out loud." Math review, test review questions, vocabulary words, French, Spanish, and science content are excellent choices for this activity.

Teachers have used this strategy to rehearse and review topics such as chemical states, historical events, biology terms, and organ functions.

Each student gets a card with an answer to a question followed by a new question. Any student begins by asking the question on his or her card, "Who has . . .?" This activity forces students to listen attentively for the question that can be answered by the response on the top of his or her card. The student with the correct response calls out "I have . . ." and then asks the next "Who has . . .?" The activity continues until a question is asked that is answered by the person who began.

A teacher may decide to prepare a particular student ahead of time or to have students work in pairs to enable learners to respond correctly and succeed in front of their colleagues.

I Have . . . Who Has?

I have: the Bastille Who has: the execution machine that beheaded people?	I have: the guillotine Who has: the queen who was unsympathetic to the people?
I have: Marie Antoinette Who has: the name for the middle class of France?	I have: the bourgeoisie Who has: the term for spending more money than you have?
I have: deficit spending Who has: the term for the "estate" of clergy?	I have: the First Estate Who has: notebooks containing grievances of the French people?
I have: cahiers Who has: the term for the "estate" of nobles and aristocrats?	I have: the Second Estate Who has: the name of the palace of the French king?

Figure 5.4

For younger students, a teacher may choose to pass cards in order (and even have them sit in a circle) the first several times this activity is used to get students accustomed to the routine. The class can also be divided into groups so that different challenges can be given. Groups constructed based on ability or level of abstraction of thought can be given different colored cards, which challenge them at their level. Cards can be laminated to save and reuse. Figures 5.4 and 5.5 provide samples used in classrooms and Figure 5.6 (page 132) provides a blackline for use with any subject.

I Have . . . Who Has?

I have: 7/10 Who has: 75%?	I have: 3/4 Who has: .25?
I have: 1/4 Who has: 66%?	I have: 2/3 Who has: 50%?
I have: .50 Who has: 60%?	I have: .60 Who has: 1/10?
I have: 10% Who has: 40%?	I have: 2/5 Who has: 70%?

Figure 5.5

I Have . . . Who Has?

I have: Who has:	I have: Who has:
I have: Who has:	I have: Who has:
I have: Who has:	I have: Who has:
I have: Who has:	I have: Who has:

Figure 5.6

Working With a More Complex Structure

Expert Jigsaw

A more complex cooperative strategy is the expert jigsaw, first outlined by Elliot Aronson (1978). Expert jigsaw is a powerful strategy, but it should be used only after students have gained experience working in cooperative learning groups with less complex structures.

Students are assigned to groups of three and assigned a number or letter (e.g., 1, 2, 3). The material to be learned is divided into three comparable parts. (Color coding the pages is a good idea.) Then, the material is distributed so that each member of the group gets only one section of it (see Fig. 5.7a).

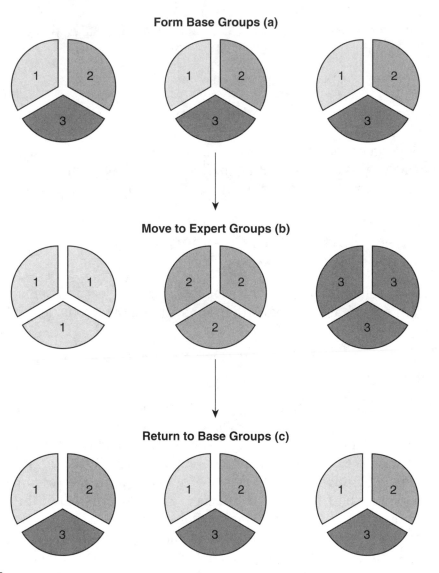

Figure 5.7

Members from each group then move to "expert" groups based on the part they have been assigned (see Fig. 5.7b). (This is where color coding proves useful.) All the members in a particular expert group have the same color and, hence, the same information. The "experts" read and discuss the material, decide on the main points, and select the best way to communicate them to their base groups.

Students then move back to their original groups, where they take turns teaching their section of the material to their group mates (see Fig. 5.7c).

Expert jigsaw may be varied as follows:

- Form groups of four students each and assign each group member a number from 1 to 4. Divide the material into only two parts. Give group members numbered 1 and 2 a section of the material; give group members numbered 3 and 4 a different section. All four students remain at the same table but work in pairs to discuss the material. After discussing the material and deciding on the main points, each pair teaches the other.

Its advantages include the following:

- Promotes positive interdependence because each person has a responsibility to the whole group
- Provides an opportunity to understand the material very thoroughly, through critical analysis and articulation, before teaching it to others
- Covers a great deal of material efficiently

The Teacher's Role in Implementing Cooperative Group Learning

Teachers planning to implement cooperative group learning should examine what they are expected to do before the lesson, during the lesson, and bringing closure to the lesson.

Before the Lesson

The first task is to determine the goals of the lesson. Cooperative learning lessons usually have two types of goals: the academic task, or curricular expectations, and the collaborative/social goal. It is important to consider both when planning your lesson.

The next task is to select the appropriate group size. This is often determined by the academic objectives or the amount of available time and resources. Groups of three or four are best for tasks that demand a diversity of skill or thinking. Pairs are best for tasks that require maximum involvement. In general, if time is short, keep the groups small. If resources are short, make the groups large.

When assigning students to groups, heterogeneous groups are recommended for most tasks. Teachers should select groups that will be beneficial to special needs students. This usually means that they are grouped with the students who are most likely to help them.

The room arrangement depends on group size. Routines should be established for arranging the furniture in clusters of two, three, and four so that students are nose to nose and toes to toes.

Other issues to consider before the lesson are materials distribution, criteria for success, and form of assessment. It also is important to consider how to build in positive interdependence, individual accountability, and a method of group processing around a collaborative skill. Initial efforts to implement cooperative learning groups can be frustrating, and it often helps to implement the process in phases, or one step at a time.

Many teachers find planning sheets useful when first designing cooperative group lessons. See Figure 5.8 (page 136) for a sample planning guide.

During the Lesson

Before the actual lesson begins, the teacher needs to prepare the students for the lesson by building in those elements that foster positive interdependence: sharing of materials, developing a group identity, and sequencing the task so that each person has a definite role to play. All these help students feel connected to the task and to each other.

The next step is to explain the academic task and expectations and to make sure that the students understand them. The students need to know the criteria for success and how they will be held individually accountable before the task begins. In many cases, it is a good idea to involve the students in developing the criteria. In addition, the teacher must clearly explain the directions for the task. Following this, the collaborative/social skill should be explained in such a way that the students see a need for practicing it.

One of the teacher's primary roles during the lesson is to provide opportunities for individual accountability. One way to do this is by randomly choosing students to answer on behalf of their groups. Another way is to have all group members sign their group's product upon completion, indicating that they have participated equally and can explain the group's conclusions if called on.

Monitoring Students

In cooperative group learning, the teacher is no longer required to be at the front of the room. The teacher's role is to move around while groups are working and to observe students' progress. The teacher may wish to make observations on a checklist, which then can be used to focus the group during debriefing. These teacher activities tend to promote accountability and allow the teacher to intervene when necessary. Apart from the usual interventions, such as those relating to discipline or keeping students on task, there may also be the need for task interventions, such as

COOPERATIVE GROUP PLANNING GUIDE

Curriculam expectations: _____

Collaborative skill: _____

Before the lesson

       Group Size   Materials

       Room Arrangement   Time Frame

During the lesson

Positive Interdependence	Academic Expectations	Task Directions	Collaborative Skill	Individual Accountability
❏ Goal ❏ Incentive ❏ Resource ❏ Sequence ❏ Role ❏ Identity ❏ Outside Force ❏ Simulation ❏ Environment				

Monitoring students

      ❏ Teacher   ❏ Student

      ❏ Formal   ❏ Informal

      ❏ Checklist   ❏ Notes

Closure

      Collaborative skill: _____

      Curriculum choice: _____

SOURCE: Adapted from *Cooperative Learning: Where Heart Meets Mind,* by Barrie Bennett, Carol Rolheiser-Bennett, and Laurie Stevahn. Toronto, Ontario: Educational Connections, 1991.

Figure 5.8

clarifying directions, reviewing procedures, teaching necessary skills, and asking and responding to questions.

When intervening, the teacher should draw on the students' skills rather than providing the answers. This builds the group's self-reliance. Students should be encouraged to follow the rule "Three before me," which means that the group must check out its question with three other sources before asking the teacher for help.

At times, direct intervention may be needed when a group is in immediate need of redirection concerning a particular collaborative/social skill. For example, a group in which one member is dominating the discussion may need some help in taking turns and allowing equal participation. As a general rule, the less intervention the better. In some cases, the teacher's best intentions may be seen as interference and ultimately may reduce the team's ability to think and solve problems on its own.

Closure

Students need to be given time for closure—time to summarize and reflect on their learning and to deal with outstanding group issues. Closure provides a chance for the teacher and the students to highlight major points, ask questions, and generate insights. Closure also should include time to process the collaborative/social skill and set plans for improvement where necessary.

The group activity may result in a presentation or product that needs to be assessed. Time is needed by the students and the teacher to assess the success of the group in achieving what was expected.

Teachers will make appropriate decisions about the configuration in the classroom based on needs and preferences of students (Gregory and Chapman 2006) Using a variety of structures will add variety and best meet the learning goals. We suggest using T.A.P.S. as a guide for grouping students for a variety of tasks and purposes. The chart on page 138 may be useful as a reminder of when and where to use the following configurations.

Total, Alone, Partners, or Small Groups.

T.A.P.S. Suggestions for Use

Total Whole class instruction All students doing the same thing	Preassessment Presenting new information Modeling new skills Guest speaker Viewing a video Using a jigsaw strategy Guest speaker Textbook(s) assignment

Alone
All students working alone may have
   a variety of tasks based on interest
   or readiness
	Preassessment
	Journal entry
	Portfolio assessing
	Self-assessment
	Independent study
	Note taking and summarizing
	Reflection
	Tickets out

Paired
All students have a partner
   Random selection (card, color, etc.)
   Teacher selection
   Students choose a partner
   Task or interest oriented
	Brainstorming
	Checking homework
	Checking for understanding
	Processing information
	Peer editing
	Peer evaluation
	Researching
	Interest in similar topic
	Planning for homework

Small groups Homogeneous for skill development Heterogeneous for cooperative groups Random or structured by teacher or students Interest or task oriented	Problem solving Group projects Learning centers Cooperative group learning assignments Portfolio conferences Group investigation Carousel brainstorming Graffiti brainstorming

SOURCE: From *Differentiating Instruction with Style* (Gregory 2005, Corwin Press).

IN CLOSING

During recent years, there has been an emphasis on moving toward a more global community, realizing that people are more interdependent than competitive. The multicultural classrooms, communities, and cities where students spend time require that the students can get along with all people in a variety of situations. The skills developed (both collaborative/social and thinking) when using cooperative structures will benefit learners in all areas of their lives.

Cooperative group learning, although a fairly easy concept to understand, is complex and time-consuming during the implementation stage. Begin by developing a climate that helps students to know one another and by building a team atmosphere among the learners. Then, teach collaborative/social skills so that students can use them when they work in groups, both inside and outside of school. Start with pairs, letting students share ideas, homework, and reflections with a partner. Design group activities that build on a mixture of concepts as appropriate, blending the multiple intelligences, a thinking skill, and a graphic organizer that shows the thinking and collaborative/social skills that can be practiced in the group.

Cooperative group learning provides the foundation on which other brain-compatible strategies can build, thus enhancing student learning and achievement.

Reflections

Respond to the questions individually in writing or with colleagues in discussion groups or at a faculty meeting.

What is PLUS about cooperative group learning?

What is MINUS about cooperative group learning?

What is INTERESTING about cooperative group learning?

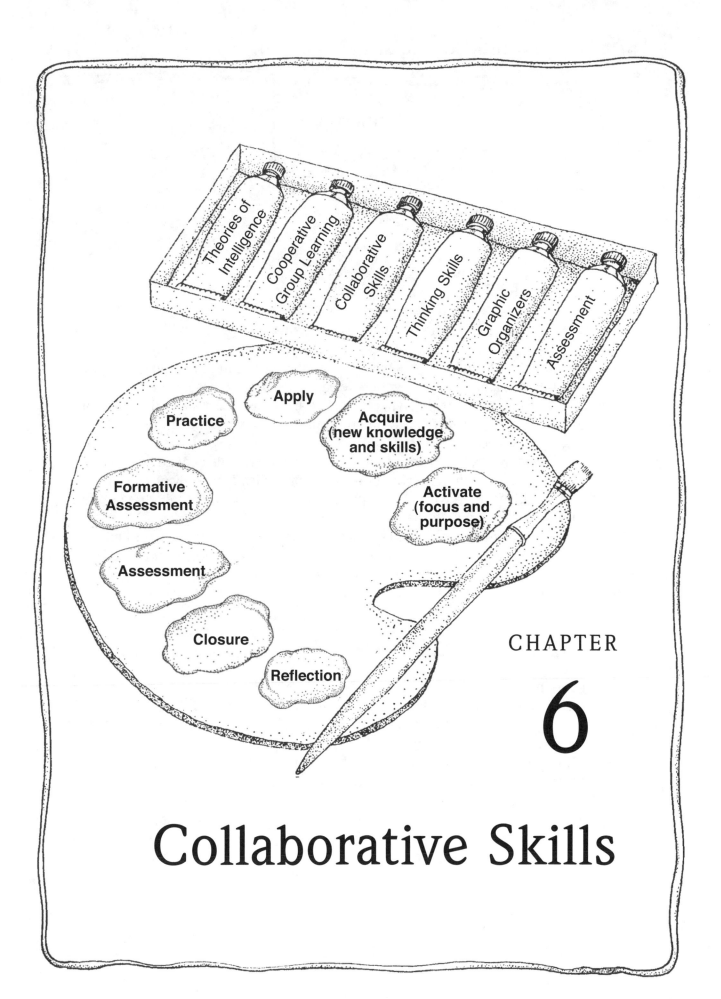

Theories of Intelligence

Cooperative Group Learning

Collaborative Skills

Thinking Skills

Graphic Organizers

Assessment

Apply

Practice

Acquire (new knowledge and skills)

Formative Assessment

Activate (focus and purpose)

Assessment

Closure

Reflection

CHAPTER

6

Collaborative Skills

CHAPTER 6

COLLABORATIVE SKILLS

WHAT ARE THEY?

Collaborative skills, sometimes called social skills, are those skills that enable students to work well in groups. They are the glue that holds cooperative group learning together. Collaborative skills, such as sharing, taking turns, and accepting diverse opinions, allow group members to function and to focus on the task and to continue learning rather than having to deal with the process and conflict. Without collaborative skills, it is difficult for a group to function well enough for academic learning to take place.

In each classroom, the need for specific collaborative skills depends on the individual group members and their experience working with others. By observing how students work together within a group, a teacher can identify which skills the students possess and which they need to develop.

Collaborative skills can be categorized into four types of skills: team building, communication, leadership, and conflict resolution. There is some overlap between the categories as skills may pertain to more than one type of function. Figure 6.1 provides basic descriptions and some examples of the types of collaborative skills.

WHY DO WE NEED THEM?

All people need to be able to interact well with others in order to form successful personal and professional relationships. The ability to work collaboratively with others is necessary not only for successful family life but also in the workplace. Many school districts recognize the importance of teamwork and collaborative skills and list these skills as desired expectations or outcomes for students. Many businesses and industries as well as government agencies that oversee labor and employment agree that the ability to work effectively in a team is a necessary competency for workers.

In addition, collaborative skills are a necessary element of emotional intelligence. These skills help students get along with others and develop positive relationships. These, in turn, promote higher self-esteem that improves students' ability to learn and fosters positive feelings about school.

No one is born with the interpersonal and/or social skills needed to get along with others. Thus, it is important to teach them to students.

Collaborative Skills

Team-Building Skills

Team-building skills are the basic skills needed to interact acceptably in any encounter of two or more individuals. They include the following:

- Being polite
- Calling people by name
- Listening attentively
- Using quiet voices
- Encouraging
- Being positive
- Praising
- Showing appreciation
- Practicing positive affirmations

Communication Skills

Communication skills are those skills needed to manage the process of working in a group by staying on task, moving toward a goal, and using time well. These skills include the following:

- Asking for help
- Clarifying ideas
- Contributing ideas
- Staying on task
- Participating equally
- Showing respect
- Being assertive
- Including everyone
- Being responsible

Leadership Skills

Leadership skills are those skills that enable group participants to fully understand, master, and retain the learning that the group is undertaking. These skills include the following:

- Extending ideas
- Paraphrasing
- Summarizing
- Elaborating
- Explaining
- Asking questions
- Checking for understanding

Conflict Resolution Skills

Conflict resolution skills are the skills that students need to challenge others' opinions and ideas in a manner that doesn't dissolve into an argument but, rather, leads to new ways of thinking. These skills include the following:

- Disagreeing agreeably
- Reaching consensus
- Seeing others' points of view
- Criticizing ideas not people
- Resolving conflicts
- Maintaining self-control

Figure 6.1

HOW DO WE TEACH THEM?

Creating Supportive Climate

For people to feel comfortable enough to work together, it is necessary to have a climate that supports risk taking and is free of threats and put-downs. Glasser (1986) stated that people need to feel that they "belong, which includes love, power, freedom and fun" (14). Glasser also pointed out that students need to feel that they are valued and have some choice and control in their own learning.

Before teaching collaborative/social skills, it is necessary to create a supportive climate through team-building activities and by establishing an atmosphere of acceptance and value for diverse opinions—both by the students and the teacher. Next, it is necessary to identify those skills the students need to improve their ability to work collaboratively.

Teaching Collaborative Skills

Once the teacher has identified a skill that a particular group or class needs, it is necessary to teach the skill through a process that ensures the students understand and see a need for the skill and have multiple opportunities to practice, process, and use the skill.

Following are descriptions of each step of the process of teaching collaborative/social skills:

Seeing a Need for the Skill

First, provide opportunities for students to see the need for the skill. There are a number of ways to ensure that students see a need for the skill. One is to capitalize on teachable moments. A teachable moment is one of those unscheduled, serendipitous occasions custom-made for a particular piece of learning. For example, a teacher who notices a group having difficulty arriving at a consensus can introduce some consensus-building skills even though this was not on the plan for the day. This allows students to see an immediate use for the learning in addition to placing the skills in their repertoires for future use.

Teachers may also schedule training in a particular skill based on personal observation and feedback from the students during a group processing. Group processing can include a group discussion about the skill or brainstorming about reasons the skill is important.

Understanding What the Skill Is

Next, promote student understanding of what the skill is and why it is important. One of the problems associated with teaching collaborative/social skills is that students often have no understanding of how the skill plays out in real-life situations.

One way to foster understanding is through the use of a T-chart, which allows the students to understand what the skill looks like and sounds like. The T-chart consists of two columns with a horizontal line across the top. One column is labeled Looks Like and the other Sounds Like. Students then brainstorm ideas for each of the columns, followed by a discussion of the examples that illustrates the targeted skills. The T-chart is posted for future reference.

As an example, a teacher teaching the skill of encouraging might say, "If we were practicing encouraging each other, what would I see you doing?" The students brainstorm examples of behaviors that demonstrate encouragement, such as nods, high fives, and thumbs-up, and these are listed under the Looks Like heading. Next, the teacher might say, "What will I hear you saying?" Once again, the students brainstorm examples that demonstrate encouragement, such as "Right on" and "That's a good idea," and these are listed under the Sounds Like heading. This is followed by discussion and clarification, and then the T-chart is posted on chart paper and displayed for reference. Figure 6.2 shows a sample T-chart for what the collaborative skill *encouraging* would look like and sound like.

T-Chart—Encouraging

Looks Like (What Will We See?)	**Sounds Like** (What Will We Hear?)
Nods of approval	That's a good idea!
Smiles	Right on!
Pats on the back	Could you tell me more?
Thumbs-up	I never thought of that.
High fives	What do you think?

Figure 6.2

The teacher should actively reinforce the desired behaviors while interacting with the groups. For example, a teacher might say, "I saw lots of nods and smiles in group one. In group two, I heard lots of 'good ideas' and 'right ons.'" Other ways of ensuring that students understand the skill are through role plays, mini lessons, simulations, puppets, guest speakers, and stories.

One very powerful strategy is to videotape the groups in action and use it in the debriefing process. This allows students to observe themselves and others in action in a way they couldn't when they were in the midst of an activity.

Practice the Skill

The third step is to provide practice situations that foster mastery of the skill. For students to practice a particular collaborative/social skill, they need to be placed in situations that put a premium on that skill. For example, the skill of disagreeing in agreeable ways or disagreeing without hurting people can be practiced in a situation that is contentious or likely to give rise to disagreement. Similarly, using quiet voices can be practiced in situations that are likely to generate lots of noise.

Process the Skill

Next, provide opportunities for students to process the skill and a set of procedures for doing it. Of all the elements of cooperative group learning, group processing is the one most often neglected, yet it is vital for students to improve in a particular skill. After practicing the skill, students need to be given time for both individual reflection and group discussion or debriefing. The teacher can provide feedback through participation in the group discussion or by using a debriefing sheet such as the one shown in Figure 6.3. (Blacklines for additional debriefing forms appear in the Blacklines section at the end of this chapter.) Students also can use debriefing sheets to provide feedback to other group members.

For example, the debriefing sheet How Well Did We Work Together? (Fig. 6.3) can be used by the teacher and/or a peer observer. The students' names are listed in the far-left column, with the targeted skills written across the column headings in the first row. The observer notes when group members exhibit different behaviors and records these on the sheet using a checkmark or other symbol. This information then serves as a discussion piece for group processing.

Other debriefing sheets include How Did I Help My Group? Observing Another Group, Giving Feedback to Another Group, Providing Feedback for Another Group's Presentation, and Group Reflection (Figures 6.4–6.8 in the Blacklines section, pages 151–155). Debriefing sheets may be completed individually, such as in a journal entry, with a partner, or in a small group.

Continuous Practice of the Skill

Once the students have become familiar with a skill, they need ample opportunities to practice it until using the skill seems natural. Learning collaborative/social skills to the point where they become second nature is not an easy task—it takes time and patience. When students first begin to practice these skills, they

How Well Did We Work Together?

Team Name: _____

Members: _____

Names	Targeted Skills		
	Used Quiet Voices	Offered Ideas	Took Turns

Suggestions for Next Time: _____

_____

_____

_____

_____

Figure 6.3

may be somewhat embarrassed. They may exaggerate the skill by being overly polite or by encouraging it to an excessive degree. There often is an air of "phony" behavior in their initial attempts, but eventually the skill becomes standard operating procedure or "part of the way we treat each other around here."

A number of strategies can be used to help students persist with a particular skill. Monitors, or peer observers, may be appointed in each group to keep the members on track. The monitor acts as an observer who provides feedback on specific behavior within the group. The teacher can also keep the group on task by preparing 5" × 7" cards with comments such as *The noise level in this group is just right—keep it up* or *The noise is getting too loud—keep it down.* Cards can be made to suit all eventualities. The teacher can drop a card on the appropriate student's desk without making any comment. In this way, the momentum of the group is maintained, but the individual student receives feedback on his or her behavior.

IN CLOSING

When we focus on teaching collaborative/social skills, we increase the chances that our students will develop the ability to work successfully with others. These skills are valued in relationships, families, schools, and organizations and businesses throughout the world. Knowing that collaborative/social skills are important to success in life and actually embedding them in our day-to-day lives in the classroom are two different things. To promote these skills in students, it is important that teachers model behaviors that reflect these skills. All adults involved in the school community, not only the teachers, need to demonstrate these skills in their everyday behaviors and integrate them into the fabric of the school.

The skills of team building, communication, leadership, and conflict resolution are as important to students as the subject content taught in schools. Students who learn to work well with others will have mastered one of the most essential skills for postschool success.

Reflections

Use the shapes and prompts to reflect on the need for collaborative skills and their implementation. You may want to compare your ideas with a colleague or your planning team. You can also use this format with students to bring closure to a lesson.

Shaping up a Review

Four things you want to remember.

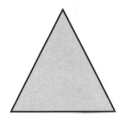

Three points of view.

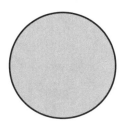

One idea that is rolling around in your mind.

BLACKLINES

HOW DID I HELP MY GROUP?

My job for this assignment was _____

_____

_____

_____

I organized myself using these steps: _____

_____

_____

_____

_____

I helped the group by _____

_____

_____

_____

_____

Next time I will _____

_____

_____

_____

Figure 6.4

OBSERVING ANOTHER GROUP

I am _____

Team I watched _____

Skill they were working on _____

What did they do to demonstrate the skill?

Things They Did	Things They Said

Outstanding   Needs More Work

```
|-------------|-------------|-------------|-------------|
1             2             3             4             5
```

Suggestions: _____

_____

_____

_____

_____

Figure 6.5

GIVING FEEDBACK TO ANOTHER GROUP

What do you remember as being most important/interesting in the presentation?

_____

_____

_____

What two new things did you learn? _____

_____

_____

_____

What was the best thing the presenters did? _____

_____

_____

_____

Another idea the group might have used is _____

_____

_____

_____

What do you want to know more about?_____

_____

_____

_____

Where might you get help? _____

_____

_____

_____

Figure 6.6

PROVIDING FEEDBACK FOR
ANOTHER GROUP'S PRESENTATION

Topic: _____

Presenters: _____

	Outstanding			Needs More Work	
General overview	1	2	3	4	5
Quality of materials	1	2	3	4	5
Creativity	1	2	3	4	5
Clarity of ideas	1	2	3	4	5
Presentation delivery	1	2	3	4	5

Positive Comments	Questions	Interesting Ideas

Figure 6.7

GROUP REFLECTION

As a group, fill in together.

What roles did your group members take? _____

_____

_____

_____

_____

Describe the steps you took in organizing. _____

_____

_____

_____

_____

What went well? What did you learn? _____

_____

_____

_____

_____

If you were working together again, what changes would you make? _____

_____

_____

_____

_____

Figure 6.8

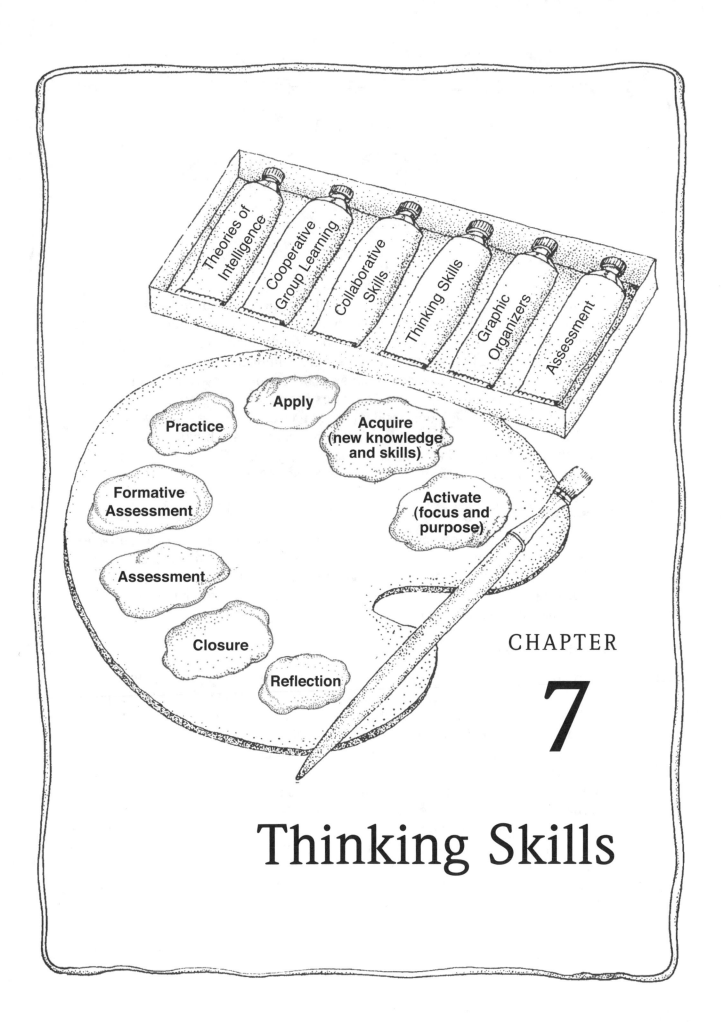

Theories of Intelligence

Cooperative Group Learning

Collaborative Skills

Thinking Skills

Graphic Organizers

Assessment

Apply

Practice

Acquire (new knowledge and skills)

Formative Assessment

Activate (focus and purpose)

Assessment

Closure

Reflection

CHAPTER

7

Thinking Skills

CHAPTER 7

THINKING SKILLS

WHAT ARE THEY?

In general terms, thinking is the exercise of the mental faculties to form ideas, reach conclusions, and solve problems. Although there is well-documented evidence that some of the higher vertebrates, such as apes and dolphins, are capable of thought, none of them is as adept as the human being. All humans are capable of thinking to some extent, and even the slowest of us can outperform the average chimpanzee. Thinking, therefore, is the ability that sets us apart from other species, and yet in many schools it is dealt with only incidentally. In previous chapters, we have described how the brain performs many of the functions that we call thinking or reasoning. In this chapter, we examine different ways of categorizing thinking skills and then look at ways of teaching thinking skills in the classroom.

Types of Thinking

Thinking skills can be categorized in many ways, but for practical purposes, they can be divided into two major groups: creative thinking and critical thinking. This distinction is somewhat arbitrary because the two types of thinking are closely and irrevocably intertwined—creative thinking has critical components and critical thinking has creative elements.

Creative Thinking

Creative thinking is divergent in nature and seeks multiple solutions to problems. *Divergent* means to move outward in many directions from a given point. This is what the brain does when it is called on to think creatively. The brain can perform this function in two ways: one, by scanning the information that is already stored in long-term memory and, two, by going out and seeking new information. In the first instance, the brain retrieves information from long-term memory and brings it into short-term, or working, memory. It is called working memory because it is the part of the brain where information is actually processed or worked on.

Information in long-term memory is not stored in complete chunks like a series of pictures in a book. It is actually stored as a collection of fragments that the brain is able to call up and reassemble into complete memories, facts, or concepts. The sequence of steps in which the information is reconstructed may be different each time the memory is recalled into working memory. This is one of the reasons that the details of some memories fade or assume greater significance over time. It also means that each time information is recalled, it is not only connected in new and different ways but it may also have fragments of different ideas attached to it. If you have ever included black socks in a load of white clothes and then tumble-dried them, you can visualize how this would look.

The brain's creative abilities depend in part on its myriad connections and cross connections. These synaptic connections form as a direct result of new experiences and learning. This maze of connections allows us to recall information into working memory and process it very quickly. When dealing with an information network of this complexity, it is inevitable that previously unrelated bits of information may be thrown together as if by accident. This linking of one idea with another seemingly unrelated idea allows us to gain insight and understanding of complex ideas. Perhaps it is the ability to recognize the potential of these connections and capitalize on them that is the mark of the creative thinker.

As teachers, we should be aware that creativity is not as random and accidental as it may seem. Much creative thought depends on the kinds of information at the brain's disposal. The brain cannot connect what it does not have. This makes a very good case for providing our students with the broadest and most diverse education possible, as opposed to narrowing the curriculum by eliminating many of the more creative programs.

One of the strange things about creative thinking and this seemingly haphazard connection of information is that many of our best ideas are more often accidental than deliberate. We seem to do our most creative thinking when the mind is slightly disengaged from the problem at hand. This may be why we get our best ideas in the shower or while brushing our teeth. Albert Einstein reported that he got many of his more brilliant notions while shaving, and Archimedes is remembered for jumping out of his bathtub shouting, "Eureka!," which in Greek means "I have found it" (*it,* in this case, being the principle of water displacement).

This often serendipitous connection of information in new and different ways combined with the addition of other ideas or fragments of information allows us to be creative and achieve understanding. When a person says, "I never thought of it that way," the statement might be quite literally true because the information may never have been recalled in that particular sequence before.

A similar phenomenon occurs when the brain seeks out new information or previously unexplored options. It collects new ideas, which then appear to swirl around in the brain looking for ways of connecting to other information to see if any useful or viable patterns are formed. Useful ideas are stored for future use and nonapplicable ideas are discarded. The process by which ideas are selected or rejected is a function of critical thinking; thus, both types of thinking are closely intertwined. In fact, creative thinking cannot exist without critical thinking.

Critical Thinking

Critical thinking is convergent in nature and seeks to narrow the field of options by applying some criteria or evaluation to the data. *Convergent* is the opposite of divergent. It means to move inward from many points and converge, or focus, on a single point. We think convergently when we focus on the alternatives generated by creative thinking and then analyze and evaluate them according to a set of criteria.

The separation of critical thinking from creative thinking works well in theory. In practice, especially for most substantive tasks, we use both types of thinking by rapidly and often unconsciously moving from divergence to convergence and back again. We use both modes of thinking to solve problems, create new technologies, make new artifacts, and establish philosophies.

Let us examine this idea further by looking at how we use critical and creative thinking to make decisions. At first glance, decision making appears to involve more critical/convergent thinking than creative/divergent thinking, but on closer examination, it appears that we need both. For example, when a person is faced with making a decision such as buying a car, he or she usually begins to think divergently by scanning the available information about all the makes and models on the market and collecting an extensive list of possible vehicles.

Many of these vehicles may be desirable, but only some are acceptable. Thus, the brain switches to the critical mode and thinks convergently by taking the unexamined mass of data and zeroing in on the more acceptable choices. It does this by applying a set of criteria to the list of options. The list of considerations might include the price and whether the car is for family or personal use, has four doors or two doors, is primarily for city or country use, and so on. The cars that do not conform to the criteria are dropped from the list. The result is a shorter list based on some fairly broad considerations, which narrows the field somewhat.

The brain then switches back to divergent thinking as the car shopper scans all the available cars that conform to his or her base set of criteria: price range, body style, and category. This produces a limited set of data from which many of the unacceptable items have been removed.

The potential buyer then switches back to the convergent mode and applies another set of criteria that may not have been considered at the outset. These criteria might include features such as fixed or folding seats, rear-wheel drive or front-wheel drive, traction control, and so on. Through a process of elimination, the individual arrives at the most logical choice, considering his or her needs, preferences, and pocketbook.

At this point, the car shopper goes out and buys the red two-door convertible that he or she wanted in the first place. (Nobody said that the ability to think well guarantees logical behavior!)

This example distorts the thinking process to some extent because it appears to be both linear and logical. In reality, decision making often is much more muddled or messy. If the process were as logical and foolproof as our example seems to appear, then it would guarantee that we all would make the right choice every time. However, in our daily lives, we sometimes make poor decisions because our emotions override our attempts at logical decision making. Despite the apparent lack of logic that sometimes goes into decision making, it is important that students understand the thinking process and realize the value of weighing options and applying criteria.

Taxonomies

Apart from critical and creative thinking, it is possible to categorize thinking in a number of other ways. These usually are called taxonomies. The most familiar of these is Bloom's taxonomy (Bloom et al. 1956), which has a wide acceptance among educators (see Fig. 7.1).

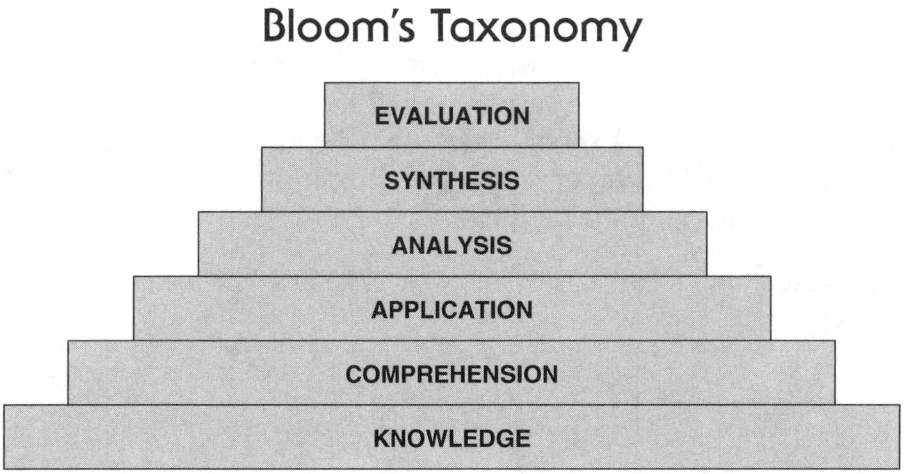

Bloom's Taxonomy

```
                    EVALUATION
                 SYNTHESIS
              ANALYSIS
           APPLICATION
        COMPREHENSION
     KNOWLEDGE
```

Figure 7.1

Bloom's taxonomy divides thinking into six categories:

- *Knowledge:* Recalling the facts and remembering previously learned information. The abilities to describe, identify, list, locate, and label are evidence of thinking at the knowledge level.
- *Comprehension:* Understanding the meaning of information or how and why events happen. The abilities to explain, give examples, summarize, and paraphrase are evidence of comprehension.
- *Application:* Transferring information or a skill learned in one situation to another circumstance or setting. Application puts knowledge and comprehension to work. The abilities to deduce, infer, predict, adapt, modify, and solve are evidence of application.
- *Analysis:* Breaking down information into its elements or components so that its structure can be understood. Understanding the structure of information is especially useful when one is comparing two complex sets of data. Knowing how things are put together also enables one to modify or adapt data to apply it to new situations or synthesize it in new ways. The abilities to subdivide, discriminate, classify, and categorize are evidence of analysis.

- *Synthesis:* Combining elements or components to create new or different structures or ideas. The skill of synthesis is predicated on the ability to analyze. In other words, one has to be able to take things apart before one can put them together in new or different ways. The abilities to induce, generalize, create, compose, combine, rearrange, design, and plan are evidence of synthesis.
- *Evaluation:* Rating or ranking the value of information according to a set of criteria. The skill of evaluation is often predicated on the skill of analysis, especially when comparing complex ideas or products. For example, to compare the relative merits of two makes of automobiles, one would first have to analyze each of them in terms of characteristics such as safety, styling, comfort, horsepower, handling, and fuel consumption. Next, one would compare the horsepower of one with the horsepower of the other, the fuel consumption of one with the fuel consumption of the other, and so on. By analyzing the data, one devises a set of criteria that forms a more valid basis for comparison. The abilities to judge, compare, contrast, criticize, justify, and conclude are evidence of evaluation.

Another taxonomy worth considering is that proposed by E. S. Quellmalz (1985) (see Fig. 7.2).

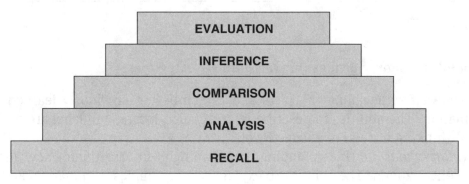

Quellmalz's Taxonomy

EVALUATION

INFERENCE

COMPARISON

ANALYSIS

RECALL

Figure 7.2

Quellmalz's taxonomy has five categories, which are similar in some ways to those in Bloom's taxonomy:

- *Recall:* Repeating or paraphrasing key facts, concepts, and principles. In order to paraphrase, or express another person's ideas in their own words, students need to connect and associate ideas with previous learning. Recall is evidence of understanding or comprehension. (Recall combines Bloom's categories of knowledge and comprehension.)

- *Analysis:* Dividing the whole into components, or parts. The components can be either the characteristics of objects or ideas or the sequence of events in actions or procedures. It is often necessary to analyze cause-and-effect relationships and the relationship of parts to the whole before evaluations and comparisons can be made. (Analysis is similar to Bloom's category of analysis.)
- *Comparison:* Explaining the similarities and differences of ideas or objects. Comparison emphasizes the information-processing skills that students require when they compare the similarities and the differences between the components that they have analyzed from the whole. (Comparison includes some of the skills in Bloom's category of analysis.)
- *Inference:* Combining the elements to make a conclusion or generalization. Hypothesizing, predicting, concluding, and synthesizing fall under this category. Inference often follows an "if-then" pattern of thinking; for example, if what we know about global warming is true, then what conclusions can we draw from it? This category of the Quellmalz taxonomy includes both inductive and deductive reasoning. In inductive tasks, the students are given the evidence or details and are required to develop a conclusion or generalization. In deductive tasks, the students are given the generalization and then are required to examine particular cases to see if the details or evidence in them conform to the pattern of the original generalization. Putting the pieces together to make a generalization is a form of synthesis. Using deductive reasoning to prove a rule is a form of application. (Inference relates to Bloom's categories of synthesis and application.)
- *Evaluation:* Judging the quality, worth, or credibility of ideas. Evaluation requires students to establish a set of criteria on which to base their decisions and then to explain the reasons that support their conclusions. It also may require students to explain or to justify their choice of a particular criterion. The explanation of criteria is unique to evaluative thinking. Assembling and explaining the interrelationships among pieces of supporting evidence is also a form of synthesis. (Evaluation relates to Bloom's categories of synthesis and evaluation.)

Although some people prefer one taxonomy over the other, both are useful. Some people find Bloom's taxonomy more useful for teaching thinking skills and Quellmalz's more helpful for designing assessment tools. Misconceptions about taxonomies and the thinking process can create difficulties for teachers. A common misconception is that taxonomies of thinking skills are arranged as a hierarchy from easy to difficult. In fact, they are categorized according to the type of thinking process required. The confusion arises when we speak of analysis, synthesis, and evaluation as being higher-order thinking. This often leads people to believe that questions or tasks based on these skills are inherently more difficult than those based on recall or comprehension. The logic of this argument seems to go as follows: If higher-order thinking is difficult, then lower-order thinking must be easy. Let us look at some questions to see if this is true.

Q: *How many bears are there in the story of Goldilocks?*
This is a recall question and for most people it is hardly a stretch.

Q: *Can you write out the periodic table of elements from memory?*
This also is a recall question, but how many of us would care to try it?

Q: *What happens when you go out in the rain?*
This question calls for a basic understanding of cause and effect. It is, in fact, a comprehension question, but it is hardly a brain teaser.

Q: *What is the theory behind quantum physics?*
This also is a comprehension question and a definite brain teaser.

Q: *Can you take this box of buttons and sort them into categories?*
Most kindergarten students perform this kind of analysis on a routine basis.

Q: *Select three well-known fairy tales and analyze them in terms of common or recurring elements.*
This also calls for analysis, but it is a bit more complex than sorting buttons.

Q: *Which is better, vanilla or strawberry ice cream?*
This is definitely a subjective evaluation of relative merit, but it is not particularly difficult.

Q: *Which is the best type of government, democracy or communism?*
This also is an evaluation question but at a much higher level of difficulty because it requires a detailed analysis of the two systems of government.

It appears that difficulty is not the criterion on which taxonomies are based. We can ask easy recall questions; we can ask difficult recall questions. We can ask easy comprehension questions; we can ask difficult ones. Taxonomies merely describe the type of thinking required by a particular question or problem.

We have examined two ways of categorizing thinking skills—critical thinking and creative thinking—and two taxonomies that divide thinking into a number of sub-skills—Bloom's and Quellmalz's. Breaking thinking down in these ways is an obvious oversimplification. When we take a look at how to teach thinking skills in the classroom, we describe additional ways to classify thinking skills—those that acquire information and those that extend information, and inductive and deductive reasoning.

WHY DO WE NEED THEM?

Thinking is what defines us as human beings and sets us apart, as far as we know, from other creatures. It is the ability to think that adds dimension and color to our daily lives. Whenever we ponder the aesthetic qualities of art, music, and literature or the nature of our interpersonal relationships, we are, in fact, engaged in critical and creative thinking. The ability to critically analyze information as a way to make decisions is the key to becoming a well-informed citizen and is the first line of defense for our democratic rights and privileges. Another compelling reason for the explicit teaching of thinking comes from the world of work. When business and industry leaders are surveyed about the skills that students need to function in the workplace, the abilities to think creatively and critically usually rank high on the list.

One of the primary goals of education is to produce well-functioning, productive, happy citizens who are capable of reaching both personal and professional goals. All these goals are predicated on the ability to think, and yet, in many schools, thinking receives a very sketchy or cursory treatment at best. So here is the dilemma: If the ability to think is such a vital skill, why is it not integrated into every subject area in the curriculum? The following section provides some suggestions on how to rectify this situation.

HOW DO WE TEACH THEM?

Thinking is an integral element of the whole curriculum, and thinking skills have applications in all subject areas. Thinking skills should be taught within the context of the regular program as opposed to being taught as a stand-alone or an add-on item to an already crowded curriculum. Students need to be explicitly taught thinking skills, to be given opportunities to practice them, and then to be given time to reflect on what they have learned through some form of metacognition. Providing students opportunities to work in small groups with other students to organize information and to apply thinking skills promotes learning because it allows students to discuss, clarify, and question the material to be learned.

All these activities tend to enhance both the level of comprehension and the level of retention of information. When students process information by working in small groups, they enhance their ability to organize information. It is this ability to organize information rather than the sheer volume of facts one knows that is the hallmark of good thinkers.

Using Taxonomies

Bloom's taxonomy is a useful starting place for introducing thinking skills to students. When a taxonomy is used in conjunction with lesson design, it guides the teacher in understanding what the students are expected to learn and how they will demonstrate that learning. For example, if the expectation for a unit in social studies is that students will evaluate the relative merits of a free market versus a controlled economy, then presumably the teacher will require the students to demonstrate the skill of evaluation as well as recall the salient facts. In such a case, the teacher might start by teaching the desired thinking skill of evaluation first and then allow the students to organize the information and draw conclusions for themselves. Because the goal of the lesson is to learn the thinking skill of evaluation, students should also be required to demonstrate this skill as part of the assessment process.

When designing a lesson with a thinking skill in mind, the expectation is that by the end of the lesson the students will have acquired some measure of the skill. This in turn leads to a series of questions, such as, How will the students demonstrate the skill? How will the evidence they produce be assessed? To what set of standards will the students be held accountable? The answers to these questions give students a clear picture of the expectations and provide the teacher with information on the skills he or she needs to teach in order for the students to meet the established criteria and be successful. Planning with the outcome in mind has a profound effect on the way material is presented to students and the type of assessment activities that the teacher designs.

A taxonomy also allows the teacher to design questions requiring higher-order thinking that are at a level of difficulty within the students' capabilities. Sometimes teachers mistakenly believe that only gifted students can handle "higher-order" thinking; however, teachers can take care to pose questions at the right level of difficulty so that all students can engage with all types of thinking.

When designing thinking-skills lessons, a teacher may want to emphasize a particular skill, but because the skills overlap, it often is difficult to isolate just one skill and teach it as a discrete skill. Therefore, thinking skills are usually taught in sequences and combinations. For example, a teacher may wish to emphasize the skill of comprehension, but comprehension also requires the ability to recall certain facts or concepts into working memory. Similarly, before students can evaluate a body of information, they must use analysis to break the whole into its parts.

It is often difficult to make fine distinctions between types of thinking. We may agonize over whether question A is an evaluation or analysis question. One way of solving this dilemma is to categorize thinking skills by whether they acquire information or extend information. Recall and comprehension may be said to acquire information, because the brain usually seeks out and consumes knowledge as a way of understanding complex issues. Application, analysis, synthesis, and evaluation may be said to extend information, because the brain uses what it has learned to make new connections, creative applications, and elegant solutions to problems. In other words, knowledge and comprehension become useful only when they are applied in new and different ways to produce additional information. We should, therefore, strive to lead our students to becoming producers of information who use knowledge to create or extend learning as opposed to consumers who merely acquire knowledge and retrieve it on demand to answer recall questions.

Metacognition

One of the keys to the successful teaching of thinking skills is metacognition:

Being conscious of our own thinking and problem solving during the act of thinking and problem solving is known as metacognition. It is a uniquely human ability occurring in the cerebral cortex of the brain. Interestingly, it has been found that good problem solvers do it; they plan a course of action before they begin a task. They monitor themselves during the execution of the plan, they consciously back up or adjust the plan, and they evaluate themselves upon completion. (Costa 1995, 11)

This conscious monitoring of one's thought processes takes the form of an internal dialogue. For example, a student might first define a problem by asking a question such as, What am I really trying do here? Then, the student searches for a possible solution, asking him or herself, Have I encountered this type of problem before? Having selected a viable strategy, the student continuously monitors his or her progress by checking it against the defined goals of the problem-solving task. At the conclusion of the activity, the student might ask questions such as, How was my use of this solution in this situation different from the last time I tried it? Can I replicate this solution and use it for other problems? Was this the best solution for this problem? What have I learned from this activity?

Metacognition is a very useful and flexible tool. Even within the context of direct teaching or a lecture, a teacher should pause every ten to fifteen minutes and give the students a chance to process the information with a partner or in small groups. The cognitive and pedagogical sciences indicate that the process of talking about new information—questioning, clarifying, and expressing the concept in one's own words—is a major tool in arriving at understanding because it is only when one has constructed personal meaning from a body of information that one can truly be said to have learned it.

If we reflect on our experiences of teaching collaborative/social skills within the context of cooperative group learning, we find that students get better at these skills only by reflecting on their past performances through some kind of debriefing or group processing activity. The same is true for thinking and metacognition. We get better at problem solving only by reflecting on our performance before, during, and after the related task.

Although metacognition usually means to reflect on one's own thinking, metacognitive strategies can be used by small groups by adapting the concept to "thinking about our thinking."

Following are four sets of reflective questions, or metaquestions, that can be used to engage students in metacognition. Once students become familiar with metacognition, they may develop their own sets of metaquestions to use to reflect on their thinking and learning.

General Problem-Solving Metaquestions

- Define the problem: What am I being asked to do or find out?
- Establish preconditions: What information have I been given?
- Scan previous learning: What strategies have I used in similar situations?

- Access information: Who or what could help me with this?
- Establish criteria: What will a successful solution look like?
- Develop a plan: What will be step one, step two, step three?
- Sequence activities into a timeline: What has to be done by when?
- Monitor the plan: How much time do I have? Should I persevere or start over?
- Evaluate the solution: How well does the solution conform to the criteria?
- Assess the performance: What helped me in this process? What hindered me? What would I do differently next time?
- Extension of knowledge: What new skills have I learned? Can I replicate this solution or apply it to other situations?

In-Lesson Metaquestions

- What are the big ideas or concepts?
- How well does this information fit with what I already know?
- What generalizations or inferences can I make from this information?
- Are there any questions or concerns that I still have?

Thinking-Level Metaquestions

- What type of thinking is built into this question (e.g., analysis, synthesis, inductive reasoning)?
- What type of thinking do I need to engage in to answer this question?

Applying/Transferring Skills Metaquestions

- Are there other uses for this knowledge or skill?
- What are some other situations where I might apply this skill?
- Can I transfer the skill as is or do I need to change it in some way?
- How could I modify or adapt this skill to suit my particular need?

Two other useful metacognitive strategies are the PMI (de Bono 1976) and Six Hat Thinking (de Bono 1985). Both were developed by Edward de Bono to provide a structure or framework for discussion that may be adapted for either individual or group reflection.

PMI

The PMI is particularly useful as a framework for group discussion after the students have been exposed to a piece of information, such as a poem, an essay, or a written commentary. It also may be used with material on audio or videotape.

The strategy works like this: After the students have read, heard, or viewed the material, they reflect upon it by considering the following question: In terms of what you have just heard, seen, or read, what did you find to be a plus (P), a minus (M), or an interesting (I) question or comment? At this point, the teacher may wish to display a number of sentence stems for each category (as shown in Fig. 7.3).

PMI

Plus
I agree with the main ideas for the following reasons . . .
This fits in with what I already know about . . .
This has given me further insight into the situation in the
   following way . . .

Minus
I do not agree with this for the following reasons . . .
This is at odds with what I know about . . .
I have questions or concerns about . . .

Interesting Questions/Comments
This is a whole new slant on the subject in terms of . . .
I have never thought of it as . . .
I can adapt some of these ideas and use them by . . .

Figure 7.3

Working individually, the students process the information they have read, seen, or heard by completing the sentence stems in each category. Following this individual reflection, they share their thoughts with a partner and then share their comments or questions with the whole group.

The PMI is especially effective when used at ten- to fifteen-minute intervals during a lecture because it provides students a means for processing and reflecting on what they are learning.

Six Hat Thinking

Six Hat Thinking is similar to the PMI but is more sophisticated. The six hats are metaphors for the types of thinking skills students can use during a discussion. Each hat has a unique color that represents a specific type of thinking. Students are assigned a specific colored hat and then use the type of thinking represented by that hat in a small-group or full-class discussion.

Following are the types of thinking represented by each of the different colored hats:

The white hat thinkers look for hard facts, figures, and data. They maintain a cool and neutral outlook on the topic or material.

 The yellow hat thinkers look for all the positive aspects. They reflect optimism, try to remain enthusiastic, and find the constructive ideas and possible benefits related to the topic/material.

 The purple hat thinkers focus on the negative aspects. They look for flaws, faults, and reasons why something won't work.

 The red hat thinkers deal with the hunches, intuitions, emotions, and feelings they have about the topic.

 The green hat thinkers use the topic or material as a springboard for creative adaptations, options, and alternatives. They look for opportunities "outside the box," or beyond the obvious.

 The blue hat thinkers draw conclusions from the material. They provide definitions of concepts and summaries of the major ideas.

Six Hat Thinking is provided as a blackline at the end of this chapter for use in a classroom. Although the hats are usually metaphorical, students, particularly younger ones, may wear colored hats during a thinking activity or discussion.

As an example of how the strategy might play out in a classroom, a teacher might assign six students to watch the same film, read the same book, or attend the same presentation. Each student is assigned a different colored hat and engages with the material according to the type of thinking represented by that hat. In this way, each student responds to the information from a different perspective. At the end of the allotted time, each student reports on the material based on the type of thinking skill represented by the assigned hat.

This strategy also can be adapted for a whole class. In this case, the students form six small groups and each member of a particular group assumes the same colored hat. At the end of the allotted time, each group processes its own information before electing a spokesperson to report to the rest of the class.

Engaging in metacognitive discussion provides students opportunities to develop their thinking skills. The role of the teacher is to provide the conditions that help students develop and internalize these metacognitive dialogues. These conditions may be facilitated through direct instruction, modeling, and practice.

Questioning Strategies

Questioning is one of the major tools in a teacher's repertoire of skills. When handled skillfully, questioning can enhance, clarify, and extend student thinking. However, the ways in which teachers pose questions to students also can detract from these abilities. As we have seen from the discussion of brain research (see chapter 1), stress can significantly hamper one's ability to think clearly.

Wait Time

One of the major causes of stress in a classroom and a major impediment to thinking is the lack of adequate time for students to formulate a response to a question. Many teachers ask a question and promptly call on a student to respond. Researchers such as Mary Budd Rowe have studied the effects of increasing the amount of time between posing a question and calling on a student to respond, often referred to as wait time. Rowe concluded that

> the quality of discourse can be markedly improved by increasing to three seconds or longer the amount of time between posing the question and the response. When teachers pose a question and pause while waiting for a response, the pauses usually are so brief, one second or less on average, that an adequate exchange of ideas and the nurturing of new ideas cannot take place. (Rowe 1987, 43)

The think-pair-share strategy has wait time built into it. In this strategy, students are first given time to *think* for themselves. Next, they *pair* with a partner and discuss their answers. Finally, they are called on to *share* their responses with the class.

This strategy relieves tension and provides ample time to formulate a response in the question-and-answer process. It reduces stress in two ways: It provides more time to think, and it provides students with an opportunity to rehearse their answers and clarify their thinking with a partner before being asked to respond in front of the whole class.

Rowe advocated a wait time of three seconds; however, wait times of ten seconds or longer are beneficial when asking questions that call for complex or multipart answers. Increased wait time is important when asking complex questions, because they require the student to marshal his or her thoughts before responding. On the other hand, recall questions about facts such as names, dates, and places usually require less wait time because the student either knows the answer and can respond immediately or doesn't know the answer, in which case wait time will not make much difference.

Black and William (1998, 2004) also conducted research on the use of wait time in secondary schools in the U.K. They found that students gave more complete and detailed answers when more wait time was given. Students, as a result of this higher level of thinking and more complete and thorough answers, had a better understanding of the materials and concepts and thus achieve higher scores on tests.

Higher-Order Questions

Another important aspect of questioning techniques involves the types of thinking skills required by the questions we ask of students. If we want students to develop higher-order thinking skills, then we need to ask questions that require them to analyze, synthesize, apply, and evaluate as opposed to questions that prompt only recall.

A useful strategy to promote higher-order thinking skills is to familiarize the students with the action verbs that signal the various types of thinking skills (see Fig. 7.4). Posting a list of action verbs helps students to recognize the required thinking.

Question Distribution

We also need to pay attention to the ways in which we distribute questions to students. This includes being sensitive to gender and asking questions of a comparable number of girls and boys. The amount of wait time afforded to girls and boys should be similar, as should the kinds of probing questions that ask for additional information or an extension of ideas. In many classrooms, teachers ask more questions of children at the front and center of the room and fewer questions of those at the sides and back. By being aware of one's habits, teachers can make a conscious effort to distribute questions in a more equitable fashion.

Keeping a plan of the students who are going to be called on is one strategy that can help teachers to keep all students engaged with the lesson. When using a pre-planned arrangement for the distribution of questions, it helps to call on individual students more than once so that the students know that they need to pay attention at all times and aren't "off the hook" once they have answered a question.

Responding to Students' Responses

Most teachers have been trained to provide positive or reinforcing comments to students' responses. These comments, such as "Well done" and "Good attempt," are usually given with the best of intentions, but in certain circumstances they can interfere with flexible or creative thinking (Kohn 1993).

Consider what happens when you ask students to respond in new, different, or original ways and then lavishly praise the very first response. When we do this, we may be sending a message to the remaining students about the type of answer we want. This can result in students shaping their responses to conform with what they perceive as "what the teacher wants." Another consequence is that some students may hesitate to volunteer ideas that differ from the answer that received praise or they may modify their responses to be more aligned to what they perceive as the right answer.

This can result in an environment in which students are unsure or reluctant to voice new or original ideas for fear that they may be unacceptable. By maintaining

Taxonomy of Thinking Skill Action Words

Knowledge

Example: Locate the state capitals on the map of the United States.

What	Name
Who	Recite
When	List
Where	Relate
Recall	Find
Locate	Identify
Repeat	Label

Comprehension

Example: Transpose *Romeo and Juliet* into a modern-day idiom.

Reword	Reconstruct
Convert	Paraphrase
Outline	Transpose
Explain	Understand
Define	Conceive
Interpret	Calculate

Application

Example: Solve the problem of fastening two objects by studying the properties of burrs.

Apply	Transform
Adapt	Employ
Transfer	Manipulate
Adopt	Utilize
Transcribe	Transplant
Solve	Relate
Use	Convert

Analysis

Example: Classify the following animals according to diet and determine their place in the food chain: shrimp, dolphin, worm, monkey, and rabbit.

Break down	Analyze
Examine	Separate
Dissect	Investigate
Scrutinize	Compartmentalize
Inspect	Classify
Sort	Take apart

Synthesis

Example: Compound the following ingredients into a smooth paste: butter, flour, milk, and honey.

Combine	Mix
Build	Compound
Originate	Structure
Regroup	Make
Conceive	Generate
Blend	Join
Develop	

Evaluation

Example: Determine the performance of the following mutual funds and select the top two: Fund A, Fund B, Fund AA, Fund BB, and Fund ABC.

Assess	Assay
Judge	Decide
Weigh	Arbitrate
Rate	Grade
Determine	Appraise
Rank	Classify

Figure 7.4

a neutral stance, the teacher encourages more diverse opinions from the students and creates an environment in which students feel free to consider and express a multitude of ideas. When the teacher's intent is to encourage a range of possible solutions, the best response is a neutral one, such as "Thank you," "Uh-huh," or

"Okay." Another way of providing a neutral response is either to paraphrase what a student has said or to ask another student to paraphrase it. This not only models attentive listening but also verifies that the answer was correctly interpreted.

Responding to students' answers by using probes or follow-up questions, such as "If what you say is true, then what are some possible consequences?" is a great way to encourage students to extend their thinking. Follow-up questions and comments can include prompts such as, "Why do you think this may have happened?" "Tell me more about that." Can you give me an example?" These types of probes promote flexible thinking and encourage students to consider questions from different points of view.

Teachers also might play the devil's advocate or have other students play the devil's advocate by taking the opposite side of an argument even though it may be an apparently indefensible position. Another possibility is to have the students reverse roles and "attack" their own answers while defending others' points of view. All these strategies tend to promote flexible thinking because they encourage students to consider alternate ways of perceiving and understanding a concept or topic.

Critical Thinking

Critical thinking and creative thinking are closely intertwined, and it is often difficult to isolate one type of thinking and label it as one or the other. In general, though, critical thinking, which is convergent in nature, includes the ability to reason deductively and inductively.

The deductive method of instruction is the one most familiar to teachers. When we teach through deductive reasoning, a concept is presented and then specific examples are examined to see if they conform to the rules or generalizations relating to the concept. For example, we might teach the concept *democracy* by introducing the students to the characteristics of democratic systems of government. To reinforce the concept, the students examine examples of various regimes to see if they conform to the critical characteristics that pertain to the concept democracy. The same pattern of instruction may be applied in all subject areas, from concepts such as place value in math to the structure of Shakespeare's sonnets in English literature to the characteristics of Expressionist paintings in visual arts.

Inductive thinking causes us to do the opposite of deductive reasoning. To learn the concept of democracy, the students first examine a number of countries that are defined as democracies; then they look for the attributes that democratic forms of government have in common, such as free elections, an elected head of state, representatives elected for a specified term, some form of cabinet structure, and multiparty representation. The students then take their lists of attributes and form a hypothesis or generalization about the critical characteristics of the concept democracy.

Inductive thinking, by definition, means to form a generalization from a set of particular facts. Inductive thinking allows students to make inferences and form hypotheses. Both inductive and deductive thinking are effective strategies; however, inductive teaching may be more brain compatible in that it enables students to construct personal meaning for themselves. Two powerful inductive thinking strategies are concept attainment and concept formation.

Concept Attainment

The concept attainment strategy was first introduced by Jerome Bruner (Bruner, Goodnow, and Austin 1967). Bruner described the way in which we learn to classify information and form concepts as a process of identifying the critical attributes and then forming generalizations. Most of our informal or unstructured learning is acquired in this way. Bruner maintained that all of us acquire understanding by examining positive and negative examples of concepts. For instance, the first animal a child encounters may be the family pet, Rover. Thereafter, the child calls all animals "dog." At some point, the parents intervene and say, "No, this is a cat. That is a dog." Eventually, after multiple exposures to a range of animals, the child learns to differentiate between the characteristics that make dogs dogs, cats cats, cows cows, and so on.

At a more sophisticated level, we might learn about abstract concepts, such as justice, by being exposed to various situations or examples of things that are deemed either fair or unfair. At the outset, a child's grasp of the concept *justice* might be fairly rudimentary and unsophisticated and along the lines of "An eye for an eye and a tooth for a tooth." But as the child encounters a wider range of examples, he or she perceives the concept in greater depth. At this point, the child becomes aware of the shadings and gray areas of many abstract concepts and extends his or her range of understanding.

The concept attainment strategy promotes the development of inductive thinking by using critical attributes to form concepts and to understand the characteristics that allow a particular item to belong to a general category. In its simplest form, it is a classification activity. The concept attainment strategy is teacher controlled, which means that the teacher presents the data as a series of positive or negative examples of the concept to be learned. These sometimes are referred to as examples and nonexamples, or Yes and No examples.

Although the formal instructional strategy of concept attainment is teacher controlled, Bruner maintained that we all work through a similar process of examining examples and nonexamples as a way of understanding either with or without the intervention of a teacher.

Following are examples of two concept attainment lessons that have been deliberately oversimplified. They are meant to demonstrate a process rather than to stand as actual lessons.

Concept Attainment Example—Insects

The introduction for a concept attainment lesson may involve a discussion, mini lecture, or video presentation that activates the students' prior knowledge of the concept. Activating prior knowledge brings information to an individual's working memory and increases the chance that new information will find a similar body of knowledge that previously has been acquired.

In a lesson on insects, the teacher may activate prior knowledge about bugs and other creepy crawlies through a discussion with the students. Then, the teacher states the objective and purpose of the lesson. For example, he or she may say, "Today we are going to learn about insects and the fact that while all insects are bugs, all bugs are not insects. Insects have critical characteristics that set them apart and allow them to belong in a group or class called insects."

Next, the teacher engages the students with the concept attainment strategy as a way of imparting information or providing input for the lesson. For example, the teacher may say, "Today we are going to learn about insects by using a process called concept attainment." The teacher then draws two columns on the chalkboard, labels each as Yes or No, and places a long strip of masking tape, sticky side out, in each column. (The tape can be used to hold pictures of examples and nonexamples.) Next, the teacher presents a picture of a common housefly. This would be a positive example of the concept and would go in the Yes column. The teacher then shows a picture of a spider. Because spiders are not insects, this would be placed in the No column. The teacher then presents pictures of various bugs, such as ants, butterflies, scorpions, and sow bugs, and places them in the Yes or No column according to their attributes (see Fig. 7.5).

Yes/No Examples

Yes	No
 Housefly	Spider 
 Butterfly	Scorpion 
 Ant	Centipede 
 Grasshopper	Sow bug 

Figure 7.5

After showing several examples, the teacher will ask the students to discuss the critical attributes of all the items in the Yes column to see what they have in common. If the students have enough information, they may form a generalization of what an insect is. To test this, the teacher could show an unlabeled example and ask, "Which column does this one belong in?" If the students are successful, the teacher can repeat the process by randomly presenting several Yes and No examples and asking the students to place them in the appropriate columns.

When the students are able to place examples in the correct columns with consistent accuracy, they revisit their original hypothesis and refine it. The teacher then asks, "What do all the creatures in the Yes column have in common?" Or in other words, What are the characteristics that allow these creatures to be included as examples of insects? The students list the characteristics they have noticed, such as all the creatures in the insect column have six legs and they all have three body segments.

If necessary, the teacher can provide the students with clues and then present more Yes and No examples until the students have identified all the critical characteristics that form the concept *insect.*

As a way of assessing progress and bringing the lesson to a close, the teacher can have students form small groups, with each group receiving a package of pictures depicting a variety of creatures. Each group then sorts the pictures into two groups: insects and noninsects.

Concept Attainment Example—Metaphors

Following is an example of a language arts application in which the Yes and No examples are presented as a way of teaching the concept *metaphor.*

First, students activate their prior knowledge by revisiting several pieces of poetry. They then discuss what they know about imagery, metaphors, similes, and analogies.

The teacher then states the lesson's objective and purpose by saying, "Today we are going to form a definition for the concept *metaphor* by using the strategy called concept attainment." As in the previous lesson on insects, the teacher makes two columns and labels them Yes and No. Next, the teacher provides an example by holding up a large sheet of paper with the words *The curtain of night brought the day to a close* printed in large clear letters. This is placed in the Yes column. This is followed by another example, *The night descended like a curtain,* placed in the No column. The process is repeated using several examples, such as the following:

- The sun flamed brightly like a huge orange ball. (No example)
- Apollo's golden chariot sank into the ocean. (Yes example)
- The bright diamond of the northern sky guides mariners to port. (Yes example)
- The North Star is useful for navigation. (No example)
- Fred gazelled around the track. (Yes example)
- Fred runs as fast as an antelope. (No example)
- My brother pigs out at mealtimes. (Yes example)
- My brother eats like a pig. (No example)

After several examples, the teacher pauses and asks the students what the Yes examples have in common that the No examples don't have. The students may hypothesize that the Yes examples are metaphors. To test this, the teacher can present an example such as *My dad has a waist like a barrel,* and ask the students if it is a Yes or No example of the concept metaphor. To further test their grasp of the concept, the teacher can present the example.

My dad barreled through the crowd and ask students to place it in the appropriate column.

If the students are able to correctly identify all of the examples, they may be ready to identify the characteristics that define the concept metaphor. They formulate a definition and then check their hypotheses against two additional examples:

- The protest was nipped in the bud by the arrival of the police. (Yes example)
- The police soon put an end to the protest. (No example)

To reinforce the concept and bring closure to the lesson, the teacher can ask the students to design their own sets of Yes and No examples and to test them out on their classmates.

Concept Attainment Applications

Some readers may wonder, "Why didn't you just tell the students the characteristics and save a whole bunch of time?" The answer is twofold. First, in a brain-compatible classroom the students are encouraged to construct knowledge for themselves as opposed to being told the facts. Second, in addition to learning about the designated concept, the students have reinforced their knowledge of critical attributes and the significance they play in the formation of concepts.

The concept attainment strategy can be used throughout the curriculum. As an example, we will look at how it can be used in the arts curriculum. A teacher may present students with examples of different styles of painting and ask, "What makes the Yes examples Neoclassical paintings and the No examples Impressionist paintings?"

Similarly in the music program, the students can listen to recordings of various styles of music as a way of differentiating traditional jazz from swing or the music of the Baroque period from more modern symphonic music.

Concept attainment can be incorporated into lesson design in a number of places, including at the beginning of a lesson to activate prior learning, during the instructional phase of the lesson to introduce a new concept, and at the end of lesson as a check for understanding.

Concept attainment is especially useful for concepts that are abstract, complex, or subject to a number of interpretations. Concepts such as justice, honor, rights, and privilege are well served by this strategy.

Concept Formation

Concept formation is an inductive thinking strategy developed by curriculum theorist Hilda Taba (1967) to assist students in developing their abilities to think inductively, categorize information, and use new information to make inferences and predict consequences. In essence, it is a classification activity in which the students either are given a set of data to sort and classify or create a data set for themselves.

Concept formation is more student centered and less teacher directed than concept attainment because students have more control over the data. What makes this strategy powerful is, in part, the discussion and interchange of ideas that take place as students make decisions about what information belongs in what category. Educational researcher Bruce Joyce described concept formation in this way:

> The purpose of the concept formation strategy is to induce students to expand the conceptual systems with which they process information. Thus, in the first phase they are required to do something with the data, which requires them to alter or expand their capacity for handling information. In other words, they have to form concepts that they subsequently use to handle new information as it comes their way. (Joyce and Weil 1972, 125)

Concept formation capitalizes on the brain's ability to recognize and construct patterns. In its simplest form, a concept is a body of information that for some reason clusters into a group or classification or, in other words, a pattern. The concept formation strategy facilitates this clustering or categorizing of information.

This is an inductive process in which students process information at a deep level of understanding and construct meaning for themselves, thereby forming the cognitive structures that "hold" the information better than those structures the teacher may provide for them.

Concept Formation Example—Systems and Processes

Following is an example of a lesson using the concept formation strategy. Parts of the lesson have been oversimplified to demonstrate a process.

In the first phase of a lesson, the teacher activates prior learning by leading a discussion about supermarkets and stores, asking questions such as, What are the different types of stores in town? What are some of the products available to us on a daily basis? How do these products get to the shelves of our local stores?

Next, the teacher states the objective and purpose for the lesson by saying, "Today we are going to look at systems and processes. We will do this by focusing on the systems and processes that allow us to have a wide variety of goods in our stores. To help us understand this information, we are going to use a thinking strategy called concept formation."

For the acquisition or instructional phase of the lesson, the students form into groups of four, and the teacher gives each group an envelope containing several slips of paper. Written on each slip is a physical location related to an area of manufacturing or retailing, such as a fish processing plant, retail fish store, lumber mill, building supply store, steel mill, or automobile showroom. The slips of paper are in no particular order. The students are directed to sort the slips into categories that make sense to all the group members. At this stage of the process, the students do not need to name the categories; they will do so later. The students are directed to look for the attributes or characteristics that allow a particular group to form.

The students then sort arrived the data, or slips, into groups. Upon completion, they are asked to explain how they at their groupings. The students may say something such as, "This group has the places where the main resources come from, such as mines, forests, and farms. Our next group has the places where raw materials are taken and made it into something. And our last group is the stores that sell the finished products."

The teacher then asks the students to name each group. In some cases, the teacher may provide this information. In this example, the groups could be labeled primary industries (source of raw materials), secondary industries (manufacturing companies), and tertiary industries (tertiary means third in rank and relates to the third step in the manufacturing-to-retail process).

To extend the discussion and provide links to other concepts, the discussion may evolve into a series of questions and answers about how economic systems work. Sample questions and possible answers include the following:

Question: *What happens to the cost of goods as they move up the chain?*
Answer: They become more expensive.

Question: *At which part of the chain is the most value added to the products?*
Answer: Probably the secondary, or manufacturing, part.

Next, the teacher assigns students to the task of searching for information about the primary industries of their home states, provinces, or countries and whether or not they have secondary industries to support them. The material generated by these investigations could then be used to predict the consequences of strong primary industries with weak or inadequate secondary industries.

Concept Formation Variation

As a variation to the prior example, in which the teacher gave the set of data to the students, the students can generate their own data. This particular variation is useful when forming concepts or generalizations that require some degree of consensus. For example, the students might use the concept formation strategy to develop a set of classroom behavioral norms. To activate prior learning about behavioral norms, the students can discuss why rules are necessary. In stating the lesson's objective and purpose, the teacher can inform the students that they are going to develop a set of behavioral rules that will help them to work better as a class using a process that is a variation of the concept formation strategy.

For the acquisition phase of the lesson, the students form groups of four to six students and each student is given five 3" × 2" sheets of paper. (This number is purely arbitrary, but five or six sheets seem to work best.) The teacher then directs the students to work individually to decide five important behaviors and to write each on a single sheet of paper. At this point, students should be advised that they will have a chance to discuss their ideas with others at a later time.

Working individually, the students generate and record their ideas. Then, the students in each group pool their sheets, place them in a central location, and sort the sheets into groups, or categories, according to the characteristics they have in common. In other words, the ideas should be categorized in ways that make sense to all the group members. The students should be informed that as they group the ideas they do not need to identify names for the categories they are forming—that will come later. (Keeping the categories unnamed as students sort items into them encourages flexible thinking. Once a category is named, students have a tendency to force items to fit into a particular group.) The students discuss their ideas and make adjustments to the categories and the data represented in each. They then name each category.

The teacher asks each group in turn to provide the name of one of its categories. For example, students may have categorized classroom behaviors as *no put-downs, no gossiping, no fighting,* and *be helpful.* These names are listed on chart paper in a location visible to all in the classroom. As a class, the students discuss any gaps and overlaps in the list and turn any negative statements into positive ones. For example, *no disrespect* could be revised to become *show respect at all times.* After additional discussion and modification, a list of recommended classroom behaviors is prepared and displayed.

As an extension of this activity, the teacher can ask the students to describe what each of the listed behaviors would look like and sound like if the students were demonstrating it.

Other Applications

The concept formation strategy can be used in a variety of subject areas. For example, students in a social studies class can generate a data set of the attributes of a good citizen or of good government. In literature, the students can generate the attributes of heroes or villains. In a biology lesson, students could categorize a data set of living organisms into their various subspecies; for example, mammals, reptiles, marsupials, and so on. The students could also use this strategy to develop a list of priorities for conserving energy or for a good education.

In a more sophisticated form of the concept formation strategy, students could be taught how to recognize the critical attributes of excellent work. For example, a teacher can gather a representative sample of student work, such as research essays or lab reports, as the data set. (All identifying information on who created the work would be removed.) The data set would include samples of excellent work, barely acceptable work, and unacceptable work. The students would sort the data into three or four groupings and discuss the attributes or lack of attributes that allow a work to belong in a particular group. From this, they would be able to generate a list of characteristics that define excellent work and not-so-good work. By completing this activity prior to a specific project or assignment, the students can gain a clear idea of the expectations and standards that will be used to evaluate their work. This provides a means to self-monitor their work by comparing it with the established criteria for excellence.

Concept attainment and concept formation are powerful and adaptable strategies that can be applied in all subject areas and at all grade levels. Once they become part of a teacher's repertoire, they become self-perpetuating, because each time they are used they generate new applications and better adaptations.

Creative Thinking

The ability to think creatively often is seen as an innate characteristic, and it sometimes appears that some people have been born creative. However, if we believe that students can be taught to behave more intelligently, then it follows that they also can be taught to think more creatively. The teacher's role is first to provide the conditions or learning climate that values and fosters creative thinking and then to teach the students tools or structures that enable them to develop their creative capabilities.

The conditions that foster creativity are typified by a relaxed and happy environment in which students enjoy the challenge of creative thinking and are encouraged to take risks and try new and different approaches to finding creative solutions. To think creatively, one should be in a state of relaxed alertness, which means that one is relaxed enough to allow his or her brain some latitude in making connections but alert enough to recognize a good idea.

One of the keys to creative thinking seems to defy common sense. The key is don't think too hard. For creative thinking, one needs to put one's brain slightly out of focus and approach a problem at a tangent. Most of us have had the experience of trying to concentrate, with great intensity, on finding a solution to a problem only to find that the solution popped into our head sometime later when we were concentrating on something else. This is a common experience when trying to recall someone's name. The name seems to be on the tip of our tongue, but we just can't seem to grasp it. So we go on with some other task, and suddenly the name pops into our mind. It appears that the brain subconsciously continues to seek an answer even when we have consciously abandoned the search.

An analogy may be found in the computer-generated three-dimensional graphics that have become popular as books and posters. The harder one stares, the less one sees. However, if you put your eyes slightly out of focus, a Stealth bomber suddenly explodes from the paper in three dimensions or a vase of flowers seems real enough to touch. The same phenomenon occurs in the creative thinking mode—the harder we concentrate, the fewer ideas we seem to get. What we need to do is loosen up, let go of the handlebars, and allow the brain to freewheel as it goes about its business of making connections.

Brainstorming

A number of techniques stimulate creative thinking. Perhaps the most widely known one is brainstorming. Brainstorming should be a freewheeling, anything goes, creative explosion. However, in practice, it often devolves into a dispute about whether an idea or suggestion belongs on the list of options. When brainstorming, any and all ideas should be accepted. Some ideas may prove to be useless, but by allowing all ideas, there is a greater chance of generating a viable solution. The initial brainstorm is not the time to discuss the viability or feasibility of a suggestion; the list can be discussed and refined once all the ideas have been generated.

Simple guidelines, such as the DOVE rules proposed by James Bellanca and Robin Fogarty (1986), help to manage the process and promote ideas:

D—Defer judgment; no put-downs
O—Opt for originality
V—Variety and vast numbers of ideas are what we are looking for
E—Expand by association; piggyback off the ideas of others

To get started, it helps to prime the pump. Giving thirty seconds of individual, quiet think time before brainstorming provides each student an opportunity to start thinking of ideas and usually results in a greater number of responses.

For the actual brainstorming, set a time limit of thirty to sixty seconds. The essence of a good brainstorm is the rapid-fire generation of ideas. When the group believes that it has a lot of time, it often slows down or debates ideas.

There are numerous variations of brainstorming, from the classic brainstorm in which people respond in turn to the carousel brainstorm in which people get up and move around the room. Each has applications to different circumstances and situations.

Classic Brainstorm

In a classic brainstorm, the students take turns responding. This is probably the least flexible form of brainstorming. It should be used when a group is being introduced to brainstorming or when some students are likely to be overwhelmed by their more exuberant classmates. It may be structured in the following way: First, revisit the DOVE guidelines to ensure that the students understand the principles of brainstorming. The participants then sit in a semicircle and elect one person as the recorder. Each person in the group is  assigned a number and responds in turn based on his or her number, with each person responding only once. The recorder writes the responses on a sheet of chart paper as they are generated so that all group members can see them. This accommodates the auditory as well as the visual learners and makes a connection between auditory and visual information for everyone. At the end of the thirty- or sixty-second time period, participants analyze the list of generated ideas and select the most appropriate solutions.

Freewheeling Brainstorm

A freewheeling brainstorm is a somewhat unstructured free-for-all in which people express their ideas as they occur and in no particular order. It allows for the release of much creative energy and the generation of many good ideas. However, it can result in an unruly situation or one in which the more reticent students are drowned out by the more vocal students.

Reverse Brainstorm

In a reverse brainstorm, the participants turn the problem around and generate a list of all the things that could work against them. The reverse brainstorm may be used in situations in which a group is having difficulties finding positive solutions. One of the quirks of human nature is that when it comes to creative thinking, people often are more adept at finding reasons why something won't work than finding reasons why something will work. The reverse brainstorm capitalizes on this phenomenon.

For example, if a group of teachers were trying to find ways to prevent students from dropping out before graduation, they might have difficulty coming up with positive ideas. By turning the question around, however, so that it reads, What can we do to encourage students to drop out? the teachers probably could generate a long list of suggestions, such as adopt an arbitrary set of rules, exclude students from all decision making, discriminate against certain subgroups in the school population, teach boring and irrelevant lessons, set tests that are inappropriate, and so on. If the teachers then reverse the list of things they *should not do,* they presumably will discover the things they *should do.*

Graffiti Brainstorm

In a graffiti brainstorm, a number of large sheets of paper are used to collect data. The sheets circulate around the room from group to group while the students remain in one place.

First, the teacher prepares a number of large sheets of chart paper with one problem written at the top of each. Students form small groups, and each group receives

a problem sheet and a different colored felt-tip pen. (Using different colored pens allows a response to be traced to a particular group.) Each group generates ideas for thirty seconds and then passes its sheet to the group at the next location so that each group has a different sheet. The groups have thirty seconds to peruse the first group's responses; then they brainstorm additional ideas for another thirty seconds. The sheets are passed again, and this procedure is repeated until the sheets are back to their original owners. The original group analyzes the ideas related to its problem data. If clarification of a particular response is needed, it can be traced to its source by color.

The graffiti brainstorm is useful in situations in which there are numerous problems requiring solutions or a problem requiring multiple solutions. It also is useful in situations that require smaller groups so that individuals can have greater participation.

Carousel Brainstorm

A carousel brainstorm is similar to a graffiti brainstorm in that it is used to generate multiple solutions. It also is useful in situations where a group needs an opportunity to get up and move around. In a carousel brainstorm, the ideas are collected on a number of sheets posted in various locations around the room. Small groups of students circulate around the room, visiting each location and recording their ideas on the sheets.

First, the teacher prepares a number of large sheets of chart paper with one problem written at the top of each sheet. Students form small groups, and each group receives a different colored felt-tip pen. Each group travels to a different location, at which they find a sheet with a problem written on it. The students record their responses for thirty seconds and then move on to a new location. They review the recorded responses and then brainstorm their own responses. This process is repeated until the groups are back at the location from which they started. (See Carousel Brainstorming in the Blacklines section at the end of this chapter.)

Give One, Take One

Give One, Take One (adapted from Silver and Strong) is an interpersonal strategy for interactive brainstorming. Each student gets a small strip of paper with numbers 1 to 10 down the side (see Give One, Take One in the Blacklines section at the end of this chapter). Each individual will jot down one or two ideas related to a topic such as

- two things you know about reptiles
- two states on the Atlantic coast
- two sources of protein

Then students walk about and give one idea and take one idea from each person they talk to. Give students a short time (perhaps sixty seconds) to keep the ideas flowing. This can also be called Give and Go or Give and Get.

This can be used as a preassessment activity to open mental files and find out what students already know about a topic or as an oral review. It is an energizer because it gets students up and moving and discussing ideas. Use a stopwatch or timer to keep things lively and increase the interaction in the amount of time given.

SCAMPER

SCAMPER is another strategy for generating creative solutions. It is similar to brainstorming but uses a specific checklist of questions designed to spur creativity. Some of the questions were first suggested in the early 1940s by Alex Osborn (1963), a pioneer teacher of creativity. Bob Eberle (1982), a noted expert on thinking strategies, later rearranged them as the following mnemonic strategy:

S ubstitute: What can we use in place of this? What materials, methods, processes, personnel, locations, and times can we use in place of this?

C ombine: What can be added to this? What materials, methods, processes, personnel, locations, and times can we add to this?

A dapt: How could I put this to another use?

M odify: How can I make this bigger, stronger, faster, more frequent, flexible, adaptable? How can I make it smaller, lighter, less bulky, cheaper?

P ut to other use: How could I use this in place of other materials, methods, process, personnel, location, time of the original?

E liminate: How can I simplify? What can I leave out?

R everse: Can I turn this process or method around? Can I start at the beginning and work backward?

To use SCAMPER, decide on a problem or challenge that requires a creative solution. Then, use the SCAMPER questions to see if the problem can be solved through substitution, combination, adaptation, modification, putting to other use, elimination, or reversal. It isn't necessary to use all the SCAMPER questions; some may not apply to a particular situation or problem. For example, students may come across a problem that provides no opportunity to eliminate but has multiple opportunities to put to other use. In such cases, they should be encouraged to go with the more promising question.

The key to using SCAMPER is to have fun with it. Remind students that the craziest ideas are sometimes the best ones.

Following is an example of applying the SCAMPER process to think of ways masking tape can be used:

S ubstitute: We can use masking tape in place of other kinds of adhesive tape, such as cellophane tape, electrical tape, and even first-aid tape.

Combine: When combined with a roller, it makes a handy dandy lint remover.

Adapt: Fold it into a loop and flatten it out and you have a two-sided tape to hang posters on your walls or to stick carpet to the floor.

Modify: Self-sticking removable notes are a modification of masking tape; the glue has been weakened and the length-to-width ratios altered.

Put to other use: Use it to hold up pant cuffs or skirt hems temporarily, or to bind packages and hold splints in place.

Eliminate: Reduce the stickiness. Some masking tape has a very weak adhesive for use on delicate surfaces. The adhesive has been modified and the tape made very thin for use in technical drawings and artwork.

Reverse: Instead of sticking tape to things, stick things to the tape; for example, postcards, Christmas cards.

Most areas of the curriculum provide opportunities to use at least some of the SCAMPER elements. The SCAMPER process can be used with everyday topics and is an ideal strategy to use with environmental issues, such as, What can we do with old cars, oil drums, plastic bottles, waste paper, and so on?

The SCAMPER format also can be used as a teacher checklist when modifying programs for students with special needs:

Substitute more appropriate materials for textbooks.

Combine thinking skills with graphic organizers.

Adapt learning materials and teaching strategies.

Modify by allowing students more time.

Put to other use: Use parent volunteers or student helpers.

Eliminate the number of distractions.

Reverse: Start with the desired end in mind and work backward from that point.

Using SCAMPER allows one to create a wide range of possible ways to view an issue, consider options, and generate solutions.

Analogies and Metaphors

We often use analogies, metaphors, and similes as away of clarifying or explaining ideas. The creative use of an analogy can help students make connections and achieve greater understanding. For example, in trying to explain the impact of composers such as Mozart or Liszt, we might use the analogy that they were the pop stars of their day. Students then are able to connect their understanding of what they already know about pop stars (they are mobbed by fans wherever they go, young women often become hysterical and faint when they appear, and they are courted by the rich, famous, and powerful) to what they have learned about Mozart and Liszt. In doing this, they can gain insight into the conditions under which many of the great composers lived. Similarly, when a teacher describes the rain forest as the lungs of the world, the students are able to understand the consequences of destroying one of the major producers of oxygen.

Synectics

One of the more creative ways to use analogies is called Synectics. This process for developing creativity is based on the use of metaphorical forms and was developed by educational theorist William Gordon (1961). The strategy works by combining uncommon images and by relating objects and ideas in nontraditional ways. With minor adaptations, we can use the strategy in the classroom. For example, if we were to ask a question such as What is life all about? we may be confronted with a sea of blank faces. However, if we asked, Why is life like an elevator? we may get responses such as, It's full of ups and downs. You don't always get to choose the people you ride with. Sometimes your elevator doesn't go all the way to the top. Sometimes somebody else is pushing your buttons. What we have done is activate the students' prior knowledge and broken their perceptual sets by getting them to create analogies. At this point, they may be ready to move to a higher level of discussion by analyzing the meaning of some of their statements about life and elevators.

The Synectics strategy may be used to clarify concepts by creating new or deeper meaning. When we create metaphors or analogies, we put a measure of space or distance between ourselves and the subject at hand. This intellectual space allows us the room to let our minds explore other ways of perceiving or understanding new or difficult concepts. Metaphors use familiar language to put unfamiliar subject matter in a recognizable context. Thus, when the heart is described as a pump, we immediately understand the heart's function and purpose.

Gordon described Synectics as making the strange seem familiar and the familiar strange (1961). To explore this idea further, consider the following examples. We might say that a molecular structure (something unfamiliar) is like a string of beads (something familiar). Conversely, we might say a painter's palette (something familiar) is like a framework for teaching strategies (something unfamiliar). Constructing metaphors is one way of achieving understanding, but sometimes we have to deconstruct them, or take them apart, as a way of checking our understanding. When we deconstruct metaphors, we are, in fact, analyzing them to see if they hold up based on all that we already understand about a subject.

If we deconstruct the analogy, *A painter's palette is like a framework for teaching strategies,* we need to examine our beliefs (perceptual set) about teaching strategies. It could be that we perceive them as a short list of discrete strategies, each of which has a distinct function and purpose in a lesson. However, if we use the intellectual distance created by the metaphor, we can think about the subject in more creative ways. Our rather narrow perceptual set is broken, and we can see a wider range of possibilities. We may now expand our thinking to capture the notion that a teacher's repertoire of instructional strategies is wide and varied like the colors on a palette. In the same way that a painter mixes and matches colors to create an endless variety of colors so, too, a teacher can mix and match strategies to create an endless variety of instructional experiences.

Personal Analogies

Synectics may be used in a number of forms, of which one is personal analogies. In personal analogies, one metaphorically creates an empathic relationship with a person, animal, plant, or inanimate object. For example, we might ask students to imagine how an atom would feel if it were accelerated to the speed of light or how the last tiger on earth might feel. When we put ourselves in a new position, we can empathize with a subject and see things from a new perspective.

We also can use personal analogies to make statements about perceptions of ourselves or others. When we perceive a person as a specific type of animal, such as a bear, it says something about our perceptions of that person. Likewise, a comment such as, Today I feel like a sponge is a succinct statement that communicates a strong message about a person's state of mind.

Direct Analogies

Another type of Synectics structure is direct analogies, which compare one class of objects or ideas with another, as in, Why is the brain like a swamp? Those familiar with the theories of neuroscientist Gerald Edelman (1987) may respond by saying, Because the brain, like a swamp, is wet and somewhat messy, no one part of a swamp is in charge, and all the systems, plants, animals, reptiles, and birds are interdependent. The swamp does not choose winners and losers, it merely supports the organisms that thrive by their own efforts or adaptations.

All these statements would be indicators that the students had made the connection between the brain as a swamp and Edelman's theory of neural Darwinism. The next step would be to deconstruct the analogy as a check for understanding and to make the similarities between the brain and the swamp more explicit.

To develop a direct analogy, select a concept that you wish to examine or clarify. Avoid the temptation to make a comparison that is too obvious, such as, Why is compound interest like a garden? Choose a comparison that is somewhat bizarre and see what happens. For example, Why is compound interest like the ocean?

Other examples include the following:

- Why is our community like a mosaic?
- Why is our country like a stew?
- Why is thinking like an onion?
- Why is school like an orchestra?

Synectics can be used in a number of phases of a lesson. It can be used at the beginning of a lesson to activate prior learning and to assess how much the students already know about a subject. In the input phase, it can be used to deepen students' understanding. Deconstructing the analogy can be particularly powerful when used at this point. Synectics can also be used as a check for understanding; if the students truly understand the concept, they will be able to create a rich and varied set of connections.

Synectics can also be used as an assessment activity, in which case the students either create a personal or conflicting analogy or generate a list of connections in a direct analogy.

When images are combined in these ways, they may seem strange and somewhat bizarre to students at first. But as students begin to express their ideas, they spark ideas in other people until the group begins to realize, for example, that our country is like a stew because there are many different ingredients, a stew has to stick together to be successful, time and energy are needed to make a stew work, and sometimes there are unpleasant things hidden in a stew.

Conflicting Analogies

An additional type of Synectics structure is to use conflicting analogies, which place two opposing ideas together, such as, Why is talent both a blessing and a curse? Many an out-of-work but talented actor could answer that one. Why are teenagers both conforming and individualistic? They all want to be different but they are slaves to brand name clothing. Why is war both creative and destructive? Most of the breakthroughs in medicine, surgery, communications have been invented in times of devastating war. Conflicting analogies cause students to examine their beliefs and reexamine their perceptual sets about a topic.

IN CLOSING

One of the key messages of this chapter is that thinking needs to pervade the whole curriculum. Students of all ages and levels of ability need to be continually engaged with higher-order thinking and problem solving. They should have a general understanding of what each skill entails; for example, analysis means to take something apart and synthesis means to put things together.

Although the general categories of thinking are universal, the ways in which they are applied depend on the subject context. Thus, the way skills are taught varies from subject to subject. For example, while the steps needed to analyze a compound in chemistry are different from the steps for analyzing a sentence in language arts, both involve some kind of "taking apart" process.

Additionally, the purpose to which thinking is applied may cause persons to look at information in different ways. For example, persons planning to write a story or play may decide to analyze some existing stories or plays to see how they are put together and then synthesize what they know by writing their own stories or plays.

Thinking skills are seldom used as stand-alone or discrete items. More often than not, they are used in sequences or combinations to solve a particular problem. For example, persons may use the skills of knowledge, recall, and comprehension to acquire new information and then understand it. Next, they might take the information apart (analysis), put it back together in a different way (synthesis), and transfer it to a new situation (application).

Although we, as teachers, may need to isolate a skill in order to help students gain an understanding of it, we also should give students the opportunity to apply the skill in a relevant context as soon as possible. Building thinking skills into the design of every lesson is one way of ensuring that students get maximum exposure to a multitude of thinking skills. Using the action words that signal different kinds of thinking (see Fig. 7.4, page 173) enhances this exposure and is a simple, yet powerful way of ensuring that students are exposed to a wide range of thinking.

The topic of thinking skills is far more complicated than the few examples presented in this chapter may lead us to believe. However, if we use them as our starting point and begin to integrate thinking across the curriculum, we have at least taken the first steps on a very long journey. When we combine thinking skills with graphic organizers, discussed in chapter 8, they form a synergistic relationship that becomes an extremely powerful instructional tool. When thinking skills, graphic organizers, and cooperative group learning (discussed in chapter 5) are combined, the synergy becomes even more powerful. The longest journey begins with the first step, and one of the simplest first steps is to encourage students to employ metacognitive strategies in their daily routines.

Reflections

Six Hat Thinking as a Metacognitive Strategy

Let's use de Bono's Six Hat Thinking strategy (see Six Hat Thinking blackline) to debrief what we have learned about thinking skills. For the purpose of this chapter, we will first wear our red thinking hats and then our green ones.

When wearing a red hat, we should think in terms of our hunches, intuitions, feelings, and emotions about thinking.

When have our green hats on, we should be looking of creative adaptations, options, or alternatives. In green hat mode, we should thinking "outside the box" and looking for practical ways to implement thinking into our everyday classroom practice.

BLACKLINES

SIX HAT THINKING

The white hat thinkers look for hard facts, figures, and data. They maintain a cool and neutral outlook on the topic or material.

The yellow hat thinkers look for all the positive aspects. They reflect optimism, try to remain enthusiastic, and find the constructive ideas and possible benefits related to the topic/material.

The purple hat thinkers focus on the negative aspects. They look for flaws, faults, and reasons why something won't work.

The red hat thinkers deal with the hunches, intuitions, emotions, and feelings they have about the topic.

The green hat thinkers use the topic or material as a springboard for creative adaptations, options, and alternatives. They look for opportunities "outside the box," or beyond the obvious.

The blue hat thinkers draw conclusions from the material. They provide definitions of concepts and summaries of the major ideas.

CAROUSEL BRAINSTORMING

Directions

1. Divide into groups of 5 or 6.

2. Stand in front of 1 piece of newsprint.

3. Choose a recorder.

4. Brainstorm responses to the posted question—quickly.

5. After 2 minutes and at the signal, move one sheet to your right.

6. Brainstorm quickly at the new sheet (2 minutes).

7. At the signal, move to the right and repeat the process.

8. When you teach the last question, go back to question #1 and repeat at each sheet of newsprint until you have brainstormed responses to all the questions.

Then see the synergy you have produced!

Give One, Take One

1. _____

2. _____

3. _____

4. _____

5. _____

6. _____

7. _____

8. _____

9. _____

10. _____

Give One, Take One

1. _____

2. _____

3. _____

4. _____

5. _____

6. _____

7. _____

8. _____

9. _____

10. _____

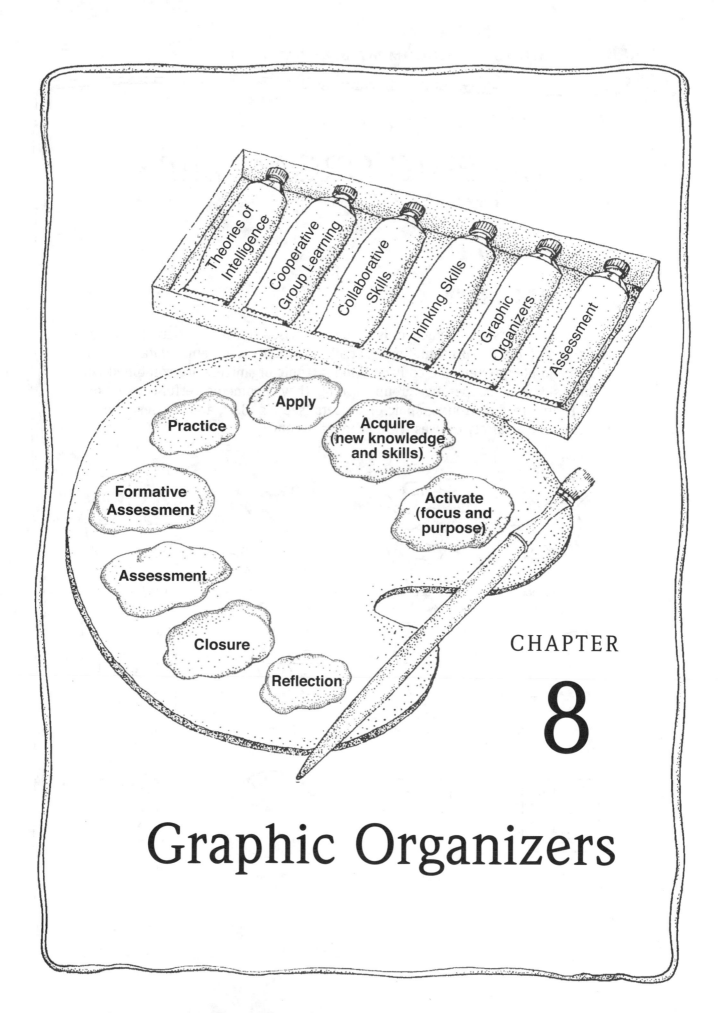

Theories of Intelligence
Cooperative Group Learning
Collaborative Skills
Thinking Skills
Graphic Organizers
Assessment

Apply

Practice

Acquire
(new knowledge
and skills)

Formative
Assessment

Activate
(focus and
purpose)

Assessment

Closure

Reflection

CHAPTER

8

Graphic Organizers

CHAPTER 8

GRAPHIC ORGANIZERS

WHAT ARE THEY?

Graphic organizers are metacognitive tools in a visual form. They are charts, diagrams, and pictorial representations that allow students to organize data into manageable and comprehensible chunks. When graphic organizers are combined with thinking skills and cooperative group learning, they become powerful instructional tools. There are numerous graphic organizers (see Fig. 8.1), and we describe several that have a variety of uses within the classroom.

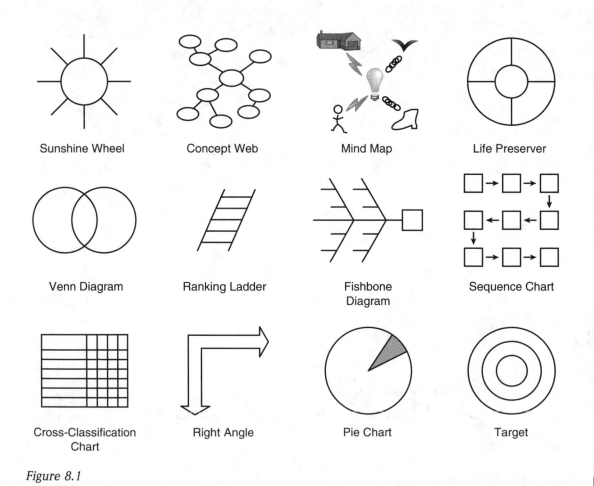

Sunshine Wheel   Concept Web   Mind Map   Life Preserver

Venn Diagram   Ranking Ladder   Fishbone Diagram   Sequence Chart

Cross-Classification Chart   Right Angle   Pie Chart   Target

Figure 8.1

Sunshine Wheel

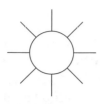

The sunshine wheel, also called a concept wheel, is a useful tool when brainstorming. This organizer, which consists of a circle with lines extending outward like the rays of sunshine, can be used when generating the attributes of a concept prior to selecting the critical attributes of the concept and forming a definition. As the attributes related to the concept are generated, they are recorded on the lines radiating from the circle.

Concept Web

The concept web, also called an attribute web or semantic map, consists of a set of linked bubbles or circles. This graphic organizer is particularly useful for brainstorming and generating ideas for concepts that have topics and subtopics or that have major and minor themes. The concept web capitalizes on the brain's ability to associate and connect ideas. As in other forms of brainstorming, the brain generates ideas and, as these are captured on paper, these ideas trigger related subtopics or subthemes. These then are joined by lines to the main idea as a way of showing their relationship.

Mind Map

The mind map may be seen as the most complex of all graphic organizers because it combines logical organization of concepts with a highly creative process.

Mind mapping was devised by Tony Buzan (1974) as a way of engaging all the brain's functions and capturing the "big picture" through pictorial images. It was first developed as a way of building on Sperry's (1968) right brain/left brain theory. The ways that a mind map organizes and displays information are predicated to some extent by the functions of the right and left brain. Getting the words onto paper is primarily a left brain activity, and it often limits one's ability to see the big picture. When we engage the right side of the brain by changing words into images, it allows us to see the big picture in terms of visual images. In doing this, we begin to see the whole concept as the sum of its interconnected parts.

Mind mapping, therefore, is useful in conceptualizing complex ideas in a visual form. It also can be used to show the organization of and relationships among the ideas found in concepts as diverse as a family, the interconnected systems in a swamp, or the organization of the criminal justice system. It also can be used to display an agenda or lecture notes in a way that allows students to recall the major chunks of information at a glance.

Life Preserver

This organizer is valuable for brainstorming individually and coming to consensus as a group. The outer circle may be divided to allow a segment for each person in the group (3, 4, 5 segments). Each person brainstorms on a question or topic by listing ideas in one section of the outer circle. After the brainstorm, students share and discuss the information and come to agreement about some key aspects of the topic, which are then listed in the center.

Venn Diagram

The Venn diagram has long been used in mathematics; in fact, it originated with a British logician, John Venn. The diagram consists of two or more intersecting circles, each representing a set or sets. Elements unique to a set are recorded in its corresponding circle, with elements shared by two sets recorded in the intersection of the corresponding circles. When three sets are being compared, the characteristics common to all three are recorded in the intersection of all three circles.

Ranking Ladder

As its name suggests, this organizer looks like a ladder. It is used to rank or prioritize a set of data, such as the priorities of a school budget or the points to consider when selecting anything from a new pair of shoes to a new government. The item of the highest priority is listed on the top rung of the ladder. The item of the least priority is listed on the bottom rung. The item in second place is written on the second rung, the item in the next-to-last place is written on the rung above the last rung, and so on. By the time all of the rungs of the ladder are filled, the items will be ranked in the order of priority. To identify the top five or ten priorities, one merely has to count down the rungs.

Fishbone Diagram

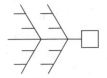

This organizer, as its name implies, looks much like a fishbone. The problem, or the desired effect, is written in the box that forms the head of the fish. The possible causes are arranged along the bones, or ribs.

Businesses and industries use this organizer when troubleshooting the probable causes of problems. They also use it when making business decisions or planning a course of action to bring about a desired effect. In business situations, most problems can be attributed to the following causes: personnel, procedure, equipment, and material. Brainstorming possible causes for a problem in terms of these four categories expands the scope of an inquiry and ensures that all the bases are covered.

Other categories may also be used for determining specific cause-effect relationships. For example, in using a fishbone diagram to determine the cause of a stock market crash, the categories could be world trends, current events, technology, and speculation.

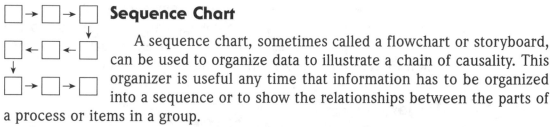

Sequence Chart

A sequence chart, sometimes called a flowchart or storyboard, can be used to organize data to illustrate a chain of causality. This organizer is useful any time that information has to be organized into a sequence or to show the relationships between the parts of a process or items in a group.

Sequence charts may be used to map out the sequence of events as a precursor to narrative writing or the development of a drama. The individual events or scenes are drawn or written on separate sheets of paper to represent each event or scene and the pieces manipulated until the most favorable sequence is found. Although *sequence chart* is the generic name for this type of organizer, it is called a *storyboard* when it is used to map out events in a story for a video or film.

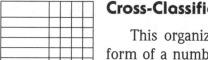

Cross-Classification Chart

This organizer, also called a cross-classification grid, takes the form of a number of intersecting horizontal and vertical lines. It is used when cross-referencing two classes of information in order to make a decision about them. One class of information is listed in the left-hand column of the grid, the other in the column headings across the top row.

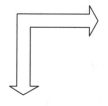

Right Angle

As its name implies, this organizer is arranged around two lines of a right angle. The items arranged in the horizontal line represent the facts about an event or topic. The items shown in the vertical line represent thoughts, feelings, reactions, or predictions about the event or topic.

The right angle is useful when we want students to change the direction of their thinking. Frequently, when students are asked about their thoughts and feelings about a topic, they respond by retelling the facts as opposed to their subjective reactions. The point of this organizer is to break the mental set that students bring to the task and cause them to examine alternate ways of viewing an event or topic.

Pie Chart

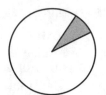

The pie chart is familiar to most students because it is frequently is used by the media to portray information visually. Pie charts are useful for showing how the parts relate to the whole. The circle, or pie, represents a whole entity or unit, and the individual "slices" represent segments, or fractions, of the whole. The pie chart often is used to visualize budget allocations, such as the amount spent for defense, social programs, education, and other services. It also is used to represent demographic information, such as the number of people who have a college degree in relation to the entire adult population or the percentages of people who attended particular sporting events in relation to the total number who attended sports events.

Target

This organizer consists of three concentric circles. It can be used to indicate or judge the merits of ideas or solutions to problems by shading the appropriate circle. A successful solution would be a bull's eye, a near miss would be the middle circle, a definite miss would be the outer circle, and completely off target would be the area outside all of the circles.

The target also can be used to provide students with a visual assessment of their work without resorting to the usual letter grades or percentages. It is useful in all subject areas and for a wide range of situations. It can be filled in by the student as a form of self-assessment or by the teacher in place of a more traditional grade.

WHY DO WE NEED THEM?

Among the brain's many functions is the ability to think. This is what sets humans apart from most other species and, if we are to believe Descartes' dictum "I think, therefore I am," it is what defines us as human beings. All of us are capable of thinking to some degree, but many students do not have the skills necessary for the more "heavy duty" creative and critical thinking needed to thrive both within and beyond the classroom.

The acquisition of these skills is too important to be left to chance. To be successful, thinking skills should be taught explicitly within the context of each subject area.

In the classroom, thinking skills should be integrated with two other instructional strategies: graphic organizers and cooperative group learning. When graphic organizers, thinking skills, and cooperative group learning are combined, they create a powerful synergy that is wholly brain compatible. Cooperative groups allow for an interchange of ideas, and the graphic organizers provide a structure or framework in which to display the internal process of thinking in an external, visual form. In a sense, they provide a "window" into students' brains and give us a way of observing and assessing students' thought processes.

In both pedagogical studies cited in the book, McTighe (1990) and McREL/ Marzano (Marzano, Pickering, and Pollack 2000) include graphic organizers and visual representations as instructional strategies that increase student achievement (see chapter 2). The Marzano study attributes a 27 percentile gain to the use of nonlinguistic visual representations, which include the use of graphic organizers (Fig. 2.1, page 48).

Graphic organizers have a number of attributes that enhance students' thinking skills. They allow students to make connections among pieces of information. This makes information easier to recall. They also allow students to break information into manageable chunks. Chunking information allows students to see the relationships among the separate pieces and is key to the formation of concepts, which leads to understanding. When all this learning takes place in small groups, students have an opportunity to exchange and compare ideas, articulate their points of view, defend their own thinking, and probe the thinking of others. These are the ways in which true learning takes place.

HOW DO WE USE THEM?

Graphic organizers capitalize on the brain's capacity for divergent and convergent thinking. When using them in the classroom, we usually start with some kind of brainstorming (divergent thinking) technique to generate ideas. The next step is to subject the ideas to critical analysis (convergent thinking) by using the appropriate graphic organizer as a framework. This usually involves activities such as grouping similar ideas, prioritizing ideas according to a set of criteria, and drawing conclusions or generalizations from the prioritized set of data. The final step is to apply the knowledge to the problem at hand or transfer it to other situations.

Although graphic organizers can be used as stand-alone items, in practice they are often used in sequence with other organizers. As an example, if students are engaged in determining the critical attributes of a concept, such as democracy, they would first use an organizer such as a concept web or a sunshine wheel to brainstorm as many of the attributes of a democracy as possible. Next, they might use a ranking ladder to prioritize the attributes in order of importance. Finally, they would select four or five attributes from the list and form a generalization or definition of democracy.

Four primary ways of using graphic organizers are to brainstorm or generate ideas, to analyze or evaluate ideas, to reflect, and to display information (see Fig. 8.2, page 204). Following are descriptions of the organizers that lend themselves to each of these functions.

Graphic Organizers to . . .

Brainstorm	Analyze	Reflect	Display
Sunshine Wheel	Venn Diagram	Right Angle	Pie Chart
Concept Web	Ranking Ladder		Target
Mind Map	Fishbone Diagram		Pie Chart & Target
Life Preserver	Sequence Chart		Combined
	Cross-Classification		
	Chart		

Figure 8.2

Graphic Organizers for Brainstorming

Graphic organizers are excellent tools to use when brainstorming ideas. Before we can organize data, we have to collect or generate them. When teaching thinking skills, we sometimes generate a set of data by using the simple, but often misused, strategy of brainstorming. In its purest sense, brainstorming is a nonjudgmental and creative way to generate ideas. In terms of brain function, the power of brainstorming is similar to the technique of word association. When one person says a particular word, it sets up an association in the mind of another person and triggers a response in the form of an idea. This starts a group of brains thinking of similar ideas, which, in turn, generates additional ideas.

In practice, the process of brainstorming often becomes bogged down as participants debate the merits of one idea over another. This stops the flow of ideas and interrupts the brain's ability to form associations by piggybacking on other people's ideas. Because brainstorming is a divergent thinking activity, it is meant to generate ideas, not analyze and debate them. The time to debate ideas follows the brainstorming stage when students switch to a convergent mode, engage in critical thinking, and analyze the list of generated ideas.

In a brainstorm, any and all ideas are accepted. Two basic strategies can enhance the quality and quantity of students' ideas. First, prime the pump. Give students thirty seconds to think about their responses before they begin to list them. (Longer time can be given as needed.) Second, use the DOVE guidelines, which encourage creativity and acceptance of ideas.

Four graphic organizers that can be used to organize the ideas generated during a brainstorming activity are the sunshine wheel, the concept web, the mind map, and the life preserver.

Sunshine Wheel

The sunshine wheel, also called a concept wheel, is a helpful graphic organizer to use when brainstorming. As ideas are generated, they are recorded along the "rays of sunshine" that give this organizer its name.

For example, we might choose to examine the attributes of a concept such as conflict as a step toward forming a definition. We begin by activating students' previous knowledge of conflict in the world around them—fights on the playground, arguments with a sibling or parent, strikes and lockouts in local industries, wars over religious ideology, and the conquest of territory. Next, students brainstorm the attributes and the words that come to mind when they think about conflict and arrange them around a center as shown in Figure 8.3.

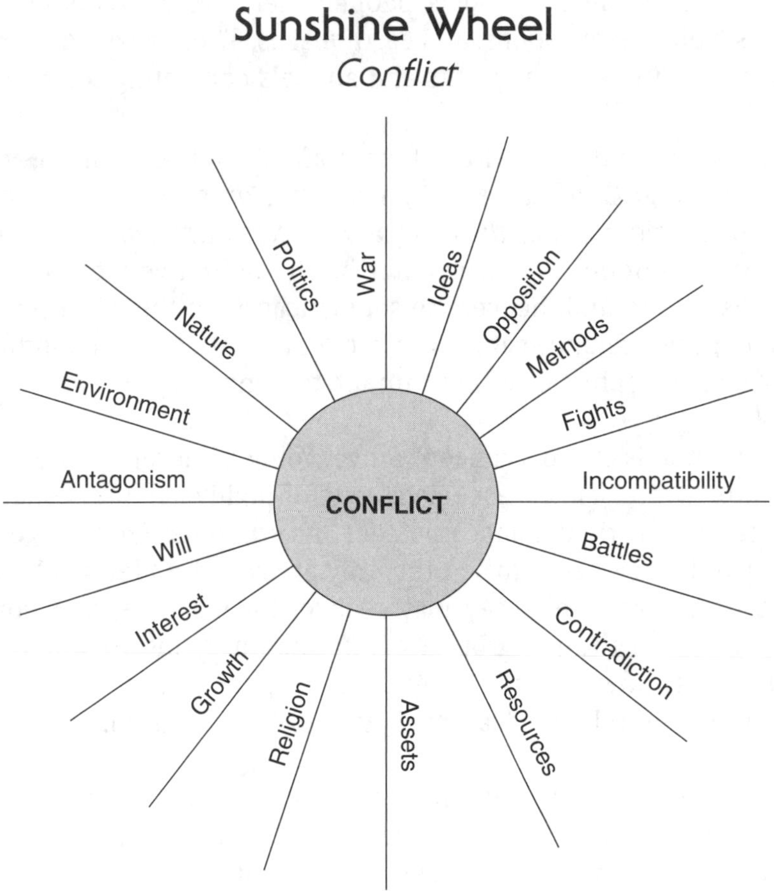

Sunshine Wheel
Conflict

Figure 8.3

Students then examine the data and, through discussion, select three to six words that usually typify conflict-related situations. These are called the *critical attributes.* Critical attributes are defined as the minimum set of characteristics that allow a particular example to belong in a certain group. At this stage, students might select attributes such as disagreement, argument, war, people, resources, and assets.

After further discussion and with some probing questions from the teacher, students may realize the following:

- Conflict usually involves a disagreement of some kind.
- Disagreements come in varying degrees, ranging from an argument to an all-out war.
- Conflict is not always about material things (e.g., assets, resources); conflict can be about ideas (e.g., religion, philosophy).
- Conflicts can be between two people or among many people (e.g., individuals, nations).
- Conflict does not always involve people; there are conflicts in nature, such as storms, volcanic eruptions, and earthquakes. There also are conflicts among entities in nature, such as plants and animals competing for survival.

After discussion, students write a first draft of their definition, which might look like the following: *Conflict may arise when two or more people or other entities disagree over ideas, methods, or the division of assets or resources.* Although this is a fairly sophisticated definition, it may not be the definitive word on the subject. The depth of discussion and, hence, the sophistication of the definition depend on the students' experience and maturity. A student's initial understanding of a concept may be fairly unsophisticated, but understanding broadens and deepens with experience.

This phenomenon is called a concept range. Young children tend to see concepts as either black or white. This is especially true of highly abstract concepts such as conflict, justice, honor, rights, and privileges. As students' knowledge and experience bases expand, they begin to see the gray areas and understand concepts at a deeper or more mature level. They may realize, for instance, that conflict is not always about fights on the playground or one nation going to war with another. For young students, however, this may be the place to start learning about the concept of conflict and related ideas, such as conflict escalation, confrontation, and resolution.

As a culminating activity to defining a concept, students check their definitions against the examples of conflict discussed at the beginning of the lesson to see if their definitions hold up in all cases. They also might check them against the definitions in the dictionary to see how closely they match.

Concept Web

The concept web may be used to brainstorm ideas in such a way as to show the relationship between various topics and subtopics. For example, a web can be used to map out the paragraphs or major events in a story. The minor incidents or details then are connected to the major ideas as a way of keeping them organized. A story about a boy and his dog and their great adventure might be mapped out using the web, as shown in Figure 8.4.

Concept Web
Story of a Boy and His Dog

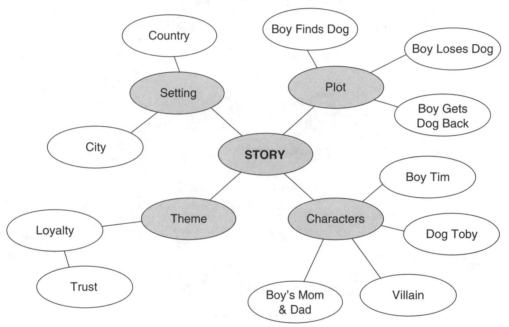

Figure 8.4

The concept web can also be used to organize data as a preliminary step for other thinking skills, such as defining, comparing and contrasting, prioritizing, and decision making. For example, we might decide to use a web to arrive at a definition for the concept *drama.* Once again, we first activate the students' prior knowledge by having them recall dramas they have experienced on television, in movies, or in live theater. The next step is to brainstorm ideas and web these ideas, as shown in Figure 8.5 (page 208).

The first attempt at brainstorming often is haphazard and seemingly disorganized. Remind students of the DOVE guidelines, because at this stage of the proceedings they will be in a divergent thinking mode and the goal is to generate as many ideas as possible. Students should be reassured that they will have a chance to refine their lists and apply their critical thinking skills later.

The next step is to refine the initial data and move closer to a definition. We take the divergent, brainstormed list and refine it by thinking convergently. One advantage of the concept web as an organizer is that it allows us to see the relationships between ideas. Our second attempt may look more organized as we begin to see relationships and logical groupings between the words (see Fig. 8.6, page 208).

Concept Web—Drama
Initial Attempt

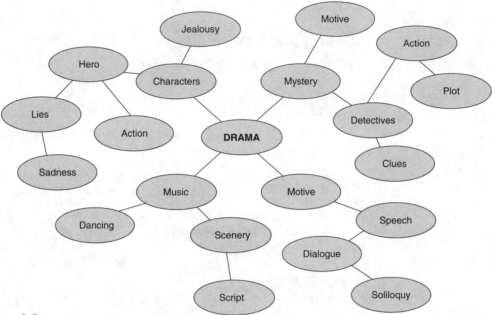

Figure 8.5

Concept Web—Drama
Refined

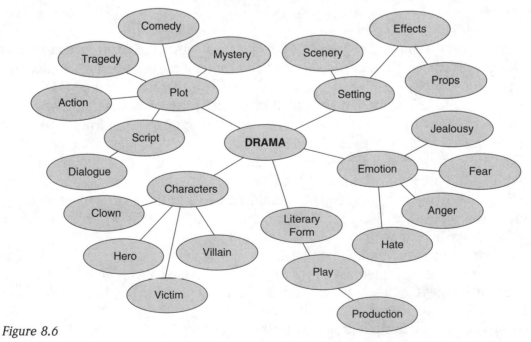

Figure 8.6

Further discussion allows us to eliminate certain attributes from our list. For instance, do all dramas need mystery, detectives, clues, lies, deceit, props, scenery, gods, goddesses, heroes, and so on? The answer is that some dramas need all these attributes and all dramas need some of them, but all dramas do not need all of them. Students will come to this realization only as a result of much discussion. When this happens, they will be ready to pare down their list of attributes to a much shorter set of critical attributes. This list might include actors, dialogue, action, story or plot, and an emotional hook, such as mystery, conflict, or a comic situation. Students now take the critical attributes and weave them into a definition, which might look like the following: *In general terms, a drama may be defined as a literary form with actors, who by means of action or dialogue convey a story or situation involving conflict, emotion, mystery, tragedy, or comedy.*

This definition no doubt will upset the drama purists, but it gets the basic idea across. Once again, we are dealing with the phenomenon of concept range. The concept drama, just like any other concept, can be understood at a number of levels, from simple to complex.

As a final step, students check their definitions by applying them to a wide range of examples of plays and movies. If there are significant difficulties with the definitions, students can be encouraged to use the dictionary to restate their definitions. At this point, some students may ask why they couldn't have used the dictionary in the first place. You can explain that they have been constructing knowledge for themselves. When people construct meaning for themselves, they understand the material at much deeper levels than when the information is given to them. You also might point out that the students have been learning a process for applied thinking. As a culminating activity, they can turn the process around and use the definitions they created to generate ideas for a drama of their own.

The concept web helps us refine our list of general attributes to a much smaller list of critical attributes or essential characteristics. The significance of critical attributes becomes apparent when one evaluates, compares, or analyzes ideas and concepts.

Mind Map

Tony Buzan (Buzan and Buzan 1994) invented mind mapping as a way of building on Sperry's right brain/left brain theory. Buzan believed one can increase the conceptualization, retention, recall, and processing of information by engaging as many parts of the brain as possible. This is what is meant by a whole-brain approach to learning. The left side of the brain deals in words and abstract symbols; the right side deals with images and pictorial symbols. The left side of the brain might conceive of a concept as an abstraction in the form of words. When this information is transferred to the right side of the brain, it may be transposed into pictures or visual images. Because the right side of the brain perceives information more panoramically or globally, it helps us visualize the concept as a whole rather than as separate pieces. By committing the visual images to paper, organizing the data, and adding color and design, we create a mind map.

By engaging in this creative process, we also increase our understanding of the original concept. As a final step, we can explain the concept to another person, using the mind map as a visual aid. This increases understanding as well as our ability to recall and explain the concept at a later date.

The first step in creating a mind map is to draw a picture to represent a concept. This central image should be made quite small to allow room on the page to draw other ideas. The next step is to free-associate, or brainstorm ideas, about the topic and to jot down all the ideas that come to mind. Using the list of ideas, draw simple pictorial images to represent each item.

Images, such as chain links, light bulbs, lightning bolts, stick figures, and hands, can be used to form connections between and among ideas (see Fig. 8.7).

Mind Map Images
For Connecting Ideas

Figure 8.7

Color and perspective can also be used to give the map dimension and impact. A word of encouragement to those who believe they cannot draw—it isn't necessary to create works of art. The simplest images often are the ones that bring the most clarity to the concept.

Encourage students to keep words to a minimum and to use key words sparingly. If they get stuck for an image, they can draw a cloud or a free-form shape as a placeholder and indicate what they want to convey. Later, when they return to the placeholder, an image may pop into their heads, allowing them to remember the idea. Or, the act of writing a word may trigger the desired image.

Figure 8.8 shows a simple mind map that depicts a child's representation of things to keep in mind in order to become a good student.

Mind Map

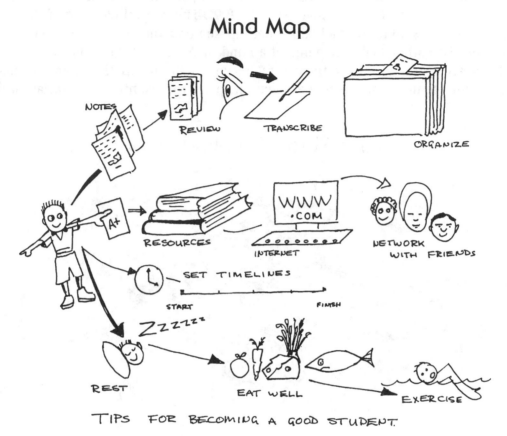

Figure 8.8

Other Uses for Mind Maps

Mind maps are useful for representing an agenda or lecture notes in a way that allows us to recall the major chunks of information at a glance. You might consider sharing the outline of a teaching unit with your students in the form of a mind map. Mind maps can also be used to represent the critical attributes of concepts or topics, such as a brain-compatible classroom.

Although mind mapping is often used as an individual activity, it adapts very well to cooperative group learning situations. This allows group members to harness the power of the brainstorm as they generate ideas for the mind map. When a mind map is developed as a group activity, there may be a tendency for some members to slack off and allow others to do the work. One way to keep all participants accountable is to state at the outset that all members must be able to articulate the main ideas and connections of the map and that any member may be called on to present it. If you delay choosing each group's presenter until the task is completed, the level of participation increases because group members realize they may be called on to stand and deliver.

To summarize the key concepts related to this particular graphic organizer, we present a mind map of a mind map (see Fig. 8.9). The central element of this map combines a representation of a brain superimposed on a map to convey the concept *mind map.* The other main elements of a mind map, such as color, beauty, design, and links, are arranged around the central image of a brain superimposed on a map. Thus, all the elements of the concept mind map are represented in pictorial form.

Mind Map of a Mind Map

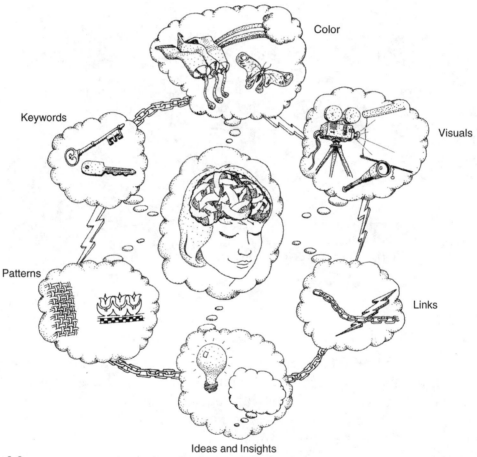

Figure 8.9

Mind mapping has applications in many subject areas. It is most useful when it is used to clarify complex ideas and to represent group deliberations or discussions in a visual form. In science, it can be used to represent cycles in nature or cause-and-effect relationships. In social studies, it can be used to depict the attributes of a family or a society. It can be used to represent visually how math and science applications are woven into the fabric of our lives. It can also be used as a culminating activity for other more formal graphic organizers. As an example, after using a fishbone diagram to determine cause and effect, a mind map could be used to depict a causal chain of events in a pictorial form.

Life Preserver

This graphic (adapted from the activity Place Mat, Bennett and Rolheiser 2001) is used to let individuals brainstorm as a group and then discuss and reach consensus if necessary. Teachers may use this organizer as a preassessment tool to find out what students know or are interested in. For example, students may be asked to brainstorm the following:

- How much you know about atoms
- What you would like to know about Arizona
- What behaviors are important when we work in a group
- What would be some good rules for our classroom

After the brainstorming, students can share their ideas and develop a collective list or come to consensus on ideas related to the topic. It could also be used to open mental files or as a review strategy. Students may jot down ideas while viewing a videotape or listening to a speaker. Pairs or groups of three, four, or five can divide the outer ring into the number of parts needed for the number of people in the group.

Figure 8.10 shows an example of three students brainstorming about what they know about winter. After brainstorming, the students would then share and discuss

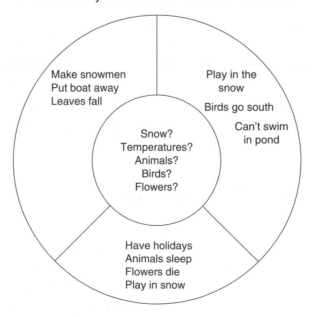

Life Preserver
What do you know about winter?

Figure 8.10

their ideas and come up with a list to investigate and place it in the center of the life preserver. They would then proceed to investigate the answers to their questions.

Another example that could be used in any classroom to establish group norms or agreements would be the life preserver shown in Figure 8.11, where four students working together first brainstormed what they felt was important to remember when working in a group.

Life Preserver
What is important to you when you work in a group?

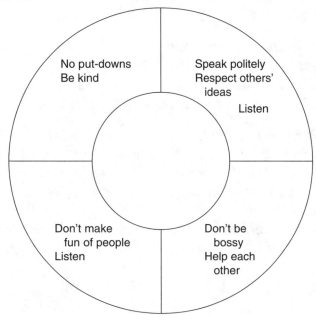

Figure 8.11

After the brainstorming, students can share their ideas in a roundtable discussion and decide what two or three rules they could live with and support. These norms or rules would be placed in the center when consensus is reached. Because these are their own expectations, they are likely to become invested in monitoring and enforcing them within the group.

Graphic Organizers for Analyzing

Venn Diagram

The ability to compare and contrast requires both convergent and divergent thinking. Once students have acquired the skill of attributing by using a concept web, they can use this skill with another graphic organizer—the Venn diagram. The Venn diagram is familiar to math teachers and to some social scientists, but it also has applications outside those disciplines. In fact, the Venn diagram is a prime example of transfer of knowledge from one subject, such as math, to applications in all disciplines.

The Venn diagram is a useful organizer to show the similarities and differences of two or more items. A circle is drawn to represent each item. The characteristics common to both items are recorded in the intersection of the circles. The characteristics unique to each item are written in the nonintersecting portion of the corresponding circle.

As an introduction to Venn diagrams, ask students to work in pairs. Instruct each pair to draw two intersecting circles and to record the similarities and differences between the two members of the pair. The nonintersecting part of each circle is to contain the differences; the intersecting part of the circles is to contain the similarities.

Imagine, if you will, a lesson in which the stated aim is to teach students about the thinking skill of evaluation by having them compare and contrast the similarities and differences between cats and dogs. This lesson bears little resemblance to what actually goes on in the classroom; it is a caricature with certain aspects exaggerated to reinforce the key points.

To get my point across, I might present the following facts: These are some differences—cats have rough tongues, dogs have smooth tongues. Cats are not amenable to training, dogs are. Cats have retractable claws, dogs don't. Most dogs like to swim, few cats do. Here are some similarities—they are both four-legged, fur-bearing domestic mammals. Next, I might ask students to write a paragraph comparing and contrasting the similarities between cats and dogs.

Now let us examine what is going on here. Does this task call for higher-order thinking, or does it merely require students to recall what I have told them about cats and dogs? The answer is, of course, that this is a recall task masquerading as an evaluation task.

The stated aim of the lesson was to teach students the skill of evaluation by comparing and contrasting. However, what actually has been achieved is that the students have recalled what they have been taught without ever having demonstrated any form of thinking for themselves. If students truly have mastered the skill of evaluation by comparing and contrasting, they will be able to generate a data set about cats and dogs by themselves using a concept web, such as the one shown in Figure 8.12 (page 216), and then organize their information using a Venn diagram, such as the one shown in Figure 8.13 (page 216), to show similarities and differences.

Ranking Ladder

The cat-and-dog example was relatively simple to organize because it did not involve a large mass of data. In some cases, however, there is so much information or so many aspects on which to base a comparison that we need a way to focus on the more significant items. We can narrow the field through prioritization. To do this, we use another graphic organizer, the ranking ladder. As its name suggests, this organizer looks like a ladder and is used to rank or prioritize a set of data.

Concept Webs
Generating Data

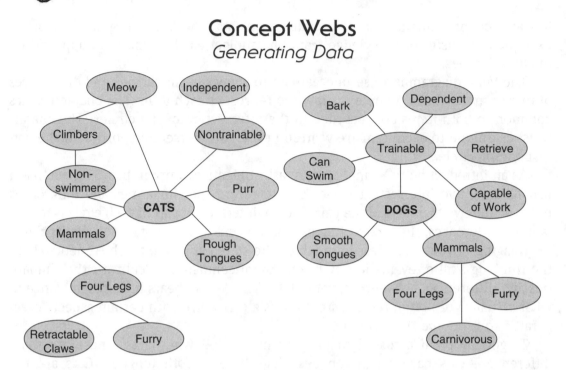

Figure 8.12

Venn Diagrams
Cats and Dogs

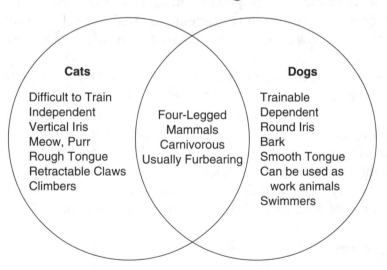

Figure 8.13

For example, the ranking ladder can be used to prioritize the data concerning two styles of painting—Classicism and Romanticism. After researching the pertinent literature, students may realize that a great deal of data can be used to compare and contrast these two styles. By using the ranking ladder with the concept web and the Venn diagram, students can organize the data, prioritize it, and select those elements that characterize both styles of paintings.

After the students have spent some time researching the data on these artistic styles, we might direct them to the following task: Use a concept web to brainstorm the words, attributes, and characteristics that come to mind when you think about Classicism and Romanticism as movements in the field of painting (see Fig. 8.14).

Concept Web
Brainstorming Ideas on Classicism and Romanticism

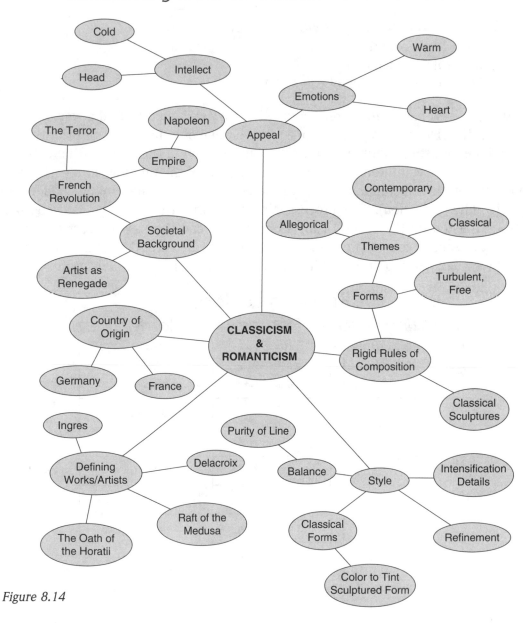

Figure 8.14

An examination of this initial brainstorm reveals that there is far more information than needed. Therefore, students need to refine their lists by deciding what to include and what to leave out. There are no hard-and-fast rules for making these decisions, and we all have different notions about what is important. After examining the web, students might come up with a short list of considerations such as the following:

- Artists whose works define the style
- Societal influences
- Form, style
- Rules of composition
- Major works that define art from each school
- Themes
- Countries where the styles were prevalent
- Political backgrounds
- Artist's role in society
- Defining characteristics of the styles

Students now have a more refined list, but they still need to find a way of shortening it further by assigning each item a relative value of importance, or priority. This can be done by using a ranking ladder. The information in the short list is reviewed and the most important item is listed on the top rung of the ranking ladder. The least important item is selected and listed on the bottom rung of the ranking ladder (see Fig. 8.15, First Selection). This process is repeated with the second-most important item being listed on the second rung from the top and the next-to-least important item on the second-to-last rung (see Fig. 8.15, Next Selection), and so on until all items have been listed on the ranking ladder (see Fig. 8.15, Final Selection).

Ranking Ladder
Prioritizing Data on Classicism and Romanticism

Defining Characteristics	Defining Characteristics	Defining Characteristics
	Defining Work	Defining Work
		Defining Artist
		Form, Style
		Themes
		Political Background
	Country of Origin	Country of Origin
Role of the Artist	Role of the Artist	Role of the Artist
First Selection	**Next Selection**	**Final Selection**

Figure 8.15

Once students have ranked the attributes from first to last, they determine the number of items they wish to consider. In the example shown in Figure 8.16, students could select the top five items: defining characteristics, defining work, defining artist, form and style, and themes. The students could select any quantity, based on the purpose for which they are making the comparison. A short essay might need five items, a doctoral thesis might require more. The similarities and differences of the top five items then are arranged on the Venn diagram as shown in Figure 8.16.

Venn Diagram
Classicism and Romanticism

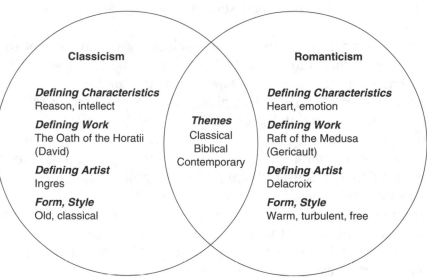

Classicism

Defining Characteristics
Reason, intellect

Defining Work
The Oath of the Horatii
(David)

Defining Artist
Ingres

Form, Style
Old, classical

Themes
Classical
Biblical
Contemporary

Romanticism

Defining Characteristics
Heart, emotion

Defining Work
Raft of the Medusa
(Gericault)

Defining Artist
Delacroix

Form, Style
Warm, turbulent, free

Figure 8.16

As teachers, we can make a number of decisions at this stage. We may decide to have students write an essay comparing and contrasting Romanticism and Classicism or we may decide that this is as far as the students need to go with this activity. If the aim were to assess whether students can compare and contrast data, there probably is enough information on the Venn diagram for us to make a valid judgment. When used like this, the Venn diagram becomes not only an instructional strategy but also an assessment tool.

Fishbone Diagram

Cause-and-effect relationships are found in the headlines of major newspapers on a daily basis. For example, we might read headlines such as the following: Faulty De-Icing Procedures Cause Plane Crash, Smoking Linked to Heart Disease, and News of Impending Election Results in Stock Market Fluctuation. The plane crash, heart disease, and stock market fluctuations are all outcomes, or effects, linked to a probable cause or a chain of causes.

There are many real-life situations when an acute problem arises to which we have to find and implement a solution immediately. A simple example might be as follows: There is a problem. The effect of the problem is water on the basement floor. The cause of the problem is a blocked drain. The solution to the problem is to clear the drain. This is an example of a quick fix to an acute problem and, in this case, it may be the correct one.

However, we may be faced with more chronic or complex problems that have a convoluted series of causes, some of which may not be immediately apparent. In these instances, we need to take time to review all the likely causes before putting a solution in place. We also need to consider the probable effects of our solution because it is possible that applying a solution may engender another set of unforeseen effects.

An example of an unforeseen effect of a solution was in the use of DDT to combat a problem with mosquitoes and other insects. The effect was that DDT poisoned the food chain, causing birth defects in many species of birds and animals. The key to using cause-and-effect thinking to solve problems is to be very clear about the desired outcome and to consider all possible effects.

To promote this kind of problem solving, we should encourage students to apply cause-and-effect thinking to increasingly complex situations. Businesses and industries routinely use causal thinking and a graphic organizer called a fishbone diagram to solve problems.

As an example of using the fishbone diagram, we can examine the possible causes for stomach pains suffered by the first-class passengers on an airplane. As a quick-fix solution, we might attribute this to food poisoning. This may or may not be the cause. To identify the actual cause, we need to broaden the scope of our inquiry. If after investigation we find that food poisoning was the cause, we need to delve deeper and find out how it happened. If we were to categorize the possible causes under our fishbone headings, they might look like those shown in Figure 8.17.

Please note that these are not all the possible causes, and as the investigation proceeds, a possible cause can be moved from one category to another. For example, a cause in the personnel category, an infected flight attendant, might be the result of a poor medical screening procedure. Or a new food supplier might be the nephew of the catering supervisor, which could make it a personnel rather than a material problem. Our purpose here is to simplify the process and encourage students to expand their thinking about possible causes by focusing on the four categories: personnel, procedures, equipment, and materials.

Each student now prepares a sheet with two columns—one for listing three probable causes and the other for listing the corresponding rationale or reasons why the cause was selected (see Fig. 8.18). Working individually, each student takes the data about the airline passengers, selects three probable causes, and writes down the reasons each was chosen. For example, a student may select bad fish as a probable cause and the rationale might be that many people are allergic to fish.

Fishbone Diagram
Identifying Cause of Food Poisoning

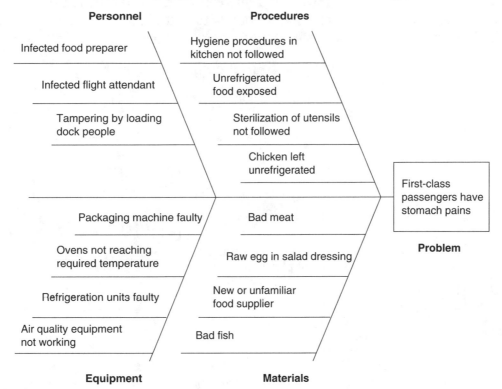

Figure 8.17

Cause-Reason Chart
Food Poisoning

Probable Cause	Reason
Bad Fish	Many people are allergic to fish
Air Quality	Sometimes makes people sick
Infected Flight Attendant	First-class passengers only ones infected

Figure 8.18

To complete the next step, the teacher or a person designated as the recorder prepares a large sheet on which to list the arguments for and against a particular cause. This is displayed at the front of the room. When this step is complete, the recorder asks for a volunteer to identify his or her first choice and the reason for selecting it. The recorder adds this cause to the master chart and puts the reason in the Arguments For column (see Fig. 8.19). If other members of the class have chosen the same cause but for a different reason, the different reasons also are added to the master list. For example, another student might also select bad fish as a probable cause but the rationale might be that fish spoils easily on airplanes.

Arguments For/Against Chart
Food Poisoning

Probable Cause	Arguments For	Arguments Against
Bad Fish	Many people allergic to fish Fish spoils easily on airplanes	

Figure 8.19

Once all the reasons for the first cause are listed, the recorder moves to the next person in the class. A new cause is given and the process is repeated.

The class will eventually have a complete list of causes and the arguments for each cause. Each student now works individually to develop arguments that refute the reasons listed, or "arguments against" the "arguments for" a specific cause. Note that no new causes or reasons should be added to the list at this time.

The "arguments against" are collected from each student in turn and added to the list using the same procedure as before. Using the fish example, the arguments against bad fish may be as follows: Although many people are allergic to fish, people who have such an allergy would not choose fish. Another argument against fish might be that only the people who ordered chicken were affected.

The arguments against, therefore, effectively eliminate fish as a probable cause. This process is repeated until the list of causes is reduced to a manageable number. Once this is achieved, the group has two options: to vote for a cause or to investigate further. If the problem is hypothetical, the group may not have access to the information necessary to determine a definitive answer. In such cases, they may choose to vote on the most likely cause. If the problem is a real situation, the group may choose to conduct further investigation to find the most likely cause or the chain of events that led to the problem.

When used in this fashion, the fishbone diagram is a powerful graphic organizer that can be used to precede a more in-depth investigation to track down and link a cause to a problem.

Sequence Chart

Many cause-and-effect relationships cannot be attributed to a single cause but rather to a chain of events. Sometimes a relatively minor event escalates into a major problem. An example from chaos theory is that when a butterfly flaps its wings in one part of the world, it sets in motion a chain of events that ends in a major storm on another continent, which in turn causes a famine. A chain of events is typified in the following old nursery rhyme.

For the Want of a Nail

For the want of a nail

The shoe was lost,

For the want of a shoe

The horse was lost,

For the want of a horse

The rider was lost,

For the want of a rider

The battle was lost,

For the want of a battle

The kingdom was lost,

And all for the want

Of a horse shoe nail.

One way of organizing data to illustrate a chain of causality is a sequence chart. This organizer is useful any time information has to be organized into a sequence. For example, if we were to establish the chain of events that led to the passengers getting sick on the airplane, we might find that there was a succession of mishaps that led to the unfortunate incident. In complex situations, the correct sequence may not be readily apparent and the events may have to be rearranged a number of times in order to arrive at the correct solution. This is an instance when using self-sticking removable notes is invaluable. The students first write all the events on self-sticking removable notes and then manipulate them to arrive at the most likely sequence.

The sequence chart can also be used in conjunction with the fishbone diagram to identify possible causes and then arrange their sequence. For example, a student doing an action research project on global warming or acid rain would have a number of causes to examine. In complex situations such as these, there is usually a chain of causes as opposed to a single cause. Once the causes have been identified, they can be sequenced into a chain of events using a sequence chart (see Fig. 8.20, page 224). Arranging the causes sequentially often shows an emerging pattern. This may allow one to predict what will happen if events go unchecked and to put solutions in place to head off the problem.

Sequence Chart
Food Poisoning

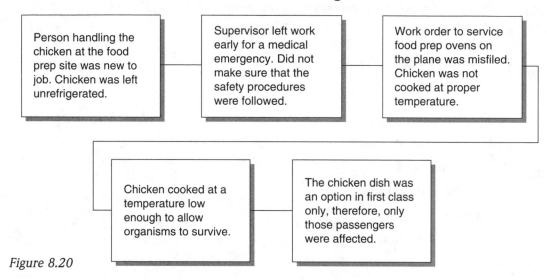

Person handling the chicken at the food prep site was new to job. Chicken was left unrefrigerated.

Supervisor left work early for a medical emergency. Did not make sure that the safety procedures were followed.

Work order to service food prep ovens on the plane was misfiled. Chicken was not cooked at proper temperature.

Chicken cooked at a temperature low enough to allow organisms to survive.

The chicken dish was an option in first class only, therefore, only those passengers were affected.

Figure 8.20

Sequence charts also may be used to show the relationships between parts of a process or items in a group. When used in this manner, they often are called flowcharts. For example, a sequence chart can be used to diagram the manufacturing-to-retail process, showing the movement from the primary source to the end of the chain at a retail outlet. An example is furniture manufacturing and distribution. The process starts with logging timber at a wooded site, moves to rough cutting at a lumber mill, then to fine milling to form moldings and laminated boards at a custom millwork factory, next to furniture making at a cabinetmaker's shop, then to a wholesale warehouser, and finally to a retail outlet.

Students can use the sequencing organizers in a variety of ways. For example, they could create a sequence chart showing the anticipated pivotal events of their lives from infancy to old age. They also might use a sequence chart to predict which choices are likely to have major consequences—for example, dropping out of school, taking up smoking, or other lifestyle choices. Sequence charts can also be adapted to depict cyclical patterns in students' lives or cyclical patterns in nature, such as weather patterns.

Cross-Classification Chart

We often are called on to make decisions or choices from a range of alternatives. These decisions range from selecting a career or buying a house to deciding what to have for dinner. When making decisions, we cycle between divergent thinking, in which we generate a list of options, and convergent thinking, in which we critically analyze the options and make a selection. For many of us, the process is unconscious, but it is helpful for students to understand the steps involved, especially when making major decisions.

Once again, we can begin to understand the decision-making process by using a variety of graphic organizers in sequence. In the following example, selecting a winter vacation destination, we use a web to brainstorm ideas, a ranking ladder to set priorities, and a cross-classification chart to overview the features of each potential destination.

We might state the objective and purpose of this lesson by saying that we are going to learn a process for making decisions by using three graphic organizers—the concept web, the ranking ladder, and the cross-classification chart. When we use a cross-classification chart for making decisions it sometimes is called a decision-making matrix.

To prime the pump for this activity and to activate prior knowledge, students can engage in a discussion of winter vacations and look at travel brochures, newspaper ads, and travel-related Internet sites. The next step would be to get into a divergent thinking mode and use a concept web or a sunshine wheel to generate a list of considerations for planning a vacation (see Fig. 8.21). Once a set of data has

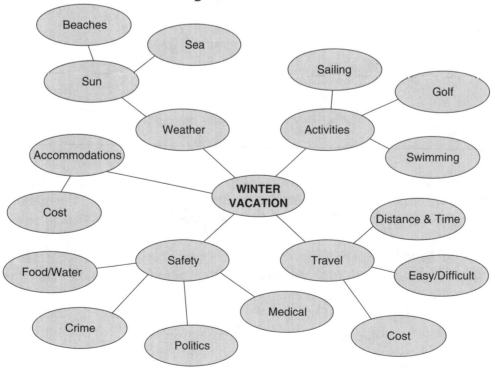

Concept Web
Planning a Winter Vacation

Figure 8.21

been generated, students should switch to a convergent mode and analyze the data. When we examine the concept web, a number of major considerations, or chunks, jump out. These cluster around safety issues, the type of accommodations required, cost, weather, available activities, and the ease or difficulty of travel given that our winter vacation is for one week.

We then take the list of considerations and transfer the information to the ranking ladder (see Fig. 8.22). In this example, the first consideration is safety. This goes on the top rung. We may not be too concerned about accommodations, so this goes on the bottom rung. As we decide on the order of priority of each item, we list it on the corresponding rung until all items have been listed.

Ranking Ladder
Prioritizing Vacation Considerations

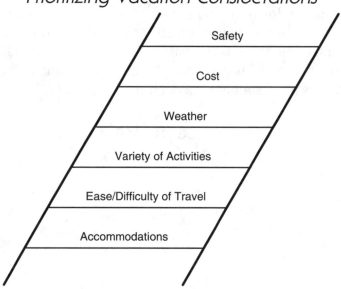

Figure 8.22

We then switch to a divergent mode and list all the possible destinations based on our information from travel brochures and other sources of information. Our list might include Alaska, the Falkland Islands, the U.S. Virgin Islands, New York, and Orlando.

We now have two kinds of information: a list of possible destinations and a list of points to consider. The next step is to transfer them to a decision-making grid in the form of a matrix (see Fig. 8.23). We then examine the suitability of each destination by checking it against our list of criteria, such as safety, cost, and weather. From this, we should come up with the most logical choice or the one that conforms to the greatest number of points on our list of criteria.

And the winner is Orlando! Please note this does not mean that we will end up in Florida. Remember, although we know that there are good and logical reasons

Decision-Making Matrix
Selecting a Destination

	Safety	Political Situation	Accommodations	Sunny, Warm Weather	Range of Activities	Cost	Ease/Difficulty of Travel
Alaska	Good	Stable	Fair	No	Fair	High	Reasonable
Falkland Islands	Fair	Stable	Poor	No	Poor	High	Restricted/ Difficult
US Virgin Islands	Good	Stable	Fair	Yes	Fair	High	Reasonable
New York	Getting Better	Stable	Good	No	Good	High	Easy
Orlando	Good	Stable	Good	Yes	Good	Medium	Easy

Figure 8.23

for making a particular decision, there always is an emotional component that defies logic. Sometimes this works in our favor, sometimes it doesn't, but at least when we go through this formal process for decision making we tend to consider a wider range of options and we also adopt a rational set of criteria.

We could extend this activity and transfer it to actual applications by having students use the process for selecting the theme for the class play or the location for the end-of-term party, or for more serious decisions such as selecting a career or college.

GRAPHIC ORGANIZER FOR REFLECTING

Right Angle

The right angle may be used by students as a reflective tool to examine their attitudes and feelings about a topic or as a precursor to writing about an event or topic in a journal entry or as a reflective essay.

For example, we might ask students to examine their thoughts and feelings about a piece of literature, a work of art, or an event only to find that they have merely regurgitated the plot, the main ideas, or the factual content. To react emotionally to a set of facts, we may need to put our minds a little out of focus. This is what the right angle is designed to do. Using this graphic organizer, we are able to turn our thoughts ninety degrees and view an event from a different perspective. The rationale for this organizer is that to concentrate on feelings, one first needs to write out the facts, making them explicit, so that they can be set aside.

Most of us can recall the fatal explosion of the space shuttle *Challenger.* For weeks prior to the scheduled launch, there had been a media frenzy about Christa McAuliffe, who was to be the first teacher in space. On the day of the crash, her students were watching the event live on television. The emotional impact on those students and anyone else who was watching was overwhelming. Because of this, most of us can recall where we were when we first heard the news. This is an example of an emotional context forever fixing a specific place and time in our memories with no apparent effort on our part.

Many years have passed since that day, and if we now wish to examine our emotions about that time, we may first have to delve into our long-term memories to bring back all the relevant facts. By recalling the facts and writing them, we do two things: One, we activate prior knowledge and bring the information into conscious, or working, memory, and two, we signal to the brain that we already have the facts, which sets the brain free to explore other avenues.

Figure 8.24 shows a right angle used to list the facts and reactions to a more recent example, the tragic events of September 11, 2001. Once the emotional reactions have been listed, students can use their lists to write a reflective paragraph or essay on how they felt.

The right angle also can be used to examine one's emotional reactions to fictional characters in literature—for example, Tom Sawyer or Captain Ahab. Similarly, it can be used to examine one's attitude and/or thoughts about historical figures, such as Julius Caesar or Abraham Lincoln, or historical events, such as the Holocaust or the Vietnam War.

One creative adaptation devised by a teacher was to reverse the process and use the right angle to list the emotions and then concentrate on the facts in a schoolyard dispute. In this way, the emotions were dealt with first, which allowed all the participants to have their say. Then, when the students were in better frames of mind, they were able to examine the facts.

Graphic Organizers for Displaying Information

Pie Chart

A pie chart, as its name implies, looks like a pie. The "pie" is divided into segments that represent halves, quarters, or any other fraction of the whole.

Students may use pie charts in a number of ways: to graph information about how they spend their allowances (see Fig. 8.25), to show what foods make up their daily food intake, or to report statistical information from a survey. In literature, pie charts can be used to graph the relative importance of various characters in a novel or play. In biology, pie charts can be used to represent the shrinking rain forest, animals and plants found in the school neighborhood, or the amounts different factors contribute to acid rain.

Right Angle
September 11, 2001

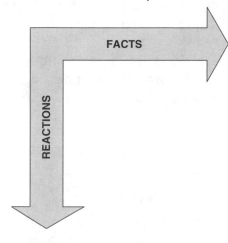

FACTS

REACTIONS

Twin Towers
Two planes
One plane hits Pentagon
One plane crashes in Pennsyivania
Nation watched
World stunned
North America brought to a standstill
Live TV coverage

Implications
Lax security
Shock and disbelief
Heroes: police and firefighters
Why us?
How should we react?
Worldwide support
Scapegoating
Revenge
Rumors and misinformation
"Hunt 'em down—smoke 'em out"

Figure 8.24

Pie Chart
How I Spend My Allowance

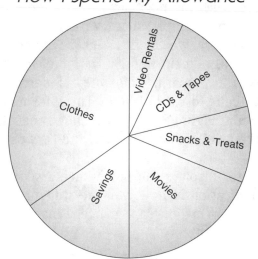

Video Rentals
CDs & Tapes
Clothes
Snacks & Treats
Savings
Movies

Figure 8.25

Target

Targets have been used for centuries to evaluate marksmanship. Everyone wants to "hit the bull's-eye." Many educators (Spence 1980; McTighe 1993; Ministry of Education 1990 [comp. by Cooper and Ward]) have used the target as an assessment tool.

The target can be used as an alternate way of assigning value to a student's work by transposing a letter grade into a visual form. If the student achieved an A, this would be recorded as a bull's-eye, a B would be the second ring from the center, and so on, as shown in Figure 8.26.

Target
Assessing Student Work

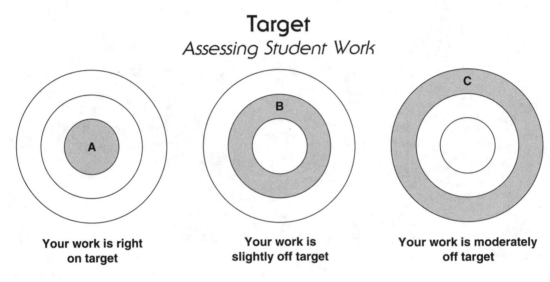

Your work is right on target   **Your work is slightly off target**   **Your work is moderately off target**

Figure 8.26

Pie Chart and Target Combined

Combining the target with the pie chart allows a more complex array of information to be displayed. For example, if we wished to provide assessment information on a student's project, we might assign 25 percent of the total grade to the selection of content, 40 percent to organization of material, 10 percent to the variety of resources used in preparing the work, 15 percent to the maps and diagrams used, and 10 percent to visual layout. The information could then be displayed visually as shown in Figure 8.27, which shows that the student did well on selecting content, not too well on organization, and very poorly at maps, diagrams, and so on.

Because this organizer displays the percentage assigned to each facet of the project as well as an indication of how well the student performed each facet, it imparts a great deal of information at a glance. What we have done is create a rubric, or rating scale, in visual form.

Pie Chart and Target Combined
Assessing Project

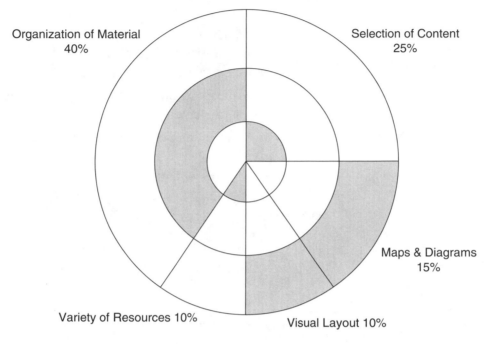

Organization of Material
40%

Selection of Content
25%

Maps & Diagrams
15%

Variety of Resources 10%

Visual Layout 10%

Figure 8.27

IN CLOSING

Graphic organizers have all the elements of brain-compatible learning. They are perceived by most students to be enjoyable, low stress, high interest, useful, and creative. They exemplify a whole-brain approach to learning and allow students to construct meaning for themselves. Graphic organizers are adaptable for all ages and across all areas of the curriculum. They are a vital part of any thinking skills program. From a teacher's point of view, they are usually fun to learn and relatively easy to implement. For most of us, graphic organizers are an infinitely rewarding element in our repertoires of instructional skills.

Graphic organizers can be used in myriad ways—as tools for brainstorming and producing ideas, for analyzing and evaluating ideas, for reflecting on ideas, and for displaying and compiling information. Because graphic organizers provide a means for students to visualize their thinking, they are valuable assets in the brain-compatible classroom.

Reflections

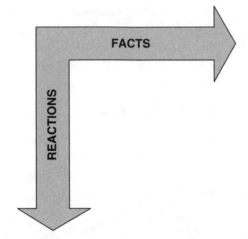

FACTS

REACTIONS

What do we know about graphic organizers and how students learn?

- Logical mathematical tool
- Taps into brain's capability for organizing information
- Increase in student achievement

Reflections

How will I use graphic organizers in my classroom?

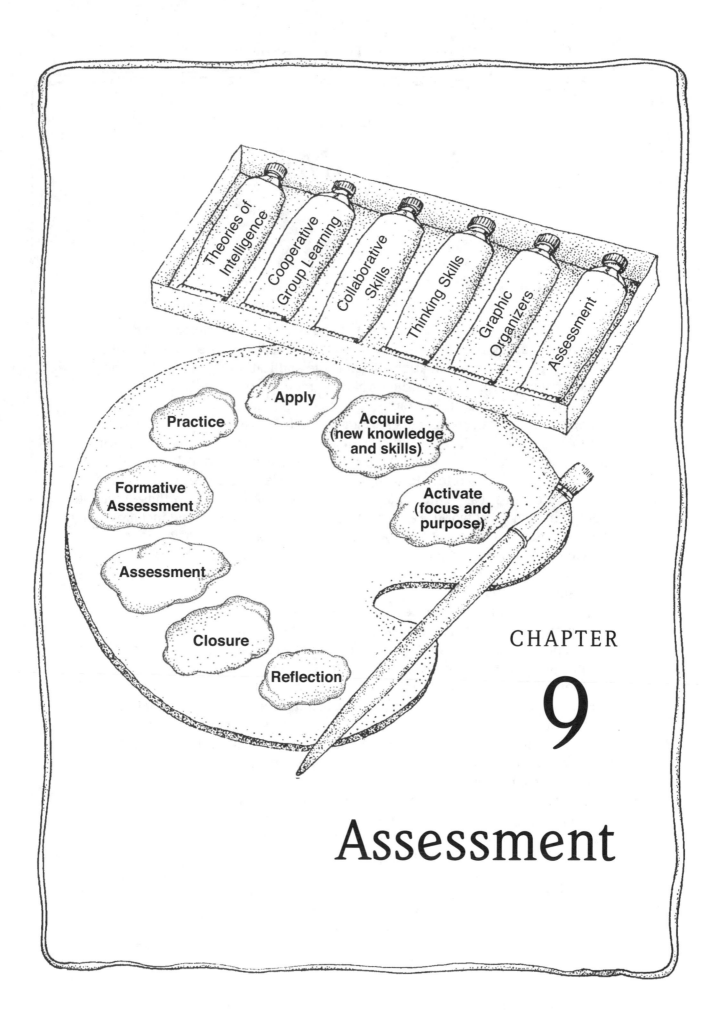

Theories of Intelligence

Cooperative Group Learning

Collaborative Skills

Thinking Skills

Graphic Organizers

Assessment

Apply

Practice

Acquire
(new knowledge
and skills)

Formative
Assessment

Activate
(focus and
purpose)

Assessment

Closure

Reflection

CHAPTER

9

Assessment

CHAPTER 9

ASSESSMENT

WHAT IS IT?

Assessment is a means of gathering data about student performance. It is a formative process that guides instruction. It provides feedback to the student and the teacher. It differs from evaluation, which is the application of judgment to the data about student performance in the form of a grade or comment.

A number of assessment terms fall under the category of brain-compatible strategies. Alternate assessments are "any and all assessments that differ from the multiple-choice, timed, one-shot approaches that characterize most standardized and many classroom assessments" (Marzano, Pickering, and Pollack 1993, 13). Authentic assessment refers to being able to use classroom learnings by applying them to problems, case studies, and situations that are similar to those students encounter in the real world. Performance assessment combines and includes many of the elements of alternate and authentic assessments. It involves a "variety of tasks and situations in which students are given opportunities to demonstrate their understanding and to thoughtfully apply knowledge, skills, and habits of mind" (Marzano et al. 1993, 13).

High-stakes, standardized tests don't fall into the category of brain-compatible assessments, but they are becoming a way of life in school districts everywhere. (Some special classroom strategies for preparing students for these types of tests are included at the end of the How Do We Do It? section of this chapter.) Traditionally, many teachers deliver information and facts and demonstrate skills and then have students "parrot" these facts and information on a variety of tests. Alternative assessments give students opportunities to move beyond recall and basic comprehension to application, synthesis, and evaluation by using knowledge and information in authentic and problem-based practices such as problems, case studies, and simulations.

The more authentic and relevant the learning and assessment tasks, the more meaningful they are to the learner. Authentic assessments ask students to perform, create, produce, or do something that could be used in a meaningful way in the real world. They require critical and/or creative thinking by the students. Teachers need to increase their instructional repertoires to include strategies such as cooperative group learning, inquiry, and case studies in order to support students in acquiring the necessary competencies to be successful in their learning tasks.

W. James Popham (2001), a long-time educator specializing in research on assessment and evaluation, suggests four rules for classroom assessment:

- Make sure classroom tests are of quality and that they actually measure growth in relationship to targeted standards.
- Use the appropriate assessment to measure the learning outcome.
- Use the test results to modify and direct the instructional process.
- Assess not only content but student affect.

Types of alternate assessment include projects, performances, observations, portfolios, learning logs, and journals. Any of these may be made more authentic by relating them to real-world applications. (All are covered in more detail in the How Do We Do It? section.)

Projects

Projects are tasks or assignments that develop students' understanding of concepts, skills, and content by immersing them in a learning experience for a designated period of time. Projects may focus on a particular area of the curriculum or a combination of disciplines. Projects are built on targeted standards. They are student-centered learning activities that are stimulating vehicles for thinking and producing. Projects may generate products such as pictures, murals, maps, plays, and performances.

Performances

Performances give students the opportunity to apply their learning in context. Students reinforce learning by doing. Performances include speeches, presentations, demonstrations, music and/or dance, and exhibitions. Performances help build in contextual learning and mastery. They allow students to measure their performance against standards and to self-correct based on feedback.

Observations

One of the most direct and immediate ways of assessing students is through observation. Much can be learned about students by monitoring their behaviors and skills, such as thinking, speaking, writing, and collaborative skills. Self-made or customized observation checklists can be used to gather and record information on student behavior. Observation checklists can also be used to give feedback to the students.

Portfolios

Student portfolios are collections of work that highlight the individual learner's competencies. Portfolios are a way for students to creatively organize their learning by collecting representative artifacts during a specific period of learning. They include examples of students' work, as well as their reflections. Portfolios show growth over time and give a much fuller picture of a student' growth than do individual and/ or isolated assessments.

Learning Logs and Journals

Logs and journals have been used for centuries to track progress, to record data, and to reflect on events and issues. Learning logs record content-based information, such as what a learner knows, is confused about, or wants to know about a specific topic or lesson. Journals give more insight into the learners' thoughts, feelings, and ideas. Both are self-reflective and encourage metacognition.

WHY DO WE NEED IT?

Although paper-and-pencil tests (including high-stakes, standardized tests) continue to play an important role in assessment, they do not provide a complete picture of student abilities. As we identify the knowledge, skills, and attitudes necessary for students in the twenty-first century (such as problem solving, effective communication, and teamwork), it becomes clear that conventional assessment practices are not sufficient.

Conventional assessments are commonly used to rank or sort students, grade and promote or retain students, reward high achievers, allow entrance into higher learning organizations, and show the quality of graduates and the credibility of schools. Standardized tests are often held up as a measure of success for the teacher, students, and school regardless of the other factors that affect the lives of learners, many of which are beyond the control of the school or teacher.

In contrast, many teachers are shifting to more learner-centered assessments and evaluations. They want to give students feedback on where they are in the learning process, increase their motivation and commitment to learning, identify their weaknesses in order to improve, predict and identify their future goals, celebrate their successes and increase their self-esteem, and promote dialogue with others.

Teachers also use assessments to evaluate curriculum and instruction; provide information for parents, other teachers, and outside agencies and organizations; and modify programs for individual learners.

We need to use more than paper-and-pencil tests if we truly want to use assessment to help students grow, to assess where they are in the learning process, to determine what they know and can do, and to measure what they understand. Paper-and-pencil tests show only a narrow range of content knowledge, not a deep understanding or application of knowledge and skills. We want students to be able to transfer the knowledge and skills they learn in school to the world beyond school and to be able to handle unique situations and challenges. Thus, they need opportunities to practice and apply these skills in schools with teachers and peer coaches who can help them analyze the process and their progress and set goals. This process is what British educational consultant Ruth Sutton (1995) referred to as value-added assessment—assessment that informs the learner of what he or she is doing, what needs to be improved, and suggestions for improvement. Value-added assessment carries the learner forward with renewed insight and strategies to achieve the desired standard.

Susan Kovalik (1991) described the elements of a brain-compatible classroom as its emotions and climate, meaningful content, choices, adequate time, immediate feedback, and enriched environment. These factors apply to assessment as well as instruction.

Emotions and Climate

Schools that are perceived as safe, nurturing places encourage students to try, experiment, fail, rethink, and try again. In many schools, assessment is based on testing in which there is only one right answer and students are evaluated based on their ability to supply it. Too often, in such situations, assessment feels like an audit or punitive measure.

Assessment is a necessary part of the growth process and should feel like such. Students need to be involved in the learning and assessment process and to have a sense of control in setting personal goals and planning next steps. They also need to feel that it is not a "gotcha" situation or one in which the teacher declares upon the task's completion that what the student produced wasn't exactly what the teacher had in mind. The criteria need to be clear, well explained, and outlined up front so that the target is clear and visible.

Timed tests have the disadvantage of sometimes overstressing the learner—the brain downshifts from the cerebral cortex to the limbic system. In such cases, the learner is overwhelmed by feelings and is not in a thinking mode to do his or her best. Learning must be challenging enough to keep the learner focused but not stressful enough to cause the learner to stop thinking and become distressed.

Meaningful Content

Relevancy and context help learners feel motivated to learn and to see meaning as they persist. In *Why Do I Have to Learn This?* Dale Parnell (1995) stated that many students do not find meaning in their school experiences and are told they will find meaning in the future. In general, the brain either pays attention to or disengages from the stimulus based on how intensely the task grabs attention. Many students have a greater impetus for learning when an activity is linked to an issue of personal relevance. Developing assessment activities such as simulations and case studies grounded in context can link what students are learning to the real world.

Choices

When we look at the multiple intelligences identified by Howard Gardner, we realize people are smart in different ways. Students need to be able to show what they know using a variety of intelligences, such as verbal/linguistic, musical/rhythmic, logical/mathematical, visual/spatial, bodily/kinesthetic, interpersonal, intrapersonal, and naturalist. To develop all intelligences, students need to learn, solve problems, and demonstrate competencies in a variety of ways.

Each learner is unique, and to honor this diversity, we need to provide opportunities for students to demonstrate their understanding in their own ways. Not all assignments are fair to each learner. Physical and language ability assessments need to be appropriate, for learners with both limited and exceptional ability.

Adequate Time

We don't all learn the same thing in the same way on the same day. To achieve mastery of content and skills, students need adequate time. Students may acquire some skills quickly; for other skills, students may need time to practice and get feedback in order to become competent. It may take several approaches or opportunities (perhaps through a variety of multiple intelligences) to integrate the knowledge or skill and file it in long-term memory.

"Sit and git" mode—when students sit and the teacher lectures—may not cause learning to take place, and saying something again "louder and slower" won't always make the concept or information any clearer. We educators have been pushed to "cover more," but this doesn't necessarily mean students learn more. They may memorize facts for a test, but if we want them to understand and retain information for transfer to other situations, students need ample time to grow dendrites and to make connections. They need time to move beyond recall to application, evaluation, and synthesis—to mastery.

Immediate Feedback

Have you ever wondered why some teenagers will endure pain and practice for hours to achieve a new trick on a skateboard? Have you ever watched kids playing a video game? Why would they sit in a dark room and manipulate a joystick and a few buttons? The answer is feedback. We all have a need to assess our own performance, to find out how well we are doing. For example, how long would you keep bowling if you never saw or heard the pins falling? How long would you continue with a journey if you had no idea whether you were going in the right direction? Feedback is an essential in the learning process.

Vince Lombardi once said that feedback is the "breakfast of champions" and that even champions have coaches. Students need a chance to receive ongoing feedback as they work on tasks. Teachers need to act as coaches, or as facilitators of learning, rather than as distributors of knowledge. Many times the teacher may circulate to monitor and give feedback to students as they work independently or in groups. If there are thirty-five students and only one teacher, the teacher is able to spend only a few seconds with each student. This is hardly enough time to modify concepts, redirect learning, or question thinking processes. Direct feedback in real situations is more relevant for learners than feedback received secondhand from the teacher. In a music performance, for example, if a student hits the wrong note, immediate feedback and self-correction can take place. Knowing that they can adjust gives learners a sense of efficacy that motivates them to continue. It is very much like a video game that gives feedback—self-correction takes place and the user can move on to a more challenging level. Black et al. (2004) found that feedback was more important than grades to increase student achievement. When grades were removed from daily work and only feedback was given, students paid attention to the feedback and the quality of their work improved and test scores increased.

In terms of brain compatibility, assessment should involve what psychologist Mihaly Csikszentmihalyi (1991) calls flow—a state of being in which a person is so immersed in a task that his or her brain does not register the passage of time or anything else in the surrounding environment. According to this theory, students often are apathetic to tasks that are too easy and may give up on tasks that are too difficult. Students perform best with tasks that are just beyond their present level of skill because they can see success if they put forth an effort.

Self-reflection is also a necessary part of the feedback process. Students must learn to reflect and to analyze what they have or have not learned, what misconceptions they have, and what actions they need to take next.

Enriched Environment

An enriched environment is pleasant and rich in resources, is stimulating but uncluttered, and is a place where student work, materials, and ideas are respected. Students are provided opportunities to work alone and with others, furniture arrangements are flexible, and access to technology is provided. Numerous displays, manipulative, and real artifacts are available, enabling students to get hands-on experience.

HOW DO WE DO IT?

Changing from traditional forms of assessments to alternate and more authentic assessments requires that teachers change more than just their assessment methods. Recognizing that we need more than test results to give us data on student growth is the first step. Currently, "accountability" means that teachers need to be clear about expectations for student accomplishments. These goals may be called any of the following depending on the district or state: outcomes, competencies, expectations, or standards.

Assessment Design

A traditional planning method involves selecting a topic or content, planning learning experiences and activities, and then designing and giving a test. In contrast, brain-compatible assessments involve determining the expectations of a task and the standards, or what the students are expected to *know* (knowledge), what they are expected to *do* (skill/performance), and what they will *value* (affect).

The second part of assessment design deals with two questions: *How* will students demonstrate their knowledge and skill? *What* is the most appropriate format to elicit this information?

After determining the standards, teachers then design the learning experience and share the standards and assessment tools with the students. It is necessary to be open and honest about the expectations so that students have a clear understanding of the target and how to achieve it.

Types of Alternative Assessments

Projects

Projects have been around for a long time and have been used in many subject areas. However, too often, the purpose and standards were not clearly articulated or intentionally embedded in the project. Projects were assigned as "busy work" that interested the students and were a change from the regular seatwork.

Projects can become a more productive vehicle for applying learning if they are used to transfer knowledge and skills and to develop understanding through hands-on, concrete activities. Projects can be engaging learning experiences and assessment tools that allow the practice of skills, the transfer of knowledge, and the demonstration of understanding. They also can create a sense of relevance and usefulness for the learner.

In all assessment tasks, the students need to be exposed to a range of projects from excellent to not-so-good. They should have a clear understanding of why the project is important and how it applies to the real world. Projects that are tied to real-world applications are more authentic and allow students to see relevance and work in a context that is of personal interest.

Projects are especially useful in allowing students to use a variety of intelligences, especially those other than logical/mathematical and verbal/ linguistic. If we want to allow students to have some freedom and choice and to feel comfortable with a task, we can let them use the eight intelligences to show what they know when doing projects. Figure 9.1 lists a variety of suggestions for projects that target each intelligence.

Performances

A speech, presentation, video, or hands-on demonstration is often the most authentic way to demonstrate understanding or competency in a subject matter or a skill. Following are tips to consider when designing a performance-based assessment.

Projects That Target Multiple Intelligences

Verbal/Linguistic
Debates
Reports
Poetry books
Storybooks
Case studies
Speeches
Pamphlets
Brochures

Bodily/Kinesthetic
Role plays
Aerobics
Dances
Mimes
Vignettes
Dramatizations

Musical/Rhythmic
Commercials
Scores (original)
Songs or raps
Background music
  to drama
Performances

Naturalist
Models
Flowcharts
Documentaries
Investigations
Exhibitions
Experiments
Photoessays

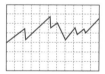

Logical/Mathematical
Action plans
Demonstrations
Problem solving
Mapping
Designing
Essays
Schedules

Intrapersonal
Logs and journals
Diaries
Autobiographies
Resumes
Portfolios

Visual/Spatial
Art portfolios
Art pieces
Murals
Illustrations
Animations
Model or dioramas
Advertisements
Mobiles

Interpersonal
Jigsaw strategies used in
  project work
Work in any area with a
  collaborative skill focus
Interview and biographical
  opportunities

Figure 9.1

- Relate the performance directly to desired outcomes or expectations.
- Develop indicators of proficient performance for each criterion and design a rubric or other assessment tool to communicate expectations and to record achievement.
- Communicate established criteria for success to students.
- Model or illustrate both excellent and not-so-good examples.
- Relate how this performance will benefit the learner and others.

Rubrics

By definition, the term *authentic assessment* refers to a situation as close to real-world conditions as possible. Most real-world tasks do not have a single correct way to do them. Consequently, they must be judged using well-defined criteria. A valuable assessment tool is the rubric, which means, in general terms, an authoritative or established rule. Specifically, a rubric consists of a fixed scale and a set of characteristics describing what performance should look like at each point on the scale. Rubrics have two major advantages: they describe expectations that are clear to teachers and parents and they provide students with a clear target.

Rubrics should be presented to the students when the performance task is assigned, with time allowed for discussion and clarification of the criteria and indicators. Also, teachers may want to include the students in the development of the rubric. Students can usually describe quality work and suggest appropriate and relevant criteria for tasks.

The best rubrics describe performance in terms of observable behavior; they are qualitative or quantitative. Consider the following examples.

The terms *no, few, adequate,* and *excellent* are vague and nonspecific. To be useful, the rubric needs to include more observable characteristics. Example 2, which includes more specific indicators, provides a clearer picture of expectations.

Rubrics, like performance tasks, may be modified after they are used. They should be debriefed with the students after using and then modified if necessary to present a clearer picture of expectations so they are more helpful in the future. Many rubrics can be designed using the Web site http://rubistar.4teachers.org.

For students to become competent, they need feedback so they can recognize where they need to make changes and what they can do in the future to make a performance better. This makes the assessment value-added, because as a result of the feedback, students are better at the task.

Example 1

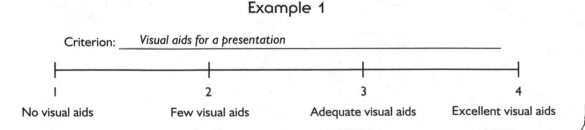

Criterion: *Visual aids for a presentation*

1	2	3	4
No visual aids	Few visual aids	Adequate visual aids	Excellent visual aids

Example 2

Criterion: _Visual aids for a presentation_

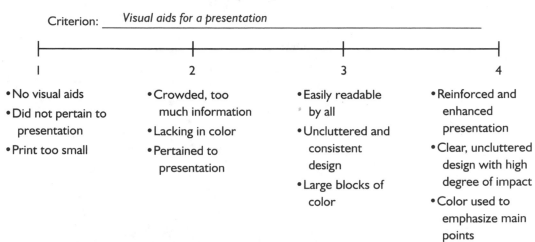

1	2	3	4
• No visual aids • Did not pertain to presentation • Print too small	• Crowded, too much information • Lacking in color • Pertained to presentation	• Easily readable by all • Uncluttered and consistent design • Large blocks of color	• Reinforced and enhanced presentation • Clear, uncluttered design with high degree of impact • Color used to emphasize main points

Targets

Like rubrics, the target is a visual/spatial tool that can be used to indicate various levels of performance (see Fig. 9.2, page 244). The target consists of three concentric circles, with each circle representing an indicator of performance. The innermost circle, or bull's-eye, represents target performance; a shaded center indicates that the student has consistently demonstrated an acceptable level of performance. The two additional circles indicate varying levels of performance, with the distance from the center indicating the distance from the target performance. A shaded middle circle indicates that the student has made significant progress. A shaded outer circle indicates that the student has made some progress. The precise interpretation of both of these levels of progress or performance can be negotiated with the student and other teachers. Clear criteria and indicators are visible at each circle of the target.

The area outside the target also can be used to indicate performance. By placing a checkmark outside the target area, the teacher can indicate that the student has made little or no progress. Students should know why this evaluation has been made and what they can do about it.

Observations

Direct observations provide teachers with the means to gather data that cannot be obtained through other forms of assessment and to give feedback to learners.

There are both advantages and disadvantages to using observation as an assessment tool. The benefits are that the teacher gets to know each student better as an individual, information is obtained that is not available through other means, and concrete information on student behavior is provided. The drawbacks are that interpretations based on observations may be subjective or biased, they are time-consuming and hard to translate to an assessment, and the teacher may have difficulty giving objective feedback.

The Target as Assessment

Topic: _____

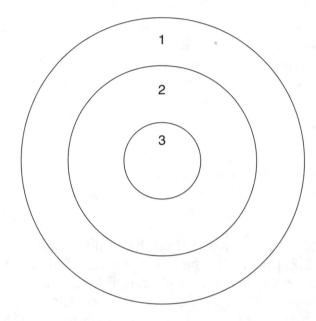

Criteria:

3 • _____

• _____

• _____

2 • _____

• _____

• _____

1 • _____

• _____

• _____

Figure 9.2

For some teachers, the advantages far outweigh the limitations. Observation provides feedback on teaching skills that testing cannot provide, allowing a teacher to hone these skills. The expertise developed through observations also helps teachers become more specific in establishing criteria, further promoting the communication of clear expectations to students.

The following tips are helpful when first using observation as a form of assessment:

- Observe only a few students at a time.
- Use a limited number of criteria.
- Develop an easy-to-use checklist.
- Use a video camera or tape recorder to collect data.
- Add self-sticking removable notes throughout the day and transfer onto the checklist at the end of the day.
- Teach students to be good observers and self-monitors.
- Give feedback in a nonevaluative way
  - I saw . . .
  - I heard . . .
  - This happened . . .

- Separate observations by specific areas
  - Work habits
  - Social behavior
  - Emotional development
  - Cognitive behavior

Observation checklists can be used to gather and record information for a variety of skills. Figure 9.3 shows a checklist used to keep track of classroom observations.

Classroom Behavior Checklist

Name							
Is Prepared for Class							
Completes Homework							
Participates in Discussions							
Shares Resources							
Uses TIme Efficiently							
Values Others							

Figure 9.3

Each student's name is written across the top row, with behaviors to monitor written in the left-hand column. Checkmarks or other symbols can be used to record observations.

Observation checklists can also be used to gather information related to specific skills, such as the use of technology. Figure 9.4 shows a checklist that can be used to collect data about the different tools the students use as they work.

Information Accessing Checklist

Name								
CD-ROMs								
Encyclopedias								
Microfiches								
Telephones								
Catalogues								
Videotapes/Audiotapes								

May cite occasion or actual information or use checkmark

Figure 9.4

Teachers can use observation checklists such as the one shown in Figure 9.5 to collect data on students' collaborative/social skills. By using the checklists daily or weekly to monitor behavior, teachers can determine if patterns, as indicated by the checkmarks, develop over time.

In addition to the teacher, the students can use checklists to assess their peers' work. This provides valuable feedback to the students and helps them develop their observation skills.

Portfolios

Portfolios are collections of student work that have been selected according to preestablished criteria and reflected on to analyze and set goals for future learning. Any of the assessment tasks or tools may be included in a portfolio.

Educator Richard Stiggins (1993) likened a portfolio to a color video with sound in contrast to a paper-and-pencil test, which is more like a black-and-white snapshot of student ability. This is because portfolios serve many purposes. Not only do they provide a means of assessment for the teacher, but they also provide valuable information to the learner. Portfolios provide a portrait, or full picture, of the learner;

let the learner show his or her strengths; and require critical and creative thinking. Portfolios encourage reflection and self-awareness and help students make judgments and decisions in goal setting. They enable students to accept ownership for the learning/assessment process, to identify growth over time, and to become more active learners. Portfolios provide students with a vehicle for assessing their learning of knowledge, skills, and values and assessing what areas need attention. They also provide a stimulus for conferences and dialogues about learning.

Social Skills Checklist

	Rarely	Usually	Often
Attendance			
• Attends regularly	_____	_____	_____
• Gets missed work	_____	_____	_____
Punctuality			
• Arrives on time	_____	_____	_____
• Keeps appointments	_____	_____	_____
Organization			
• Keeps notes neat	_____	_____	_____
• Keeps up to date	_____	_____	_____
• Has materials in class	_____	_____	_____
Effort			
• Works consistently	_____	_____	_____
• Works to improve	_____	_____	_____
• Works for quality	_____	_____	_____
• Participates actively	_____	_____	_____

Figure 9.5

It is important to examine many factors, such as purpose, procedures, and expectations, prior to making the decision to use portfolio assessments. Figure 9.6 (page 248) presents an overview of the different areas that need to be examined in deciding to use portfolio assessments and in determining how best to use them.

Teacher Decision Making

Why will I use a portfolio?

In what subject area?

How will I manage it?

    Type

    Storage

    Facilitation

    Conferencing

What are my expectations?

    Content

    Process

How will I assess and evaluate?

    Criteria

    Grading or not

    Peer

    Self

Figure 9.6

Portfolios and Different Disciplines

Math

- Journals/logs
- Mind maps
- Charts and graphs
- Best test
- Most improved test
- Problem-solving explanations
- Relevance of math in everyday life
- Pictographs

Family Studies

- Family trees
- Autobiographies
- Reports
- Logs/journals
- Favorite recipes/foods
- Family traditions
- Trends and directions
- Career reflections

History

- Essays
- Editorials
- Journals
- Charts
- Newspaper articles
- Research reports
- Investigations
- Graphic organizers
- Interviews
- Community outreach

Music

- Audiotapes
- Videotapes
- Essays on a variety of topics
- Personal compositions
- Reflections
- Mind maps
- Predictions

Science

- Lab reports
- Reaction papers
- Diagrams
- Research papers
- Mind maps
- Career opportunities
- Uses in the real world

Visual Arts

- Sketch books
- Line drawings
- Pen and wash drawings
- Watercolor paintings
- Acrylic paintings
- Oil paintings
- Photos of models
- Sculptures

Figure 9.7

Portfolios lend themselves to any subject area. Figure 9.7 shows how portfolios can be used in a variety of disciplines.

The Portfolio Process

The portfolio process involves five primary steps: selecting a container, collecting artifacts, determining criteria for artifact selection and assessment, reflecting on the process and learning, and projecting how to use the learning. Following are descriptions of each step.

Selecting a Container

The first step in the portfolio process is to select a container for storing work samples that is appropriate for the type of portfolio and/or subject area. Any of the following can be used as containers:

- Folder
- Computer disk (or other form of electronic storage)
- Work box
- Shoe box

- Three-hole binder
- Oversize folder
- Commercially designed holder
- Accordion file

Collecting Artifacts

The second step in the portfolio process is for students to collect artifacts of their work. Items can include the following:

- Homework
- Projects
- Written pieces
- Graphic organizers

- Tests
- Assignments
- Reflections
- Cassettes/videos

Students also can be encouraged to profile their multiple intelligences in a portfolio. Artifacts that reflect different intelligences are listed in Figure 9.8.

Determining Criteria for Artifact Selection and Assessment

The third step in the portfolio process is to determine the criteria to be used to select and assess artifacts. The sequence in this step depends on teacher preference. Some teachers decide on the criteria before collecting the artifacts in order to limit the collection. Others collect artifacts first, then determine the criteria for further selection of individual artifacts and assessment. Examples of artifacts based on specific criteria include the following:

- Best piece/something I'm proud of
- Work in progress
- Student or teacher selection
- Most improved piece/most difficult
- Special
- Shows growth

Sample Artifacts for Multiple Intelligences

Verbal/Linguistic
- Notes
- Logs, journals
- Anecdotal comments
- Book reviews
- Letters
- Descriptive notes
- Comments on tests
- Projects

Bodily/Kinesthetic
- Video presentations
- Dramas
- Mimes
- Demonstrations
- Field trips
- Choreographs

Musical/Rhythmic
- Creative responses
- Poems, raps, lyrics
- Audiotapes and videotapes
- Discographies
- Photographs of instruments made

Naturalist
- Models
- Experiments
- Investigations
- Photoessays

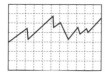

Logical/Mathematical
- Graphic organizers
- Sequence planning charts
- Lab reports
- Problem-solving notes
- Puzzles
- Photos from science fair

Intrapersonal
- Goal setting
- Study notes
- Self-assessments
- Reflection logs
- Journals

Visual/Spatial
- Diagrams
- Artwork
- Graphs
- Graphic organizers
- Mind maps
- Planning charts

Interpersonal
- Notes to and from peers
- Notes to and from teacher
- Parents' comments
- Peer tutor notes
- Peer assessments
- Conference notes

Figure 9.8

Artifact Registry

Type of Portfolio: _____

Purpose of Portfolio: _____

List the artifacts you have selected and state why you chose them.

Item	Rationale

Figure 9.9

Students can use a variety of teacher-made sheets to determine what they want to collect in their portfolios and to keep track of the items they are including in their portfolios. This can be done by keeping an artifact registry, such as the one shown in Figure 9.9. Students log their artifacts and explain their rationale for selecting them.

Reflections for Portfolio

I chose this piece because . . .	Please notice . . .
It would have helped me if . . .	What surprised me was . . .
If I were to do this again I would . . .	I learned . . .

Figure 9.10

Reflecting on the Process and Learning

The fourth step in the portfolio process is to decide what to examine critically and creatively. Students reflect on and examine specific artifacts or the portfolio process and what they did and learned. Reflections can take many forms. For example, students can attach a short note or written reflection to the artifact or complete a prepared form (see Fig. 9.10). Suggested questions include the following:

- What did I learn or notice?
- What would I do differently?
- What are my strengths/weaknesses?
- What are the pluses and minuses?

Projecting How to Use Learning

The fifth step in the portfolio process is to project—to decide how learning can be incorporated to set goals for future endeavors. Students can either write their goals or discuss them verbally during a conference. Sample goal-related questions include the following:

- What do I need to consider?
- What do I need to do next?
- What do I need to focus on?
- What do I need to improve?
- What do I need to celebrate?

Sample Timeline

The time needed for the portfolio process varies based on the desired objectives and the learners' needs. Following is a timeline that shows sample times for each step of the process.

- Weeks 1–5: *Select* a container as a working portfolio (e.g., storage box, video, three-ring binder) and *collect* everything into it.
- Weeks 6–8: *Determine criteria* to be used to assess artifacts and select seven to ten items (e.g., photos of models, videos of performances, written records, anecdotes).
- Weeks 9–10: *Reflect* on artifacts and learning process. Make deletions or additions to portfolio, prepare written reflections, polish where necessary, and include reflections in the final portfolio.
- Weeks 11–12: *Project* how to use learning in the future. Hold conferences and set goals for the next unit or for future work.

Portfolio Conference

Conferencing with others about the portfolio contents and process is a way to enhance the portfolio process. Conferences are meetings between a student and other selected persons for the purpose of presenting the portfolio, reviewing its contents, and discussing the related learning processes. Participants can include the teacher, classmates, and parents or other adults. Conferences can be done at the outset of the portfolio process, at any stage during the process, or at its culmination. The learner explains his or her portfolio and outlines the successes, areas that need attention, and goals for the future. Others, whether they are parents or peers, give feedback and perceptions that may be helpful to the learner.

Conferencing may be formal or informal. Prior to the conference, the portfolio holder plans the presentation and anticipates questions. The other participants in the conference prepare questions to ask the portfolio holder and develop constructive feedback to share. During the conference, the participants engage in dialogue and feedback. After the conference, students reflect on the feedback and set goals for the future. Reflection may include writing a journal entry or discussion with a partner. Conference participants can also give feedback after the conference using a form such as the one shown in Figure 9.11 (page 256).

Learning Logs and Journals

We learn not only from experience but also by reflecting on experience. Through metacognition, students learn to assess their growth toward the established standards. When students write about their learnings, they prove to themselves that they are learning.

Learning logs can be used after introducing a topic to describe reactions, explain relationships, reflect, and ask questions. For example, students can write something they know now that they didn't know before that is the result of the learning experience or write their reactions to an activity. Did they like it? Why? Why not?

Following are tips for using learning logs:

- Allow students to present information in a visual form—graphs, charts, webs, sketches, etc. (Logs do not always have to be verbal/linguistic.)
- Collect entries in a folder, booklet, box, or disk to provide a review or a reference for students and parents during conferences.
- Give students an opportunity to share, reinforce, and present ideas that they hadn't thought about before.
- Create a class log. Students in large groups can share learnings and develop logs of their collective wisdom.

Following are questions and lead-in statements that help students to focus on core issues for learning log entries related to what they are learning:

- What is clear?
- I wonder . . .
- What is confusing?
- What would I like to learn?
- Now I think . . .
- What puzzles me is . . .
- This reminds me of . . .
- Why would I use . . .
- I still need to know . . .

Portfolio Conference Feedback

Title:_____

I enjoyed this piece because _____
_____
_____
_____
_____
_____

I learned that _____
_____
_____
_____
_____
_____

A suggestion I have is _____
_____
_____
_____
_____
_____
_____

A question I have is _____
_____
_____
_____
_____
_____

Figure 9.11

These stems also can be used on "exit slips," or pieces of paper that students fill in and submit before they leave class. Exit slips provide students an immediate opportunity to reflect and to share with the teacher what they know and what needs clarification.

Split-Page Approach

FACTS	REACTIONS
The Berlin Wall came down in 1989.	I wonder how it felt to be there. Why did they put it up in the first place?
Log	**Journal**

Other topics for exit slips include the following:

- 3 - Three things I learned today
- 2 - Two insights or surprises
- 1 - One question I still have

Logs and journals may be used together in a split-page approach. On the log side, just the facts are listed, including tasks, times, and activities. On the journal side, students record their reactions, reflections, learning, feelings, and frustrations, as well as questions.

Varying Assessment Tools

No matter what the curriculum design, teachers need to focus on the purpose and begin with the expectation, or desired outcome, in mind. What do we want students to know, to be able to do, or to be like?

As teachers focus on competencies and expectations embedded in the curriculum, they need to collect data over time using a variety of instruments. Using an instrument only one time or using only one instrument may not give an accurate or full picture of a student's learning. For example, if effective communication is the expectation, then data can be collected from observations, presentations, journal entries, and portfolio reflections.

One way to identify expectations and consider options for collecting data is through a matrix (see Fig. 9.12, page 258). By listing the expectations in the left-hand column and checking the appropriate assessment strategies, teachers can identify the tools they are most familiar with and use most often and those they rarely use that could be used.

Curriculum Choices

The standards that students are working toward may be clustered or grouped to design learning activities that are meaningful, related to the real world, and motivational. It is best to make planning for instruction, curriculum, and assessment

Consider the Expectations or Standards

Select at least three tools for data collection.

Consider the Expectations	Anecdotals	Observations	Journals	Checklists	Presentations	Exhibitions	Portfolios	Projects	Speeches	Tests

Figure 9.12

a unified process rather than treat each as separate and discrete. They work together, complete with ongoing feedback, to keep students focused on their growth. If we want students to understand and apply their knowledge and skills in context, we need to use projects, case studies, integrated learning, role plays and simulations, community service learning, and inquiry or problem-based learning to embed the standards in a practical and creative way.

Following are brief descriptions of these curriculum and assessment choices.

Project Learning

Project learning immerses the students in a particular activity for a significant period of time. Project learning allows students to apply skills and develop understanding from a number of subject areas and to focus on a particular task or culminating performance. A culminating activity for a project usually takes the form of a performance or a product. A performance might include a demonstration of skill, as in a dance recital, an audiovisual presentation, or a family arts display. A product could be anything from an extended essay to a remodeled bathroom to a household budget for a family of four.

To design a successful learning project, first tap into the student's area of interest. Second, design a project that involves a number of subject areas and expectations, as well as a range of skills. This can be facilitated through a process of consultation with the student and other teachers. Third, decide on the evaluation criteria up front. This has a number of advantages—both teachers and students have a clear picture of the expectations, and it signals to the teachers those skills they may need to teach the students to ensure successful completion of the project.

Case Studies

Case studies have long been used in learning situations related to business, industry, and legal issues. They can easily be incorporated into the classroom for a wide variety of issues. A case or scenario is prepared and presented to the students. The issues are often ambiguous and need to be examined, questioned, and explored in order for the students to determine the truth. Students investigate and clarify the issues by discussing and debating their ideas. Many relevant issues that concern young people can be explored through case studies, such as moral and ethical decisions.

In terms of brain compatibility, case studies allow the students to examine an issue and their own ideas in depth, to use analogies to make connections, and to transfer their learning to other situations.

Integrated Learning

Integrated learning involves the explicit connection between various subject areas of the curriculum. The various models of integrated learning usually involve a central theme or organizer that acts as a framework on which to build an integrated series of lessons or units. The organizer may be a common theme, such as transportation, space, or relationships, or a set of skills, such as inductive reasoning, analyzing for bias, or determining cause and effect.

As a way of integrating the curriculum, a group of teachers might examine their particular curriculum areas to identify learning outcomes and expectations they have in common, such as the ability to access, organize, and display information. They then collectively decide on a comprehensive culminating activity that will act as a vehicle for learning in a number of curriculum areas. For example, accessing information might involve computer science and library resources, organizing information could involve language arts and math, and displaying information could involve graphic and performing arts.

Integrated learning capitalizes on the brain's ability to identify and construct patterns by connecting information.

Role Plays and Simulations

Role plays and simulations allow students to enact hypothetical situations. In a role play, the students are given a scenario, such as an interview or a confrontation. The students are assigned different roles, such as interviewer, candidate, aggressor, or victim, and a set of characteristics or personality traits associated with their character. They then act out the scene according to a set of predetermined guidelines. The role play is followed by a debriefing in which the audience and players clarify the main points of the situation.

In a simulation, the students assume the identities of various characters and replicate a situation, such as an archeological dig, a team survival exercise, or a great moment in history. Following the simulation, the students debrief the main points and consolidate their learning.

Role plays and simulations tap into the brain's emotional circuits by creating a context or mental "file" of information. The file contains not only the emotions associated with the simulation but also the academic content of the lesson. The brain is not very good at recalling unrelated facts, but it is particularly adept at recalling emotions; whenever the emotional context is recalled, the related information accompanies it. This is a very efficient way of ensuring the retention of information over extended periods of time.

Community Service Learning

Community service learning usually involves some form of cooperative (co-op) program between the school and the local community. Co-op programs are a form of inservice training where students work in local industries and businesses and begin to apply the knowledge and skills they have learned in school.

For example, a chemistry student may spend time in a local laboratory, a biology student may work at a veterinarian's office, and an English major may do a stint at the local newspaper. The key factor for school personnel is to find placements where the students will be engaged in meaningful work that provides a link between theory and practice. When they are immersed in a co-op program, students get to see, hear, and feel concrete examples of abstract concepts they learned in the classroom.

Active learning, which involves the physical manipulation of concrete examples, facilitates the learning of abstract concepts by tapping into a greater range of neural circuits. The more neural circuits one can involve in a learning activity, the greater the chance new learning will connect to previous ideas and thus foster understanding.

Inquiry/Problem-Based Learning

Inquiry/problem-based learning is built around an investigation, research, or inquiry, either for answers or questions or for solutions to problems. After an initial exploration of a topic or area of study, an individual student or group of students starts off with a general, nonspecific question, such as, Why are animals becoming extinct? Students brainstorm responses to the question, starting with a more specific question, such as, What do I already know or think I know about the topic? This leads to a generation of subquestions, such as, Which class of animals is becoming extinct? What are some of the causes of extinction? Is the rate of extinction growing? Once these questions are formed, students explore and identify resources such as databases, Internet sites, journals, articles, texts, and persons knowledgeable about the topic. The results of the inquiry are presented in a report, such as an audiovisual presentation, speech, exhibition, or portfolio.

Inquiry allows students to construct meaning through exploration and a search for information. Presenting their findings allows students to refine the information and understand it at a deeper level.

Designing Down

A chart, such as the one shown in Figure 9.13 (page 262), can be used to design down from the competencies or expectations to the curriculum choice. The steps in designing down are as follows:

1. Consider what overall concepts, skills, and competencies you want the students to achieve.

2. Determine, within one or more disciplines or subjects, the specific expectations in each area.

3. Select the curriculum choice to be used: project, case study, simulation or role play, community service, or inquiry/problem.

4. Identify the task or focus to be used within the curriculum choice.

5. Select the assessment tools to be used to collect data.

Designing Down

1. Concepts, Skills, and Competencies

Concepts, Big Ideas	Technology Skills	Thinking Skills
	Collaborative Skills	Multiple Intelligences

2. Subject or Discipline Expectations (may be one or several if integration is used)

Language Arts	Social Studies	Science	_____

3. Curriculum Choices

Project	Case Study	Simulation/ Role Play	Community Service	Inquiry or Problem

4. Focus or Task

5. Assessment Tools

Checklists	Observations	Feedback Forms	Portfolios	Rubrics	Target Criteria	Metacognitive: Logs, Journals

Figure 9.13

High-Stakes, Standardized Tests

Regardless of their usefulness as brain-compatible assessments and evaluations, high-stakes, standardized tests have become a part of teachers' lives in school districts everywhere. Teachers must be cognizant of standards, test procedures, and strategies for helping every learner succeed on "the test."

Standards can be a two-edged sword. They provide teachers with clear expectations for designing the instructional process. Because of their knowledge and skills, teachers can make a tremendous difference in what and how students learn. However, test results may be used to measure the success of students, teachers, and schools when in reality the results depend on many factors that affect the lives of learners, some of which are beyond the control of the teacher and school.

Preparing for the Test

Testing can cause great anxiety and emotional hijacking for teachers and students. Often, teachers feel they can't use interactive, brain-compatible process strategies in their classrooms because they feel pressure to prepare for the test.

A study by Smith, Lee, and Newmann (2001) was conducted to examine instructional practices in the third and fifth grades in Chicago. The results were clear. The scores that students achieved as a result of teachers who used more didactic strategies fell 3.9 percent below the city average in math and 3.4 percent in reading, whereas those students whose teachers used more interactive strategies scored 5.1 percent higher than the city average in math and 5.2 percent in reading.

Teachers who used frequent and excessive review found that students scored 4.8 percent lower than the city average in math and 4.9 percent in reading. Those teachers who reviewed less frequently (thus using more time for instruction) increased scores by 4.2 percent over the city average in math and 4.1 percent in reading.

"Drill and kill" does not necessarily improve results on tests. Teachers will facilitate reviewing time with students. However, it was found to be more beneficial for student learning when teachers had students prepare reviews developing their own questions to ask in pairs or small groups. There are three or four rehearsals in this process: preparing their own questions, being sure of the correct answers, explaining their thinking to others and answering questions prepared by other students. Having students create an "I have, who has?" game or a People Search can be a good homework strategy for review and use next day in class. Research found that students were more engaged, created better questions and were motivated to challenge themselves and others (Foos et al. 1994, King 1992, Bainbridge and Pantaleo 1999, pp. 165–167).

During the Test

As part of the Black and William research (2004), it was found that students who were encouraged to make notes during tests regarding what terms were confusing for them did better.

After the Test

After the test students and teacher should take time to address the questions that were most challenging for the students. Working with partners students can review the questions and create quality answers. Reteaching can also be done to avoid gaps in learning. "Teach, test, and hope for the best" does help in the long term for students.

To prepare students to feel more efficacious and confident about taking the test and to eliminate some of the emotional hijacking that prevents children from performing up to their potential, teachers may consider the following techniques.

Enhancing Brain Waves: Getting Ready for the TEST

"We Are What We Eat"

We have long known that well-nourished learners do better in school. Foods that help to focus attention and to sustain ongoing energy contain protein, unsaturated fats, complex carbohydrates, and sugars. Foods high in proteins include the following:

- Milk
- Cheese
- Yogurt
- Eggs
- Nuts
- Meats
- Poultry

Foods high in complex carbohydrates include these:

- Vegetables
- Fruits
- Whole-grain products

Students (or parents) should be encouraged to prepare a high-protein breakfast, which would include some of the above-suggested foods. Students should avoid foods

- high in saturated fats that can interfere with optimum brain functioning
- high in excess simple sugars such as candy, cookies, sodas, and sugared cereals that sometimes interfere with students' ability to pay attention to a task
- high in caffeine such as coffee, cola drinks, and chocolate that may interfere with concentration and make students nervous

Teachers may also want to use some of their "cupcake money" (from fund-raising) to purchase appropriate snacks (veggie or fruit trays, granola bars, cheese and crackers, etc.) so they are available for breaks on test days to keep energy levels up and brains fueled. Parents can be enlisted to help with preparation.

Water, Water Everywhere . . .

Water is essential for healthy brains. Dehydration is often related to poor learning. The brain is made up of a higher percentage of water than any other organ and needs constant replenishing (Jensen 1998; Sprenger 2002).

When the water content of the blood drops, the salt concentration increases. If salt levels are high, the cells release fluids into the bloodstream. This raises the blood pressure and stress levels. Within five minutes of drinking water, there is a noticeable decline in corticoids and ACTH, hormones associated with high stress levels. Students become less attentive and often more lethargic when they are dehydrated. Children need water often, not juices or soft drinks, which can act as diuretics.

Get Moving

We know that physical movement can raise the level of oxygen and glucose to the brain (Jensen 1998; Hannaford 1995). Movement lowers the level of cortisol, a stress hormone, in the bloodstream.

You can lead students in energizing movement breaks, using arm and leg crossover activities that can help integrate left and right hemispheres of the brain, such as moving to music and touching the right elbow to the left knee, or pat your head and rub your belly. Music also increases endorphin levels and energizes the listener. Take the students for a walk in the fresh air, giving them a chance to chat with a partner in order to lower stress and increase energy. Teach students relaxation techniques such as deep breathing and counting to ten.

Music, Relaxation, Alertness, and Visualization

Studies (Campbell 1998) show that playing Mozart for ten minutes before a test improved spatial temporal reasoning. Baroque music or music with a pulse of about sixty beats per minute also slows down the brain waves to the alpha range, enhancing alertness and general well-being (Boyd and Bowes 2001).

Teachers can help students with guided visualization, asking them to sit quietly and to imagine themselves relaxed and alert, answering all the questions, using strategies for memory retrieval such as mnemonics, diagrams, and graphic organizers.

Affirmations

Teachers can help students "pump themselves up" before a difficult or challenging endeavor like athletes and sports competitors do. Energizing cheers can help with their feelings of efficacy before a test. Students can help prepare for a successful test by chanting "Yes we can! Yes we can!" or other chants:

We can, we can, we know we can We can, we can, we should

We can, we can, we know we can We're ready! We're good!

The following simple song can be sung to the tune of "If you're happy and you know it":

> Well you're smart and you know it, clap your hands Well you're smart and you know it, clap your hands
>
> Well you're smart and you know it and you really want to show it
>
> Well you're smart and you know it, clap your hands!

Verse 2

> So you're ready and you know it, stomp your feet!

Verse 3

> Now you're thinking and you know it, shout SUCCESS!

Positive Environment

Students usually do better in the room where they learned the material (Baddeley 1990) and with the instructor who taught them somewhere in their visual field. This facilitates access to episodic memory used as a recall tool. Students will remember the location and experiences of learning and be more able to access those memories. They are also less stressed in familiar places rather than sterile study halls or gyms.

Teachers also need to consider the learning styles of their students and recognize that some students may like to be closer to the natural light of a window. Some students are easily distracted and announcements over the loudspeaker may take them off task. All students have the right to have their physical and psychological needs met. Water, bathroom access, a smile, or positive gesture should be given to students when they look perplexed to relieve stress so those students are able to think.

Test Strategies

Teach students to use techniques that will assist with memory process as well as build confidence.

"Dump sheet"

When students are trying to hold information in short-term memory, they may be unable to access information that is stored in long-term memory. Some teachers allow them to "dump the information" on a blank piece of paper so that they can concentrate on the test. The information that they have been trying to hold may not

Memory Pathways
Suitable Assessment Processes

Semantic	Episodic	Procedural	Automatic	Emotional
Graphic organizers	Props/costumes	Allow them to show you	Trigger words	Reflection and writing down responses
Short answers	Bulletin boards	Demonstration exhibition	Use songs, raps, rhymes, etc. to access memories	Celebrate learning and sharing
Contextual clues	Room location			
Matching	Presence of their teacher	Ask students to explain as they do a task		Cue feelings
	Recall role play			

Figure 9.14

even be on the test, but by getting it "off their mind," they are able to deal with questions that are on the test. This gives students the confidence that they need to accept the challenge offered by the test and helps them avoid the undue stress in trying to recall or remember needed information and processes.

Mnemonics

Teaching students to use memory hooks such as mnemonics can help them cope with retaining and accessing large amounts of unconnected information. "Memory pegs" is a strategy that hooks an idea or item to be remembered to a rhyming word. Other techniques include involving the items to be remembered in a story, rap or song, poem, or chant (see also Chapman and King 2000). Remind students to think about when and where they learned the information and access the memory pathway that they used. Figure 9.14 suggests assessment practices that use different pathways and techniques (Sprenger 2002).

IN CLOSING

Students who start school now and graduate in the years to come will face a very different world from that of today. We can't accurately predict what that will be, but we can predict some of the attributes that will enable students to be successful. They will need to have the skills to be lifelong learners who can adapt and change with the situations, challenges, and circumstances they encounter. They also will need teamwork, technology, and thinking skills.

As we continue to learn more about how people learn, we need to continue to question our practices in schools. We need to rethink our assessment practices in relation to the competencies we want our students to achieve. In recognition of what we know about brain compatibility, we must create a supportive and non-threatening environment in which the criteria are clear and understood by the learner. We need to broaden our understanding of the variety of assessment tools that can be used to collect data on student learning. We need to provide a rich environment and adequate time to explore and develop understanding.

Assessment needs to be an integral part of the instructional process and a vehicle for providing the necessary information for continuous improvement. We need to embed learning and assessment in meaningful contexts, such as problems, projects, and inquiries, so students can see the relevancy of their learning. We need to give students adequate time to reach mastery and to receive feedback. We need to provide opportunities for metacognition so students can reflect, identify their new learning, and set personal goals.

By paying attention to the elements of brain-compatible assessment strategies and designing curriculum with the competencies in mind, we increase our chances of reaching more learners and giving them the necessary opportunities to achieve the standards.

GLOSSARY

amygdala. Part of the limbic system, this is the gatekeeper of emotions. It is survival oriented and monitors incoming sensory information in terms of its threat potential. In certain circumstances it can override the thinking parts of the brain and cause the body to engage in survival tactics.

automatic memory. A relatively recent discovery, it is sometimes equated with conditioned response because a specific stimulus always triggers the same reaction. Examples include memorizing multiplication tables, the alphabet, words of songs, etc.

axon. Part of a neuron, this is a long fiber that extends from the cell body. Its purpose is to carry information in the form of nerve impulses.

base group. A group of three or four students, usually heterogeneous, who work together for extended periods.

brainstorm. An idea-generating strategy often used for team problem solving.

carousel brainstorm. A form of walkabout in which problems are written on large sheets of paper posted around the room. Groups of four move from sheet to sheet and brainstorm solutions to each problem.

cerebral cortex. The upper part of the brain, it is heavily folded in on itself as a way of conserving space in the cranial cavity. It is the part of the brain associated with academic learning.

climate setting. Setting the emotional climate of the classroom by engaging in a range of inclusion activities that make students feel as if they belong.

collaborative/social skills. The skills that individuals need in order to work as a group. These skills include team building, conflict resolution, leadership, and group management.

concept attainment. An inductive thinking strategy in which students attain an understanding of a concept by comparing examples of the concept with nonexamples.

concept formation. An inductive thinking strategy in which students organize critical attributes of a concept into groups, or chunks, and then develop generalizations from the organized data.

declarative memory. Term used by neuroscientists for information stored over time for future use. Forms include semantic, episodic, procedural, automatic, and emotional memories.

deductive thinking. A type of thinking in which an established rule or generalization is examined in terms of its critical attributes or particular examples for the purpose of proving or disproving it.

dendrite. A hairlike fiber that extends from the cell body of a neuron. It combines with other dendrites in a weblike formation for the purpose of receiving incoming messages from other brain cells.

downshifting. See emotional hijacking.

emotional hijacking. An emotional reaction to stress that causes control over brain functions to shift from the cerebral cortex to the emotional brain (limbic system). Also known as downshifting.

emotional intelligence theory. A theory of intelligence that states that certain characteristics, such as self-awareness, managing emotions, self-motivation, empathy, and social arts, constitute a different but important way of being smart.

emotional memory. Created from experiences with an emotional component, such as happiness, sadness, fear, or loathing. When an emotional memory is recalled, it may be strong enough to interfere with other memory systems, and in extreme cases, it may render learning all but impossible.

endorphin. A type of neurotransmitter that in combination with other neurotransmitters can enhance feelings of pleasure and dull feelings of pain.

episodic memory. Often called spatial or contextual memory because it usually is recalled by focusing on the context or event that caused the memory to be formed.

expert jigsaw. A way of processing large amounts of information by dividing it up among groups of students. Individuals in each group are responsible for learning a specific part and then teaching it to their peers.

fight-or-flight response. A survival-oriented response to stress in which the body responds with either aggression (fight) or the desire to flee (flight).

fishbone diagram. A problem-solving graphic organizer that examines contributing factors for the purpose of determining cause and effect.

four corners. A cooperative group strategy in which the four corners of a room are designated as different views on a topic and students form groups at the corner representative of their view.

glial cell. A type of brain cell that provides support structures and nutrients for the other brain cells (neurons). Glial cells also form the myelin sheaths that cover mature neurons.

graffiti brainstorm. A form of brainstorming used to collect multiple solutions to a number of different problems. Groups list ideas on large sheets of paper and then circulate to each sheet, adding ideas to the other groups' lists.

graphic organizer. A visual way of organizing information or ideas.

heterogeneous group. A group of students with a wide range of abilities, characteristics, and needs.

homogeneous group. A group of students who share a similar attribute, such as the same level of ability.

inclusion strategies. Team-building activities that help students to feel part of a group.

inductive thinking. A type of thinking strategy in which generalizations or rules are formed by examining individual pieces of evidence or critical attributes.

journal. Written recollections and reflections that focus on emotional reactions to events; usually longer and more subjective than a log.

KWL. An advance organizer used to list what students know (K), what they want to know (W), and what they have learned (L).

log. Recorded observations about events; usually short and objective.

metacognition. A reflective practice in which students think about their thought processes.

mind map. A graphic organizer that enhances learning through the use of symbolic representations as opposed to words.

multiple intelligences theory. A theory proposed by Howard Gardner that states all people have multiple forms of intelligence.

neuron. A brain cell associated with processing information. It consists of a cell body, with a network of dendrites, and a long fiberlike axon that divides into a series of branches called axon terminals.

neurotransmitter. A chemical messenger that transmits information from one neuron to the next.

numbered heads. A cooperative group strategy in which students are assigned a number or letter, which then is used to track their participation in a group activity or project.

paraphrase passport. A cooperative group activity in which students paraphrase the words of another student before adding their own comments.

people search. A walkabout in which students have a preset list of questions, to which they find a different person to answer each question. It may be used as an icebreaker or as a pretest of student knowledge prior to teaching a lesson or review.

peptide. A type of neurotransmitter, its function is to modulate a broad spectrum of approach-avoidance and pleasure-pain responses.

procedural memory. Associated with motor learning, it is sometimes called muscle memory and is used when playing the piano, typing, riding a bike, and so on.

role playing. A strategy in which students take on the attributes of certain characters in a short play or scenario. Each student acts out his or her role according to a predetermined set of rules.

round robin. Cooperative group structure in which students respond in turn.

roundtable round robin. Cooperative structure in which students respond in turn using paper or other material that is passed from student to student.

rubric. An assessment framework that describes the general criteria for a task. Rubrics often include detailed indicators that describe the defining characteristics of excellent work, work that meets the appropriate standards, and substandard work.

SCAMPER. A creative thinking strategy in which students consider alternate ways of viewing an artifact or idea by generating ways they could substitute, combine, adapt, put to other use, eliminate, or reverse its uses.

semantic memory. Refers to the type of memorization associated with "book learning" or school learning and is used to recall lists, dates, names, places, and other facts.

simple structure. Any cooperative group learning structure that involves minimal organization and is easy to learn (e.g., numbered heads or paraphrase passport).

synapse. The gap between the axon terminal of one neuron and the dendrite of another neuron. A message is passed when the neurotransmitters from the sending neuron cross the synaptic gap and are taken up by the dendrites of the receiving neuron.

Synectics. A thinking strategy based on the creation of metaphors.

T-chart. A way of organizing information visually using a chart formed by a horizontal line across the top and a vertical line down the center in the shape of the letter T.

talking chips. A cooperative group strategy designed to control the amount of input a student has into a group activity. Students are assigned a specific number of chips or markers (usually four) and use a chip for the opportunity to make a response. When all of a student's chips have been used, the student can make no further responses.

think-pair-share. A questioning-response strategy in which a question is posed, students think about their responses, then pair with a partner to share responses, and finally share with the class as a whole.

think time. A strategy used in conjunction with wait time. After a teacher has selected a student to answer a question, he or she is given a period of time in which to think and formulate an answer.

triune brain theory. A theory postulated by Dr. Paul MacLean in which the brain is said to have developed in three stages: reptilian, limbic system (often called the emotional brain), and cerebral cortex.

Venn diagram. A graphic organizer consisting of two (or more) intersecting circles. It may be used to sort data into categories such as similar and dissimilar or like and unlike.

wait time. The amount of time that a teacher allows between asking a question and calling on a student to answer.

BIBLIOGRAPHY

Advanced Learning Technologies, University of Kansas Center for Research on Learning. 2001. Rubistar. http://rubistar.4teachers.org

Andre, T. 1979. Does answering higher-level questions while reading facilitate productive learning? *Review of Educational Research* 49: 280–318.

Aronson, E. 1978. *The jigsaw classroom.* Beverly Hills, CA: Sage.

Baddeley, A. 1990. *Human memory.* Boston: Allyn & Bacon.

Bellanca, J. 1990a. *The cooperative think tank.* Arlington Heights, IL: IRI/SkyLight Training and Publishing.

———. 1990b. *Keep Them Thinking Level III.* Arlington Heights, IL: IRI/SkyLight Publishing.

———. 1992. *The Cooperative Think Tank II.* Arlington Heights, IL: IRI/SkyLight Training and Publishing.

Bellanca, J. and R. Fogarty. 1986a. *Catch them thinking: A handbook of classroom strategies.* Arlington Heights, IL: IRI/SkyLight Training and Publishing.

———. 1986b. *Teach them thinking.* Arlington Heights, IL: IRI/SkyLight Training and Publishing.

———. 1991. *Blueprints for thinking in the cooperative classroom.* Arlington Heights, IL: IRI/SkyLight Training and Publishing.

Bellanca, J., C. Chapman, and E. Swartz. 1994. *Multiple Assessments for Multiple Intelligences.* Arlington Heights, IL: IRI/SkyLight Training and Publishing.

Bennett, B. and C. Rolheiser. 2001. *Beyond Monet: The artful science of instructional integration.* Toronto, Ontario: Bookation.

Bennett, B., C. Rolheiser-Bennett, and L. Stevahn. 1991. *Cooperative learning: Where heart meets mind.* Toronto, Ontario: Educational Connections.

Black, P., C., Harrison, C., Lee, B., Marshall, and D. Williams, 2004. Working inside the black box: Assessment for learning in the classroom. *Phi Delta Kappan* 86(1): 8–21.

Bloom, B. S., et al. 1956. *Taxonomy of educational objectives handbook 1: Cognitive domain.* New York: David McKay.

Boyd, B., and K. Bowes. 2001. *The brain in the news.* Washington, DC: Dana Press.

Brooks, J. and M. Brooks. 1993. *In search of understanding: The case for constructivist classrooms.* Alexandria, VA: Association for Supervision and Curriculum Development.

Bruner J. S., J. Goodnow, and G. Austin. 1967. *A study of thinking.* New York: Science Editions.

Burke, K. 1993. *The Mindful School: How to Assess Authentic Learning.* Arlington Heights, IL: IRI/SkyLight Training and Publishing.

Burke, K., R. Fogarty, and S. Belgrad. 1994. *The Mindful School: The Portfolio Connection.* Arlington Heights, IL: IRI/SkyLight Training and Publishing.

Burns, E. T. 1991. *Our children, our future.* Dallas, TX: Marco Polo.

Buzan, T. 1974. *Use both sides of your brain.* New York: Dutton.

Buzan, T. and B. Buzan. 1994. *The mind map book.* New York: NAL-Dutton.

Caine, R. N. and G. Caine. 1994. *Making connections: Teaching and the human brain.* Reading, MA: Addison-Wesley.

———. 1997. *Education on the edge of possibility.* Alexandria, VA: Association for Supervision and Curriculum Development.

Campbell, D. 1998. *The Mozart effect.* New York: Avon.

Chapman, C. 1993. *If the shoe fits . . . : How to develop multiple intelligences in the classroom.* Arlington Heights, IL: IRI/SkyLight Training and Publishing.

Chapman, C., and R. King. 2000. *Test success in the brain compatible classroom.* Tucson, AZ: Zephyr Press.

————. 2003a. *Differentiated Instructional Strategies for Reading in the Content Areas.* Thousand Oaks, CA: Corwin Press.

————. R. 2003b. *Differentiated instructional strategies for writing in the content areas.* Thousand Oaks, CA: Corwin Press.

Costa, A. L. 1991. *The school as a home for the mind.* Arlington Heights, IL: IRI/SkyLight Training and Publishing.

————. 1995. *Teaching for intelligent behavior: Outstanding strategies for strengthening your students' thinking skills.* Bellevue, WA: Bureau of Education and Research.

————. 1996. Workshop presented at the Teaching for Intelligence conference sponsored by the Bureau of Education and Research of Bellevue, Washington, held in Toronto, Canada, December 6.

Csikszentmihalyi, M. 1991. *Flow: The psychology of optimal experience.* New York: HarperCollins.

Damasio, A. 1994. *Descartes' error: Emotion, reason, and the human brain.* New York: Putnam.

de Bono, E. 1976. *Teaching thinking.* New York: Penguin.

————. 1985. *Six thinking hats.* Boston, MA: Little, Brown.

————. 1987. *CoRT Thinking Program.* Elmsford, NY: Pergamon.

Dewey, J. 1938. *Experience and Education.* New York: Collier Books.

Diamond, M. 1988. *Enriching heredity. The impact of the environment on the anatomy of the brain.* New York: Free Press.

Eberle, B. 1982. *SCAMPER: Games for imagination development.* Buffalo, NY: D.O.K.

Edelman, G. M. 1987. *Neural Darwinism: The theory of neuronal group selection.* New York: Basic Books.

————. 1992. *Bright air, brilliant fire: On the matter of the mind.* New York: Basic Books.

Ekwall, E. E., and J. L. Shanker. 1988. *Diagnosis and remediation of the disabled reader.* 3d ed. Boston: Allyn & Bacon.

Elias, M. 1997. *Promoting social and emotional learning guidelines for educators.* Alexandria, VA: Association for Supervision and Curriculum Development.

Elias, M. and H. Arnold, 2006. *The educator's guide to emotional intelligence and academic achievement: Social-emotional learning in the classroom.* Thousand Oaks, CA: Corwin Press.

Emotional Intelligence: A New Vision for Educators (video). 1996. Port Chester, NY: National Professional Resources.

Fogarty, R. 1994. *The Mindful School: How to Teach for Metacognitive Reflection.* Arlington Heights, IL: IRI/SkyLight Training and Publishing.

————. 1997a. *Problem-Based Learning and Other Curriculum Models for the Multiple Intelligences Classroom.* Arlington Heights, IL: IRI/SkyLight Training and Publishing.

————. 1997b. *Brain-Compatible Classrooms.* Arlington Heights, IL: IRI/SkyLight Training and Publishing.

————. 2002. *Brain-Compatible Classrooms.* 2d ed. Arlington Heights, IL: SkyLight Training and Publishing.

Fogarty, R. and J. Bellanca. 1986. *Teach Them Thinking.* Arlington Heights, IL: IRI/SkyLight Training and Publishing.

Fogarty, R. and J. Bellanca. 1993. *Patterns for thinking, patterns for transfer.* 2d ed. Arlington Heights, IL: IRI/SkyLight Training and Publishing.

Fogarty, R. and S. Berman. 1997. *Project Learning for the Multiple Intelligences Classroom.* Arlington Heights, IL: IRI/SkyLight Training and Publishing.

Fogarty, R., D. Perkins, and J. Barell. 1993. *The Mindful School: How to Teach for Transfer.* Arlington Heights, IL: IRI/SkyLight Training and Publishing.

Fogarty, R. and J. Stoehr. 1995. *Integrating Curricula with Multiple Intelligences.* Arlington Heights, IL: IRI/SkyLight Training and Publishing.

Fullan, M. 1993. *Change forces.* New York: Falmer Press.

———. 2003. *The moral imperative of school leadership.* Thousand Oaks, CA: Corwin Press.

Gardner, H. 1983. *Frames of mind: The theory of multiple intelligences.* New York: Basic Books.

———. 1991. *The unschooled mind: How children think and how schools should teach.* New York: Basic Books.

Gibbs, J. 1995. *Tribes: A new way of learning and being together.* Santa Rosa, CA: CenterSource Systems.

Given, B. K. (2002). *The brain's natural learning systems.* Alexandria, VA: Association for Supervision and Curriculum Development.

Glasser, W. 1986. *Control theory in the classroom.* New York: HarperCollins.

———. 1990. *The quality school.* New York: HarperCollins.

Goldberg, E. 2001. *The executive brain: Frontal lobes and the civilized mind.* New York: Oxford.

Goleman, D. 1995. *Emotional intelligence.* New York: Bantam Books.

Goodlad, J. I. 1984. *A place called school.* New York: McGraw-Hill.

Gordon, W. 1961. *Synectics.* New York: Harper & Row.

Greenough, W., and B. J. Anderson. 1991. Cerebellar synaptic plasticity: Relation to learning versus neural activity. *Annals of the New York Academy of Science* 627: 231–47.

Gregory, G. 2003. *Differentiated instructional strategies in practice: Training, implementation, and supervision.* Thousand Oaks, CA: Corwin Press.

———. 2005. *Differentiating instruction with style: Aligning teacher and learner intelligences for maximum achievement.* Thousand Oaks, CA: Corwin Press.

Gregory, G., and C. Chapman. 2002. *Differentiated instructional strategies: One size doesn't fit all.* Thousand Oaks, CA: Corwin Press.

———. 2006. *Differentiated instructional strategies: One size doesn't fit all (2nd. ed.).* Thousand Oaks, CA: Corwin Press.

Gregory, G., and L. Kuzmich. 2004. *Differentiated literacy strategies for student growth and achievement in grades K-6.* Thousand Oaks, CA: Corwin Press.

———. 2005. *Differentiated literacy strategies for student growth and achievement in grades 7–12.* Thousand Oaks, CA: Corwin Press.

Hannaford, C. 1995. *Smart moves: Why learning is not all in your head.* Arlington, VA: Great Ocean Publishers.

Healy, J. M. 1990. *Endangered minds: Why our children don't think and what we can do about it.* New York: Simon & Schuster.

Herbert, N. 1993. *The elemental mind.* New York: Dutton Books.

Hill, S. and J. Hancock. 1993. *Reading and writing communities.* Armadale, Australia: Eleanor Curtin.

Hoffman, M. L. 1984. Empathy, social cognition, and moral action. In *Moral behavior and development: Advances in theory, research and applications,* edited by W. Kurtines and J. Gerwitz. New York: John Wiley.

Hunter, M. 1982. *Mastery teaching: Increasing instructional effectiveness in elementary, secondary schools, colleges, and universities.* Thousand Oaks, CA: Corwin Press,

Hunter, R. 2004. *Madeline Hunter's mastery teaching: Increasing instructional effectiveness in elementary and secondary schools.* Thousand Oaks, CA: Corwin Press.

Jacobs, B., M. Schall, and A. B. Scheibel. 1993. A quantitative dendritic analysis of Wernicke's area in humans: Gender, hemispheric and environmental factors. *Journal of Comparative Neurology 3271*: 97–111.

Jensen, E. 1996. *Completing the puzzle: A brain-based approach to learning.* Del Mar, CA: Turning Point Publishing.

———. 1998. *Teaching with the brain in mind.* Alexandria, VA: Association for Supervision and Curriculum Development.

Johnson, D. W., R. T. Johnson, and E. J. Holubec. 1984. *Circles of learning.* Alexandria, VA: Association for Supervision and Curriculum Development.

———. 1988. *Cooperation in the classroom.* Edina, MN: Interaction Book.

Jones, R. 1995. Smart brains: Neuroscientists explore the mystery of what makes us human. *American School Board Journal* (November): 22–26.

Joyce, B., and B. Showers. 1988. *Student achievement through staff development.* White Plains, NY: Longman.

Joyce, B., and M. Weil. 1972. *Models of teaching.* Englewood Cliffs, NJ: Prentice Hall.

Joyce, B., J. Wolf, and E. F Calhoun. 1993 *The self-renewing school.* Alexandria, VA: Association for Supervision and Curriculum Development.

Kagan, S. 1990. *Cooperative learning.* San Clemente, CA: Kagan Cooperative.

———. 1992. *Cooperative learning structures.* San Clemente, CA: Kagan Cooperative.

Kaufeldt, M. 1999. *Begin with the brain: Orchestrating the learner-centered classroom.* Tucson, AZ: Zephyr Press.

Kohn, A. 1993. *Punished by rewards.* Boston, MA: Houghton Mifflin.

Kovalik, S. J. 1991. *Kid's eye view of science.* Oak Creek, AZ: Center for the Future of Public Education.

Lazear, D. 1991a. *Seven ways of knowing.* Arlington Heights, IL: IRI/SkyLight Training and Publishing.

———. 1991b. *Seven ways of teaching.* Arlington Heights, IL: IRI/SkyLight Training and Publishing.

Lou, Y., P. C. Alorami, J. C. Spence, C. Paulsen, B. Chambers, and S. d'Apollonio. 1996. Within-class grouping: A meta-analysis. *Review of Educational Research* 66(4): 423–458.

MacLean, P. 1978. A mind of three minds: Educating the triune brain. In *Education and the brain, 77th National Society for the Study of Education Yearbook,* edited by J. Chall and A. Mirsky. Chicago: University of Chicago Press.

Margulies, N. 1991. *Mapping inner space: Learning and teaching mind mapping.* Tucson, AZ: Zephyr Press.

Marzano, R. J., D. Pickering, and J. McTighe. 1993. *Assessing student outcomes: Performance assessment using the dimensions of learning model.* New York: Elsevier.

Marzano, R., D. Pickering, and J. Pollack. 2000. *Classroom instruction that works.* Alexandria, VA: Association for Supervision and Curriculum Development.

McTighe, J. 1990. *Better thinking and learning.* Baltimore: Maryland State Department of Education.

McTighe, J. 1993. *Performance assessment in the classroom.* Videotape, Program 2: Creating performance tasks. Sandy, UT. *Journal of Education.*

Miller, G. 1956. The magical number seven, plus or minus two: Some limits on our capacity for processing information. *Psychological Review* 63: 81–97.

Ministry of Education, Ontario. 1990. *Basic English, OAIP.* Queen's Park, Toronto, Ontario: The Queen's Printer. (Comp. by Cooper & Ward)

Opie, I. A., and R. Opie, eds. 1955. *Oxford nursery rhyme book.* Oxford: Oxford University Press.

Osborn, A. 1963. *Applied imagination.* New York: Charles Scribner & Sons.

Parnell, D. 1995. *Why do I have to learn this? Teaching the way people learn best.* Waco, TX: Cord Communications.

Perkins, D., and G. Salomon. 1988. Teaching for transfer. *Educational Leadership* 46(1): 22–23.

———. 1990. *The science and art of transfer.* Retrieved April 7, 2006, from http://learnweb.harvard.edu/alps/thinking/docs/trancost.pdf

Peterson, L. R., and M. J. Peterson. 1959. Short-term retention of individual verbal items. *Journal of Experimental Psychology* 58: 193–198.

Popham, W. J. 2001. *The truth about testing.* Alexandria, VA: Association for Supervision and Curriculum Development.

Quellmalz, E. S. 1985. Developing reasoning skills. In *Teaching thinking skills: Theory and practice,* edited by J. R. Baron and R. J. Sternberg. New York: Freeman.

Ratey, J. 2001. *A user's guide to the brain.* New York: Pantheon Books.

Redfield, D. L., and E. W. Rousseau. 1981. A meta-analysis of experimental research on teacher questioning behavior. *Educational Leadership* 42: 40–46.

Resnick, L. B. 1987. *Education and learning to think.* Washington, DC: National Academy Press.

Restak, R. 1994. *The modular brain.* New York: Vintage.

Rolheiser, C., B. Bower, and L. Stevahn. 2000. *The portfolio organizer.* Alexandria, VA: Association for Supervision and Curriculum Development.

Ronis, D. 2000. *Brain-compatible assessments.* Arlington Heights, IL: SkyLight Training and Publishing.

Rosenholtz, S. J. 1991. *Teachers' workplace: The organizational context of schooling.* New York: Teachers College Press.

Rowe, M. B. 1987. Wait time: Slowing down may be a way of speeding up. *Educator 11*: 43.

Scheibel, A. B. 1994. *You can continuously improve your mind and your memory.* San Francisco, CA: Bottom Line Press.

———. 1995. Speech at Second Annual Symposium on the Human Brain, held at UCLA–Berkeley, Berkeley, CA, October 7.

Schlechty, P. C. 1990. *Schools for the twenty-first century.* San Francisco, CA: Jossey-Bass.

Schmoker, M. 1996. Results: The key to continuous school improvement. Alexandria, VA: Association for Supervision and Curriculum Development.

Sharan, S., and Y. Sharan. 1976. *Small-group teaching.* Englewood Cliffs, NJ: Educational Technology Publications.

Shoda, Y., W. Mischel, and P. K. Peake. 1990. Predicting adolescent cognitive and self-regulatory competencies from preschool delay of gratification. *Developmental Psychology* 26: 978–986.

Slavin, R. E. 1981. Synthesis of research on cooperative learning. *Educational Leadership* 38: 633–650.

Smith, J. B., V. E. Lee, and F. M. Newmann. 2001. *Instruction and achievement in Chicago elementary schools.* Available at www.consortium-chicago.org/publications/p0f01.html

Sousa, D. 2006. *How the brain learns: A classroom teacher's guide.* 3d ed. Thousand Oaks, CA: Corwin Press.

Spence, S. 1980. *Social skills training with children and adolescents.* Berkshire, England: NFER Publishing Company.

Sperry, R. 1968. Hemisphere disconnection and unity consciousness awareness. *American Psychologist 23:* 723–733.

Sprenger, M. 1999. *Learning and memory: The brain in action.* Alexandria, VA: Association for Supervision Curriculum Development.

———. 2002. *Becoming a "wiz" at brain-based teaching: How to make every year your best year.* Thousand Oaks, CA: Corwin Press.

———. 2003. *Differentiation through learning styles and memory.* Thousand Oaks, CA: Corwin Press.

Sternberg, R. J. 1996. *Successful intelligence: How practical and creative intelligence determine success in life.* New York: Simon & Schuster.

Stiggins, R. 1993. Authentic Assessment workshop presented at the Train the Trainers conference held in Toronto, Canada, May 5.

Stone, C. L. 1983. A meta-analysis of advance organizer studies. *Journal of Experimental Education 54:* 194–199.

Sutton, R. 1995. *Assessment for learning.* Salford, UK: RS Publications.

Sylwester, R. 1995. *A celebration of neurons: An educator's guide to the human brain.* Alexandria, VA: Association for Supervision and Curriculum Development.

———. 1998. *The downshifting dilemma: A commentary and proposal.* Seattle: New Horizons for Learning.

———. 2000. *A biological brain in a cultural classroom: Applying biological research to classroom management.* Thousand Oaks, CA: Corwin Press.

Taba, H. 1967. *Teacher's handbook for elementary social studies.* Reading, MA: Addison-Wesley.

Taylor, M. D. 1976. *Roll of thunder, hear my cry.* New York: Dial.

Thayer, R. E. 1989. *The biopsychology of mood and arousal.* New York: Oxford University Press.

Tilton, L. 1996. *Inclusion: A fresh look—Practical strategies to help all students succeed.* Shorewood, MN: Covington Cove Publications.

Vincent, J. D. 1990. *The biology of emotions.* Cambridge, MA: Basil Blackwell.

Wiggins, G., and J. McTighe. 2005. *Understanding by design* (2d ed., expanded), Alexandria, VA: Association for Supervision and Curriculum Development.

Williams, R. B. 1993. *More than 50 ways to build team consensus.* Arlington Heights, IL: IRI/SkyLight Training and Publishing.

Wolfe, P. 1998. Correspondence with authors.

———. 2001. *Brain matters: Translating research into classroom practice.* Alexandria, VA: Association for Supervision and Curriculum Development.

Wolfe, P., and P. Nevills. 2004. *Building the reading brain, PreK-3.* Thousand Oaks, CA: Corwin Press.

Wolfe, P., and M. Sorgen. 1990. Mind, memory and learning: Implications for the classroom. Self-published.

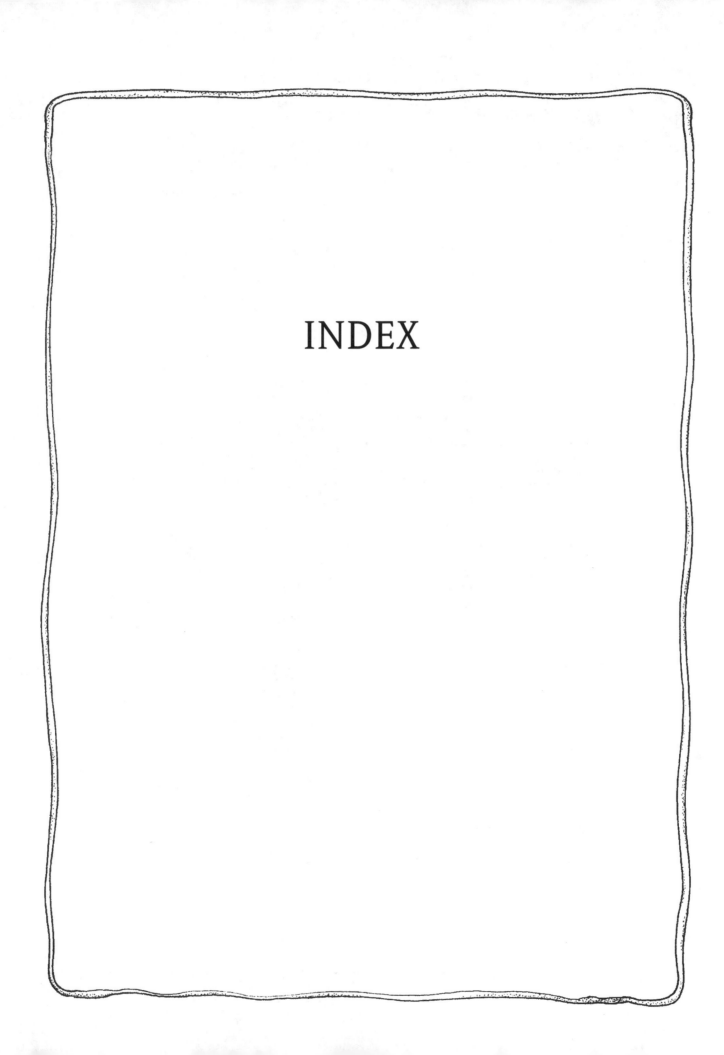

INDEX

CORWIN PRESS

The Corwin Press logo—a raven striding across an open book—represents the union of courage and learning. Corwin Press is committed to improving education for all learners by publishing books and other professional development resources for those serving the field of PreK–12 education. By providing practical, hands-on materials, Corwin Press continues to carry out the promise of its motto: **"Helping Educators Do Their Work Better."**